Postbop Jazz in the 1960s

POSTBOP JAZZ
IN THE 1960s

*The Compositions of Wayne Shorter,
Herbie Hancock, and Chick Corea*

Keith Waters

OXFORD
UNIVERSITY PRESS

Oxford University Press is a department of the University of Oxford. It furthers
the University's objective of excellence in research, scholarship, and education
by publishing worldwide. Oxford is a registered trade mark of Oxford University
Press in the UK and certain other countries.

Published in the United States of America by Oxford University Press
198 Madison Avenue, New York, NY 10016, United States of America.

© Oxford University Press 2019

CIP data is on file at the Library of Congress
ISBN 978-0-19-060457-8

9 8 7 6 5 4 3 2 1

Printed by Sheridan Books, Inc., United States of America

To my fellow members of the Jazz Piano Collective: Steve Larson, Henry Martin, and Steve Strunk.

CONTENTS

MUSICAL EXAMPLES

INTRODUCTION AND ACKNOWLEDGMENTS

This book is dedicated to a repertory of jazz compositions from the 1960s, a repertory I describe as postbop. It features a number of compositions by Wayne Shorter, Herbie Hancock, and Chick Corea, along with those of Booker Little, Joe Henderson, and Woody Shaw. I suggest that these compositions depart from or transform some earlier principles of tonal jazz compositions, and require different analytical methods.

Chapter 1 describes features of postbop composition of the 1960s. It illustrates how some principles of postbop compositions intersect those of with earlier compositions, and provides some broad methods for considering features and problems associated with tonal jazz and modal jazz. Chapter 2 regards the work of Wayne Shorter, emphasizing "Penelope," "El Gaucho," "Pinocchio," and "Face of the Deep." Chapter 3 is devoted to Herbie Hancock's "King Cobra," "Dolphin Dance," and "Jessica." Chapter 4 examines Chick Corea's "Windows," "Inner Space," and "Song of the Wind." Chapter 5 features other postbop compositions by trumpeter Booker Little, saxophonist Joe Henderson, and trumpeter Woody Shaw. Finally, chapter 6 offers some further analytical ideas and reflects on some larger questions of jazz's evolution.

I selected the compositions for this book for different and, at times, conflicting reasons. Particularly with the Shorter, Hancock, and Corea chapters, I was interested in investigating compositions likely familiar to experienced jazz players and listeners (Shorter's "El Gaucho," Hancock's "Dolphin Dance," Corea's "Windows") as well as some compositions perhaps less familiar (Shorter's "Face of the Deep," Hancock's "King Cobra," and Corea's "Song of the Wind"). Those perhaps less familiar compositions are also in many cases experimental or ambitious (or both), and offer unusual features of harmony, melody, or form. I also selected some compositions that offered writing for three or more horns (Shorter's "Face of the Deep,"

Hancock's "King Cobra" and "Jessica," Little's "We Speak") in order to exhibit some details of voicings and arranging in that format.

I do not wish to suggest that every 1960s composition by these composers invites the same analytical perspectives used here. In some cases I selected compositions and not others precisely because those perspectives seemed fruitful. Some readers might therefore find my argument circular: these are postbop compositions because they rely on the features that I described as postbop. But the intent here is to provide a location for a repertory, one that requires different views. There are likely other approaches and views, and many compositions unexamined here may require them.

Talking about jazz composition is problematic. Given the improvisational nature of jazz, lead sheet renditions of compositions are at best idealized versions of compositions that may differ markedly from performance to performance (and even within one performance).[1] Even copyright deposits of lead sheets by the composers themselves (which I discuss throughout this book) may relate to recordings of those compositions in only tenuous ways. Unlike musical scores of Western European music, lead sheets offer plans, not scripts. Nevertheless, examining jazz compositions—even through an idealized lead sheet—casts light on aesthetic priorities. The compositions illustrate how composers refashioned harmonic syntax to evoke ambiguity or clarity. As bebop composers adopted a newer improvisational language into the melodies of their compositions, so too did postbop composers appropriate newer aspects of melodic vocabulary into their own compositions. Formal designs departed from AABA and ABAC song forms. But the use of notated music here is meant merely to complement, not replace, the experience of listening to the recordings.

In this book I rely on nomenclature for chord symbols familiar to jazz musicians. In many cases those symbols merely supply the chord quality and variety of seventh (for example, Dm7 or DM7) and I assume the reader's broader knowledge of appropriate extensions for those harmonies. In some cases, I include extensions (or additional information) when they

---

1. I repeat here what I wrote in the introduction to *The Studio Recordings of the Miles Davis Quintet, 1965–68* (New York: Oxford University Press, 2011), xi: "I am aware of problems of ontology that arise from the idea of 'the composition,' that the notion of 'the composition' itself suggests a fixed and idealized entity at odds with the ways in which players freely and flexibly construct head statements. Rather than tend to those particular and interesting philosophical problems, I will use the term *composition* (or, as jazz musicians typically say, the *head* or *tune*) in the way that jazz musicians generally do—that the head relies on flexibly constructed statements of melody, harmony, bass, and rhythm, and subsequent statements preserve certain contours but may alter others."

support the melodic structure or offer alternatives that may not necessarily be inferred by readers (such as DM7♯11 or D7alt). In some cases I use slash chords to indicate harmonies that shift above bass pedal points. There are multiple methods to indicate harmonies or harmonic classes, and many of the lead sheets created by these jazz composers show them grappling with appropriate symbols for a dynamically emerging harmonic language.

To indicate intervallic distances (for melodic or bass motion) I use M for major intervals, m for minor intervals, and A and d for augmented and diminished intervals, respectively. M3 is therefore equivalent to the distance of a major third, m3 to a minor third. For convenience, I use these symbols even in the case of enharmonic equivalence: for example, the pitches C-E-A♭ form a M3 succession, even though notationally E-A♭ forms a d4. Elsewhere, I have used interval-class sizes for these distances (i.e., using ic4 instead of M3 to represent four semitones), but specific/generic intervals (such as M3) will be familiar to more readers. In most cases, I use these intervals for ascending and descending motion (i.e., descending M3 rather than ascending m6). The single exception is P4 and P5: there I distinguish between ascending fourth and ascending fifth motion.[2]

Some readers might note that my discussion of skeletal melody bears some resemblance to the reductive techniques of Schenkerian analysis. My aims, however, are different. They do not make the same claims about tonal structure, structural levels, or organic coherence that Schenkerian analysis does. My intent is to show how melodic pathways sometimes express broader axis progressions or stepwise motion, creating an ongoing continuity.

This book includes and develops some material I have published elsewhere. The Hancock chapter further explores some ideas originally presented in an article entitled "Modes, Scales, Functional, and Nonfunctional Harmony in the Compositions of Herbie Hancock." The article "'Giant Steps' and the ic4 Legacy" explores how major third transpositional schemes appear in Hancock's "Dolphin Dance," Shorter's "El Toro," and "Pinocchio." A number of ideas related to modal jazz and circular tunes (as well as Shorter's "Pinocchio") appear in the book *The Studio Recordings of the Miles Davis Quintet, 1965–68.* Finally, the analyses from the Chick Corea chapter appear in "Chick Corea and Postbop Harmony."[3]

2. The discussion of Corea's "Windows" (chapter 4) points to an ascending P5 sequence of minor harmonies.

3. Keith Waters, "Modes, Scales, Functional Harmony, and Non-Functional Harmony in the Compositions of Herbie Hancock," *Journal of Music Theory* 49, no. 2 (2005): 333–57; "'Giant Steps' and the ic4 Legacy," *Intégral* 24 (2010): 135–62; *The Studio Recordings*

I am unable to list all the individuals who helped me think through many of the ideas in this book. But I have profited immensely from informal conversations with Allan Chase, Marc Copland, Dave Hanson, Andy LaVerne, Brian Levy, and Dave Liebman. Clay Downham, Bruce Dudley, Tom Hojnacki, Henry Martin, Keith Salley, and Micheal Sebulsky read drafts of some chapters and provided excellent suggestions for improvement. In spring 2016 and again 2018, I taught a doctoral seminar on Postbop Jazz that made use of significant portions of this book, and I am deeply grateful to all the class members (in 2016: Ed Brazeale, Greg Harris, Otto Lee, Matt Michaud, Paulo Oliveira, Josh Reed, Rafael Rodriguez, Ben Sieben, Ryan van Scoyk, Heath Walton, and Paul Zaborec; in 2018: Brian Casey, Clay Downham, Sean Edwards, Hugh Ragin, Jonathan Saraga, David Smith, Charles Wofford) who worked through the analyses and offered numerous suggestions for clarification or correction.

I also would like to thank Larry Applebaum, senior librarian at the Library of Congress, for helping provide access to many of the copyright deposit lead sheets. I also owe a debt of gratitude to Lindsay Woppert of Hal Leonard and Luca Balbo of Music Sales for their work in helping me obtain reprint permissions for most of the lead sheets used in the text. I also thank Lauren Brockie of Gelfand, Rennert, and Feldman for her attempts to obtain copyright permissions for the Hancock compositions discussed. Since she was ultimately unsuccessful in those attempts, I have had to rely here on explanatory diagrams (rather than lead sheets) for the Hancock compositions in order to avoid any copyright infringements. Finally, I owe a special debt of gratitude to Henry Martin, Steven Strunk, and Steve Larson. From 1998 until the untimely deaths of Steve Larson in 2011 and Steven Strunk in 2012, the four of us performed, collaborated, and presented lectures together, maintaining a friendship that allowed frequent opportunities to discuss jazz, jazz harmony, and jazz improvisation. In Strunk and Larson we have lost too soon two very profound musical thinkers. It is our quartet—The Jazz Piano Collective—to whom this book is dedicated.

of the Miles Davis Quintet, 1965–68 (New York: Oxford University Press, 2011); "Chick Corea and Postbop Harmony," *Music Theory Spectrum* 38, no. 1 (2016): 37–57.

A NOTE ON TERMINOLOGY

Some of the terms used in this book will be familiar to some readers. Others I have coined to call attention to specific techniques. The following terms are used throughout the book in order to clarify some of the postbop practices discussed.

Aeolian progression: The use of a first inversion M7 harmony (or second inversion m7 harmony) in a progression of two or more chords with the same bass note (pedal point). That first inversion M7 harmony may be heard as an Aeolian harmony or a subset of an Aeolian collection (for example, CM7/E from E Aeolian). Most often the Aeolian harmony is the second chord in the progression, as in mm. 31–32 of Hancock's "Dolphin Dance" (Esus13-CM7/E).

Axis movement (Axis motion, Axis progression): Sequential harmonic, melodic, or bass motion by a single interval (m2, M2, m3, M3, etc.). Coltrane's "Giant Steps" uses the M3 harmonic axis throughout (tonicized by intervening V or ii-V progressions), and most consistently uses the M3 melodic axis in mm. 8–15. In mm. 8–15 of "Giant Steps" (and in other cases, as in the Introduction to Corea's "Inner Space") a M3 melodic axis is elaborated by other pitches. In most cases, axis harmonic progressions preserve the same chord type (such as M7) when moving through the axis.

A double-axis progression arises through pairs of chords transposed systematically. For example, mm. 21–24 of Woody Shaw's "Moontrane" creates a broader m3 axis progression with the chords Gm7-Fm7-B♭m7-A♭m7-C♯m7-Bm7. That double-axis progression is indicated in this book as m3 (−M2, +P4): m3 indicates the motion across two harmonies, and the figures in parentheses indicate direction (+ for up, − for down) and distance for the consecutive harmonies within the pair.

Hexatonic (augmented) collection (Hexatonic scale): A symmetrical collection that consistently alternates half steps and minor thirds (or their enharmonic equivalents). There are only four distinct collections relative to the members of a completed six-note scale: one that contains C/C♯, one that contains C♯/D, one that contains D/E♭, and one that contains D♯/E. All other completed scalar versions duplicate the pitches of those four.

Octatonic (diminished) collection (Octatonic scale): A symmetrical collection that consistently alternates half steps and whole steps (or their enharmonic equivalents). There are only three distinct collections relative to the members of a completed eight-note scale: one that contains C/C♯, one that contains C♯/D, and one that contains D/E♭. All other completed scalar versions duplicate the pitches of those three.

Pentatonic encircling: A group of three pitches belonging to the same pentatonic collection (such as C-D-F), the first two of which create a gap (such as C-F) filled in by the third pitch (D). This is related to the idea of chromatic encircling (E♭-C♯-D), but occurs instead in a pentatonic environment.

Skeletal melody: An underlying pattern of melodic pitches, usually at metrical downbeats and at changes in harmony. In some cases, the skeletal melody creates axis motion (Hancock's "Jessica," Introduction and mm. 15–18 of Corea's "Inner Space," mm. 24–36 of Corea's "Song of the Wind"). In some cases, the skeletal melody creates stepwise motion (mm. 1–9 of Hancock's "Dolphin Dance," mm. 17–24 of Corea's "Windows").

Upper-structure progression: A harmonic progression in which movement in the chords' upper voices imply harmonic progressions not reflected by the bass. For example, the progression to the bridge of Jobim's "Dindi" moves Dm7-B♭m6-Dm7. The B♭m6 chord is contained in the upper structure of an A7alt chord. Thus the upper structure suggests a conventional (i-V-i) pathway while the bass (B♭ instead of A) does not. A different upper-structure progression occurs in the bridge to Shorter's "Penelope" (see chapter 2). Its melodic progression moves through a m3 axis (A-F♯-D♯) while the harmony moves B♭M7-GM7-F♯sus13. The upper structure of F♯sus13 is related to EM7, so that upper structure pathway moves through the m3 axis (B♭M7-GM7-EM7) while the F♯ bass of the final chord does not.

V′, ii′-V′: The use of the prime symbol (′) refers to a tritone substitution harmony. For example, while ii7-V7 of C major refers to Dm7-G7, ii′7-V′7 in C major refers to A♭m7-D♭7.

Postbop Jazz in the 1960s

CHAPTER 1
Postbop

In 2010 I was asked to contribute the "Postbop" entry to the *Grove Dictionary of American Music*. The task seemed challenging in several ways. On one hand, postbop is a term that has only recently moved to a more central position in jazz scholarship.[1] On the other hand, postbop has resisted an agreed-upon definition with a fixed set of principles. In that way it resembles other terms such as modal jazz or free jazz: many jazz listeners have acquired a sense of what they mean, but they frequently mean very different things to different listeners. So to define postbop in 400 words—or less—was daunting.

In the end, the definition focused upon the improvisational techniques of artists of the late 1950s and 1960s. It began:

> *Postbop.* Term that loosely refers to a body of music that emerged in the late 1950s and 60s that combined principles of bop, hard bop, modal jazz, and free jazz. Much of this music maintained standard bop and hard bop elements, including a "head—solos—head" format and accompanimental textures such as walking bass. But the music also departed from earlier traditions in the following ways: a slower harmonic rhythm characteristic of modal jazz, techniques for playing "inside" and "outside" the underlying harmonic structure, an interactive (or conversational) approach to rhythm section accompaniment, unusual harmonic progressions, use of harmonic or metric superimposition, unusual underlying formal designs for head statements and chorus structure improvisation,

---

1. See, for example, Jeremy Yudkin, *Miles Davis, Miles Smiles, and the Invention of Post Bop* (Bloomington: Indiana University Press, 2008).

or the abandonment entirely of underlying chorus structure beneath improvisation. The recordings of the Ornette Coleman Quartet (*The Shape of Jazz to Come*, 1959), Miles Davis Sextet (*Kind of Blue*, 1959), Bill Evans Trio (*Portrait in Jazz*, 1959), the John Coltrane Quartet (*Live at the Village Vanguard*, 1961), and Eric Dolphy (*Far Cry*, 1961) are significant in that they maintain some inherited conventions of small group improvisation while enriching those conventions by establishing a degree of contact with the emerging free jazz movement. For many of these artists the notion of openness became a significant aesthetic principle.

Following a discussion of Miles Davis's Second Classic Quintet (1963–68), the definition concluded:

> All of this suggests that distinctions between free and more traditional jazz idioms are frequently not particularly crisp, and that both approaches influenced compositional and improvisational solutions. Many of the innovations forged by these players remain fundamental to small group improvisation today.[2]

My use of the term postbop differs in this book. It stresses ideas implicit but not fleshed out in the above definition. My concern here is not so much improvisational *techniques* as it is on particular jazz *compositions* of the 1960s. My thesis is that during this decade many principles of jazz composition changed. There arose an important body of small-group postbop compositions that revised and rethought traditional harmonic progressions, formal structures, and melodic designs. Their composers frequently abandoned 32-bar AABA and ABAC song forms housing cadential patterns toward the end of 8-bar sections. And often they did so in compositions whose harmonic rhythm was consistent and faster than the slower-moving or static harmonic progressions often regarded as modal. So my use of the term postbop here, referring to jazz composition, is more restrictive and exclusive than the one stated above, which attends more to improvisational techniques at the intersections of hard bop, modal, and free jazz practices.

The point of the book is to examine significant postbop compositions and composers whose contributions were wide-ranging and influential. The emphasis is on Wayne Shorter, Herbie Hancock, and Chick Corea, but I also regard others, such as Booker Little, Joe Henderson, and Woody Shaw. All

2. Keith Waters, "Postbop," entry in the *Grove Dictionary of American Music*, 2nd ed., vol. 6, ed. by Hiroshi Garrett (New York: Oxford University Press, 2013), 575.

these composers helped shape an emerging aesthetic that often highlighted ambiguity of tonality, form, and/or melody. It would be misleading to describe them as a "school" of composers. Instead, my intention is to locate points of contact, overlapping solutions, and aesthetic principles. The result, I hope, will highlight their accomplishments, provide some methods for analysis, and suggest that many of their compositional principles were absorbed into jazz compositions after 1960. Many of the compositions under discussion remain standard jazz compositions.

Rather than a single fixed definition of postbop composition, the above implies a series of family resemblances that include expanded forms, enhanced options for harmonic progression, and phrase groupings that depart from conventional 4- and 8-bar frameworks. Like most artistic trends, these ideas arose from forces that were evolutionary in a dynamic manner. So, even if transformative, postbop compositions nevertheless maintained connections with earlier styles and practices. This is especially true with harmony and tonality. For example, these composers imported newer harmonic resources into their vocabulary, but they also made use of conventional harmonies (appearing with a generally regular harmonic rhythm) that progressed in unconventional manners. In contrast to "tonal jazz" through the 1950s (referring both to the American popular songs favored by jazz artists, as well as compositions written by jazz performers),[3] postbop composers also at times used traditional progressions in ways that undermined a sense of an overall single key. Thus, while continuity prevailed in some dimensions, alterations and transformations occurred in others. The following summarizes some of the techniques of postbop composition:

1) Axis progressions (sequential harmonic, melodic, or bass progressions by single interval such as M3 or m3);
2) a) Harmonies that progress in locally functional ways, but within compositions in which a single tonic is uncertain, or
   b) Absence or suppression of functional harmonic progressions (such as V-I or ii-V-I) and/or use of alternative cadential progressions;
3) Common structure progressions, sometimes using stepwise motion in the bass (for example, BM7#11-CM7#11-DM7#11);

---

3. Henry Martin and James McGowan both adopt the term tonal jazz: see Martin's "Schenker and the Tonal Jazz Repertory," *Tijdschrift voor Muziektheorie* 16, no. 1 (2011): 1–20 and McGowan's "Dynamic Consonance in Selected Piano Performances of Tonal Jazz," PhD diss., University of Rochester, 2005. For more on tonal jazz, see later in this chapter.

4) Bass pedal points beneath shifting harmonies;

5) Characteristic harmonies, such as sus chords and slash chords, along with harmonies characteristic of earlier styles (major, minor, dominant, half-diminished); and

6) Harmonic rhythm with chord changes every half-measure, measure, or every two measures (occasionally alternating with sections of slower harmonic rhythm).

Many of the above characteristics are also common to the seminal works of Miles Davis and the John Coltrane Quartet often described as "modal" jazz (absence or suppression of functional progressions, bass pedal points over shifting harmonies, and characteristic harmonies such as sus chords and slash chords). But the final characteristic in the list above—the principle of generally regular harmonic rhythm—distinguishes postbop compositions from the so-called modal jazz compositions of Davis and Coltrane, which involve slower harmonic rhythm. Instead, postbop compositions maintained the regular harmonic rhythm of earlier song form, bebop, and hard bop compositions. But they did so without always maintaining the same conventions of cadence, form, and tonality.

The above point suggests degrees of continuity and discontinuity with tonal jazz traditions. Those who prefer to highlight elements of continuity may think a label such as postbop to be unnecessary. My position here is that the procedures of these postbop composers departed from those continuities in meaningful ways. This aligns this book with the work of writers such as Ron Miller and Wayne Naus, who emphasize significant and deep breaks with tradition in the hands of jazz composers after 1960.[4] But on the other hand, I should stress that some aspects of postbop harmony (and harmonic progression) might be thought of as transforming, rather than abandoning, earlier conventions. For example, some of the analyses in this book will use principles of harmonic substitution to show how unusual progressions transform more typical ones. Some analyses will show how one dimension of the music (such as melody) may take a familiar pathway while another dimension (such as harmony) does not. This helps explain, if only partially, something of the magic of this repertory: it often sounds inevitable or familiar, but defies predictability and cliché.

4. Ron Miller, *Modal Jazz: Composition & Harmony*, 2 vols. (Rottenburg: Advance Music: 1996), and Wayne Naus, *Beyond Functional Harmony* (Rottenburg: Advance Music, 1998).

PRECEDENTS

It is tempting to point to the many innovations of 1959 as an important catalyst for developments in 1960s postbop composition. Many writers have identified 1959 as a pivotal watershed year, in light of significant recordings such as John Coltrane's *Giant Steps* and Miles Davis's *Kind of Blue*.[5] Coltrane's composition "Giant Steps," in addition to some of his other compositions and arrangements during the late 1950s, explored transposition by M3 in systematic ways. Such axis progressions (that is, melodic or harmonic transposition by consistent interval) provided postbop composers with particular organizational methods, ones that sometimes bypassed more conventional tonal designs. The use of shifting harmonies above static bass pedal points, heard in Coltrane's "Naima" (also from *Giant Steps*), resonated for emerging postbop composers and tapped into an expanding vocabulary of pedal point chords (sometimes referred to as "slash" chords to describe their nomenclature: upper structure separated from bass pitch by a slash). Davis's *Kind of Blue* (along with his collaborations with Gil Evans) and Coltrane's 1960s recordings emphasized harmonic techniques that, while not new, would provide emerging postbop composers with significant points of departure. The use of fourth chords (including the so-called "So What" chord, consisting of perfect fourths with a M3 as the top interval), as well as sus chords (suspended fourth chords), provided more open and potentially more ambiguous sonorities than third-based chords.

From the standpoint of form, the Davis and Coltrane recordings were likely influential. "Giant Steps" was a single-section 16-bar composition without the repeated internal sections (such as AABA or ABAC) of song forms. Many of the compositions discussed in this book are single-section, and many of them expanded far beyond 16-bar designs, allowing a larger canvas and ongoing narrative without the internal repetition of constituent 8-bar sections heard in song forms. In addition, circular tunes, such

5. Darius Brubeck, "1959: The Beginning of Beyond," in *The Cambridge Companion to Jazz* (Cambridge: Cambridge University Press, 2002), 177–201. Brubeck provides some antecedents both for "Giant Steps" and *Kind of Blue* and cites additional significant recordings, publications, and events of 1959. For more on antecedents to "Giant Steps," see David Demsey, "Chromatic Third Relations in the Music of John Coltrane," *Annual Review of Jazz Studies* 5 (1991): 145–80, and Lewis Porter, *John Coltrane: His Life and Music* (Ann Arbor: University of Michigan Press, 1998), esp. 145–55. For a discussion of the precedents for Davis's so-called modal music, see Barry Kernfeld, "Adderley, Coltrane, and Davis at the Twilight of Bebop: The Search for Melodic Coherence," PhD diss., Cornell University, 1981, and Ashley Kahn, *Kind of Blue: The Making of the Miles Davis Masterpiece* (New York: Da Capo Press, 2000).

as "Blue in Green" (*Kind of Blue*) offered ways to heighten formal ambiguity by masking the returns to the top of the form, either through harmonic, melodic, or metrical groupings.[6]

But it would be misleading to suggest the 1959 recordings of Davis and Coltrane as the sole precedents for postbop composition. Tonal jazz compositions (American popular songs, as well as those written by jazz artists) typically exhibited an overall key within a song form, even when the first harmony differed from the closing harmony.[7] (For example, Irving Berlin's "Blue Skies" begins on the relative minor of the closing tonic harmony; George Gershwin's "Nice Work If You Can Get It" begins with a chain of dominant seventh chords, with the unambiguous tonic arriving only toward the end of the A section.) B sections offered interior modulations to closely or distantly related keys, but they operated within a global tonality, confirmed by cadences (often a half cadence on V or a full cadence on I) at the end of an 8-bar section.

There were early challenges to this single-key tradition. If the first four (or five) bars of Jerome Kern's "All the Things You Are" (1939) imply A♭ major (through vi-ii-V-I), that key is quickly challenged as the end of the first A section moves to C major (mm. 6–8). The second A (A′) section transposes mm. 1–8 up by fifth, ending on G major (mm. 14–16), and the B section corroborates G major before moving to E major. A linking harmony (m. 24) returns to the opening four bars, and only here in the final A″ section does the continuation unequivocally state A♭ major. Thus a clear section-ending cadence within A♭ appears only in the final bars of this composition. It is notable that the harmonic pathway—twisting and inconsistently supporting the final A♭ key at the ends of the interior A and B sections—occurs in a framework that challenges the usual 8-bar regularity of most song forms: the final A section is twelve, rather than eight bars.[8]

6. See Waters, *The Studio Recordings*, 74–76. It describes circular compositions as "composed in such a manner that, following the initial statement of the head, the top of the repeating chorus structure no longer sounds like the beginning of the form." It goes on to describe formal overlaps arising either through harmony (the m. 1 harmony continues a harmonic process begun near the end of the form), melody (the melody at m. 1 continues a melodic process begun near the end of the form), or hypermeter (irregular metric groupings suggest a continuation into the top of the form).

7. Ragtime compositions and early jazz compositions with ragtime strains usually express a single key until the modulation to the subdominant at the final strain.

8. For further discussion of "All The Things You Are," see Allen Forte, *The American Popular Ballad of the Golden Era, 1924–1950* (Princeton: Princeton University Press, 1995), 73–79, and Henry Martin, "Jazz Harmony: A Syntactic Background," *Annual Review of Jazz Studies* 4 (1988): 15–19.

David Raksin's "Laura" (written for the 1944 film *Laura*) is a 32-bar ABAC composition. The first half of the composition implies G major as its key, but does so surreptitiously. A series of stepwise downward ii-V-I sequences in G, F, and E♭ initially support the opening chromatic melody. Measures 13–16 imply G major through Am7 D7 Bm7(♭5) E7, linking back to the opening A minor harmony at the return to the second half. It includes the same stepwise sequence to E♭ before the second ending unequivocally moves to C major. The overall composition implies two keys (G and C major) rather than one, offering further challenges to the single-key tradition of American popular song.

By the late 1940s and early 1950s, bebop jazz composers were writing works whose harmonies frequently progressed conventionally (and in a manner that often suggested individual keys), yet the sense of an overall tonic was unclear. Thelonious Monk's "Ruby My Dear" (recorded initially in 1947) arguably implies a key of E♭ major, but the key is never confirmed by end-of-section cadences. The melodic/harmonic sequences of the A section are locally tonal (i.e., provide ii-V or ii-V-I progressions in different keys), but they do not collectively support a single underlying key. The A sections to Dizzy Gillespie's "Con Alma" (1954) likewise rely on melodic and harmonic sequences that are locally tonal: they tonicize E, E♭, D♭, and C. The idea of a single overarching tonic can only be determined on a first chord or last chord determination, rather than on any key-defining characteristics within the entire progression.

Other features heard in some postbop compositions had precedents earlier than 1959. Even within compositions whose overall tonality is generally clear, sequences of common-structure harmonies can undermine, if temporarily, a sense of key. For example, Bud Powell's "Un Poco Loco" (1951) includes a passage that uses a series of a common-structure harmonies: in mm. 9–16, the progression E♭M7♭5 D♭M7♭5 G♭M7♭5 CM7♭5 appears in parallel motion to the melody.

Some of Powell's compositions also offered an expanded harmonic vocabulary. "Un Poco Loco" (1951) tonicizes a major seventh harmony, with both raised eleventh and lowered ninth (at mm. 7–8 and 21–24). Powell's harmonic vocabulary is enhanced, but to a degree: some non-standard harmonies use standard upper structures with unconventional pitches in the bass.[9]

9. For example, the CM7(♭9, ♯11) voicing frequently used by Powell in "Un Poco Loco" is consistent with the upper structure of an A13 harmony (G-B-C♯-F♯). Even earlier precedents for nonstandard harmonies can be heard in Miles Davis's 1949–1950 recordings, later released as *Birth of the Cool*: the harmony heard at m. 40 of "Deception" (0:46) is a D major triad above an E♭ triad. Endings of compositions seemed to be a

In addition, there are any number of precedents for phrase groupings outside the conventional practice of 4- and 8-bar sections, beyond extensions at the ends of song forms ("I Got Rhythm" includes a 2-bar tag; "All the Things You Are" includes an additional four bars in its final A section). Even Charles Trenet's 1946 French chanson "La Mer" (imported into English as "Beyond the Sea") rendered consistent 6-bar phrases in a manner scarcely noticeable.

My point here is not to claim in all cases a direct one-to-one correspondence between postbop compositions of the 1960s and earlier ones. Such lines of direct influence are often difficult to substantiate. But it is more important to acknowledge that any number of earlier compositions embedded aesthetic and technical principles of likely interest to those composing in the 1960s. Therefore postbop composers tapped into broader ongoing traditions, highlighted by the landmark recordings of 1959, but with many techniques appearing well before that year. The 1960s compositions of Shorter, Hancock, Corea, and others often foregrounded these principles of tonal ambiguity, as well as of harmony, melody, and form.

TONAL, MODAL, AND POSTBOP JAZZ

Tonal Jazz. I use the term tonal jazz here to apply to jazz works that rely on particular harmonic procedures: functional harmonic progressions (often V-I or ii-V-I) that typically place cadences at important formal junctures. In addition, these works exhibit a fundamentally monotonal (single-key) environment, even when other keys might be implied or stated within that global key. Thus, tonal principles operate locally (through chord-to-chord successions) and globally (by expressing a single overall key). This description of tonal jazz addresses many jazz works up through the late 1950s, although the above commentary discussed how some pre-1950s compositions ("All the Things Your Are," "Laura") eroded those procedures. Tonal jazz, as used here, applies more aptly to repertories for small-group improvisation, than to larger, more-composed works for larger ensembles.

Undoubtedly, the use of the term tonal jazz to characterize traditions through the 1960s is broad and coarse. The term bypasses the finer stylistic distinctions that typically frame questions of jazz evolution. Such questions of style attend to details of improvisational technique, rhythm, accompaniment, instrumentation, and texture, as well as on the ways in which the

fertile location for nonstandard chords: the final harmony of Mulligan's "Venus de Milo" (also from *Birth of the Cool*) is indicated as $E\flat M7\sharp9$, the coda to the Brown/Roach Quintet's version of "Powell's Prances" (1956) begins with a C triad above a $D\flat$ bass.

music responded to or expressed larger social and cultural currents. The term tonal jazz implies broad similarities in harmonic progression and tonal organization that persist across multiple styles, despite improvisational, rhythmic, textural—or sociocultural—differences. Tonal jazz thus applies to the harmonic designs of jazz composition—its vocabulary (chord type) and syntax (chord progressions and techniques of closure)—rather than to style.

Nevertheless, the term tonal jazz does paper over some changes across styles, particularly details of harmonic rhythm and harmonic voicings. In his "Harmony" entry for *The New Grove Dictionary of Jazz*, Steven Strunk called attention to changes in harmonic rhythm through the 1950s: "The development of jazz harmony from early styles through the 1950s may thus be characterized as a general movement from simple to complex chord progressions and from a relaxed to a rapid rate of harmonic change."[10] Charlie Parker's "Blues for Alice," for example, provides an example of accelerated harmonic rhythm within a composition that still maintains the signal arrival points of a more conventional 12-bar blues.

Further, a more detailed account of progressive changes to tonal jazz through the 1950s would need to address stylistic (and individual) developments in harmonic extensions, alterations, and substitutions. If general classes of harmonies (major, minor, dominant, diminished, and half-diminished[11]) persevered in jazz and standard compositions, its specific vocabulary—harmonic voicings, extensions, alterations, and substitutions—varied greatly according to performer and style. Further, some syntactic conventions expanded through the 1950s.

10. Steven Strunk, "Harmony," entry in *The New Grove Dictionary of Jazz*, ed. by Barry Kernfeld (London: Macmillan: 1988), 494.

11. For a discussion of fundamental harmonies in jazz, see Laurent Cugny, *Analyser le jazz* (Paris: Outre Mesure, 2009), especially 168–74. Cugny cites John Mehegan, who identified five fundamental harmonies: Major 7th, Minor 7th, Dominant 7th, Diminished 7th, and Half-diminished 7th. To this, Cugny adds the Minor chord with Major 7th. Dariusz Terefenko instead sorts harmonies into four categories with functional implications: Major (tonic and predominant function), Minor (tonic and predominant function), Dominant 7th (dominant function), and Intermediary (predominant, dominant, and tonic: this category includes both fully and half-diminished sevenths) in *Jazz Theory: From Basic to Advanced Study* (New York: Routledge 2014), 39–42.

Historically, the half-diminished chord was sometimes labeled differently by different musicians. In his autobiography, Dizzy Gillespie referred to it as a minor sixth chord with the sixth in the bass, a harmony he learned from Thelonious Monk. See Dizzy Gillespie and Al Fraser, *To Be or Not to Bop* (Garden City, NY: Doubleday & Company, 1979), 134–35. The use of diminished triads or fully diminished seventh chords seems to have gradually receded in practice. For a discussion of the transformation of the original opening harmony to "Stella by Starlight" (from a diminished sonority on the tonic pitch to a half-diminished sonority on ♯IV), see Allen Forte, "The Real 'Stella' and the 'Real' 'Stella': A Response to 'Alternate Takes'," *Annual Review of Jazz Studies* 9 (1997–1998): 93–101.

For example, the use of tritone substitution with its downward half-step bass resolution fulfilled functional and cadential roles previously reserved for descending fifth bass motion. Changes in harmonic complexity and harmonic rhythm, then, as well as expanded possibilities for functional harmonies, responded to stylistic changes even while broader syntactic principles prevailed. Thus the term tonal jazz should in no sense be considered a static one. It merely addresses how overarching tonal principles (in particular, syntactic progressions and processes of closure usually occurring at or near the ends of 8-bar sections) largely persevered through the 1950s, despite shaded differences.

Most characterizations of tonal jazz harmony rely on at least two ingredients: a way to locate scale-step identity within a key (usually through Roman numerals) and a means to characterize cadences and progressions (usually through functional categories such as tonic, subdominant or predominant, and dominant). In the case of tonicization or modulation, these same principles apply to secondary keys. The following includes the work of two jazz theorists who provide a nuanced view of tonal jazz that moves beyond those two ingredients.

Dariusz Terefenko has described a series of paradigms for song form compositions in the standard-tune repertory.[12] He uses the term "phrase model" as a means to show how jazz standards rely on departure and return to a tonic harmony. (This is true even when compositions begin off-tonic, such as in "Autumn Leaves" or "I Hear a Rhapsody"). He is quick to acknowledge that these harmonic prototypes are flexible enough to allow harmonic and rhythmic variety. But his (diatonic and chromatic) phrase models are intended to show how single-key jazz standards (i.e., tonal jazz works) group into categories, typically by their opening and closing harmonic moves. He provides 13 phrase models. Nine models begin on tonic (I) and four begin off tonic. Table 1.1 summarizes them and includes some of his standard-tune examples. Note that the harmonic paradigms provided allow for further elaboration: for example, the opening to "Take the A Train" and "Mood Indigo" (Phrase Model 1) both elaborate the opening I-ii-V motion with a V7/V (or II7) harmony that follows I and precedes ii.

The models essentially classify song openings, since all phrase models conclude similarly (except for Phrase Model 13) in order to affirm the tonic key. It is tempting to add to these paradigms, including compositions

12. Terefenko, *Jazz Theory*. His discussion of phrase models appears at 289–322.

Table 1.1 TEREFENKO'S PHRASE MODELS

Phrase Models 1–5 (Diatonic Phrase Models)

Phrase Model 1: Begins I-ii-V, ends ii-V-I ("Take the A Train," "Mood Indigo," "Bye-Bye Blackbird")

Phrase Model 2: Begins ii-V (or II-V), ends ii-V-I ("Beautiful Love," "If I Were a Bell," "Our Love Is Here to Stay")

Phrase Model 3: Begins IV, ends ii-V-I ("Just Friends," "Love for Sale," "Remember")

Phrase Model 4: Begins I-vi-ii-V (an elaboration of Phrase Model 1, but with enough examples to justify a new model), ends ii-V-I ("I Got Rhythm," "A Foggy Day," "Stars Fell on Alabama")

Phrase Model 5: Begins vi, ends ii-V-I ("Blue Skies," "How Deep Is the Ocean," "I Hear a Rhapsody")

Phrase Models 6–13: Chromatic Phrase Models

Phrase Model 6: Begins I-ii/II-V/II-II (or I-ii/ii-V/ii-ii), ends ii-V-I ("But Beautiful," "Don't Blame Me," "East of the Sun")

Phrase Model 7: Begins I-ii/vi-V/vi-vi, ends ii-V-I ("Come Rain or Come Shine," "Georgia," "There Will Never Be Another You")

Phrase Model 8: Begins I-IV (often IV7), ends ii-V-I ("If You Could See Me Now," "Tenderly," "Willow Weep for Me")

Phrase Model 9: Begins I-ii/♭VI-V/♭VI-♭VI, ends ii-V-I ("Here's That Rainy Day," "You Stepped Out of a Dream," "What's New")

Phrase Model 10: Begins I-ii/♭II-V/♭II, ends ii-V-I ("Darn That Dream," "We'll Be Together Again," "Out of Nowhere")

Phrase Model 11: Begins I-ii/♭VII-V/♭VII-♭VII (usually continues to) ii/♭VI-V/♭VI-♭VI, ends ii-V-I ("How High the Moon," "Midnight Sun," "Star Eyes")

Phrase Model 12: Begins I-ii/iii-V/iii, ends ii-V-I ("I Remember You," "I Thought About You," "Someone to Watch Over Me")

Phrase Model 13 (Incomplete, Ends on V, often used in bridges): V/vi-V/ii-V/V-V (Bridge to "I Got Rhythm," "Nice Work If You Can Get It," bridge to "Perdido")

with chromatic bass motion from the first to fourth scale degree ("Ain't Misbehavin'," "Bewitched, Bothered, and Bewildered," "Mean to Me"). Terefenko also classifies bridge sections to AABA song forms (as well as the B and/or C sections of ABAC forms) by the key relative to the global tonic.[13]

The 13 phrase models provide one means to classify the tonal jazz repertory, or at least its AABA and ABAC song-form jazz standards. They rely on opening and closing harmonic motions, motions that frame the intermediary destinations that Terefenko refers to as "harmonic departures."

---

13. Terefenko, *Jazz Theory*, 326–30. Terefenko states that IV is the most common tonicized area at the beginning of a bridge section in AABA forms.

Not all his models include the cadences that occur near or at the ends of 8-bar phrases (half, full, or modulatory into a B or C section, usually at m. 7 or 8 of the phrase) and regulate the tonal flow. Most of his phrase models apply in major as well as minor keys. However, the vast majority of his phrase model examples (he includes far more compositions than those indicated above) are in major, rather than minor, keys. It illustrates a statistical likelihood for tonal jazz, an emphasis on major key over minor key works.

In a 1979 article Steven Strunk captures the landscape of harmonies and harmonic progressions that aid in articulating a single primary tonic key, and that may imported into subsidiary key areas.[14] His focus is on bebop compositions, by which he describes "not only the pieces composed by the performers themselves, but also those popular songs which, because of their harmonic structure, were selected as suitable vehicles for improvisation." He sets up a series of categories for harmonies that include substitutions. Some of these equate to standard functional categories of tonic, subdominant, and dominant, as indicated in Example 1.1.

Example 1.1. Strunk's I, IV, and V Sets

I set: I, iii7, vi7, ♯ivᵒ (in minor, i, IIIM7, VIM7)
IV set: IV, ii7 (in minor, iv, iiᵒ)
V set: V, vii°7, viiᵒ, ♭II7 (♭II7 also represented as V′, indicating tritone substitution)

In addition, he includes two other categories. The first is the iv set (Example 1.2), arising from "subdominant modal intensification." In a major key, these harmonies inflect the diatonic sixth scale degree to a flatted sixth scale degree, which then typically resolves downward by half-step to the fifth scale degree (often with a resolution to I or V). The conventional progression iv→VII7-I, then, is regarded as a progression that moves from the iv set (iv→VII7) to the I set.[15] This provides an alternative to considering iv→VII7 as a secondary ii-V group that necessarily implies ♭III. This iv set requires a major key environment, since its

Backdoor
V₇

14. Steven Strunk, "The Harmony of Early Bop: A Layered Approach," *Journal of Jazz Studies* 6 (1979): 4–53.
15. This idea of modally inflecting the subdominant IV chord (changing it to minor iv) is consistent with Strunk's early training at Berklee College of Music. Other jazz musicians informally refer to iv→VII as a "back-door" ii-V progression.

role is to transform that environment with harmonies borrowed from the parallel minor.

His final category is the ♯ii °7 set (Example 1.3): in the key of C, for example, this harmony is D♯ °7, and usually leads to C major (or to Dm7: in the latter case, the chord is sometimes instead represented as E♭ °7). Some analysts refer to this chord as a "common-tone" diminished seventh, which calls attention to the (at least one) common tone between it and its resolution, and distinguishes it from a vii°7-type chord, which typically has no common tones between it and its resolution. This category admits four substitutions, all dominant seventh chords obtained by lowering by half step any single pitch of the ♯ii °7 chord. In the key of C, for example, this yields D7, F7, A♭7, and B7. In the event these harmonies proceed directly to C, they may be heard as derived from D♯°7, with similar voice-leading tendencies. This provides a way of interpreting and equating harmonic moves such as I↓VI7-I ("I'm Beginning to See the Light," mm. 1–5) or I-VII7-I ("Groovin' High," mm. 1–5, or "Meditation," mm. 1–5).

Example 1.3. Strunk's ♯ii °7 Set

The ♯ii °7 set: ♯ii °7, II7, IV7, ♭VI7, VII7

If conventional views of harmony insist that dominant seventh chords typically operate as V7 chords of a stated or implied key,[16] Strunk's ♯ii °7 set admits a more flexible view, one sensitive to a jazz context. This set describes II7, IV7, ♭VI7, and VII7 (in the key of C, the network of chords containing D7, F7, A♭7, B7) as embellishing I in particular circumstances, rather than as secondary dominant chords that necessarily imply other keys, such as V7/V (i.e., D7), V7/♭VII (F7), V7/♭II (A♭7), or V7/iii (B7). Naturally, context is significant in every case: if the progression CM7-A♭7-CM7 represents the use of the ♯ii °7 set for A♭7, the progression

---

16. There are obvious exceptions, such as the use of dominant seventh chords on I and IV in blues idioms.

CM7-A♭7-G7-C indicates A♭7 as a tritone substitution for V7/V, indicated by Strunk as V'7/V.

Substitutions *within* all five sets (I, IV, V, iv, ♯ii °7) arise through common-tone principles, with the common tones preserving voice-leading tendencies of the chords for which they substitute. The ♭II7 harmony (or V'7), for example, maintains the third and seventh of the V7 chord. In the case of extended tertian harmonies, common tones are maximized: vii°7 shares all its pitches with V7♭9; vii^∅ all its pitches with V9.

Strunk also describes contrapuntal functions of chords. That is, bass motion may create passing, neighboring, or incomplete neighboring motion, all of which may be diatonic or chromatic. For example, with the progression iii-ii-I, the ii chord creates diatonic passing motion; with iii-♭iii-ii, the ♭iii chord creates chromatic passing motion. His example of a chromatic incomplete neighboring chord is the G♯7 harmony in the progression D-G♯7-A7.

Strunk's five substitution sets (I, IV, V, iv, ♯ii °7) therefore allow for further elaborations and expansions that explain many, if not most, of the chord-to-chord successions in the bebop repertory. One such elaboration appears in the opening progression to "Groovin' High," E♭M7-Am7-D7-E♭M7. In addition to the I chord (E♭M7) and a substitute from the ♯ii °7 set (D7), Strunk regards Am7 as an elaboration of D7.

These sets, then, provide a broad view of tonal jazz processes, and they expand a view of tonal function limited only to three categories of tonic, subdominant (or predominant), and dominant. Further, they can activate not only the primary tonic key of a composition, but secondary keys as well.

Of the eight compositions that Strunk fully analyzes in his article, seven of them are in major keys, and only one in a minor key. As with the Terefenko examples, it suggests a preponderance of major key compositions in jazz works through the 1950s.

Terefenko's phrase models and Strunk's substitution sets focus on general principles of tonal jazz, specifically harmonic progressions in single-key compositions through the 1950s. They are less concerned with details of harmonic rhythm, voicings, and characteristic extensions that often serve as markers of (either a general or an individual) style for jazz through the 1950s. Like most views of tonal jazz, both take as a starting point a single key, activated by harmonies on scale steps (indicated by Roman numerals) and a general view of harmonic progression that corresponds to tonic, subdominant (or predominant), and dominant. These apply not only to the main key of a composition, but also to subsidiary keys, either implied or stated. But in addition they offer a more fine-grained approach to tonal jazz through thirteen models that classify some song-form harmonic paradigms (Terefenko) or five harmonic categories that permit substitutions and elaborations (Strunk). Since harmonic conventions of tonal jazz compositions take place within a global regulating key, these writers offer a view of jazz tonality that is centripetal. *Cohesive*

Postbop composers inherited this legacy, but expanded it so that many of their compositions exhibited centrifugal forces, ones that did not always exhibit single-key design principles. Further, the decline in the use of standard tonal progressions is borne out by a statistical corpus study of jazz compositions from 1924 to 1968. In their study, Yuri Broze and Daniel Shanahan observed a marked historical decline in the use of dominant seventh harmonies as well as in the use of ii-V, V-I, and ii-V-I progressions.[17]

Modal Jazz. Like many other stylistic or technical terms related to jazz, modal jazz involves a network of features. Although the term itself refers to the notion that modes (or scales) provide the available pitches for improvisers (or accompanists), not all of its specific features involve the use of modes. Historians and analysts have singled out the late 1950s work of Miles Davis, in particular "So What" and "Flamenco Sketches" from *Kind of Blue* (1959), and sought precedents in earlier works such as "Milestones" (*Milestones*, 1958), as well as his 1957 soundtrack to the French film *Ascenseur pour l'échafaud* (*Elevator to the Scaffold*).[18] In addition, the John Coltrane Quartet recordings between 1960 and 1964, such as "Acknowledgement" (from *A Love Supreme*), "Impressions," "India," and "My Favorite Things" are considered exemplars of modal jazz.

Modal Jazz

Davis's interviews during the late 1950s, as well as pianist Bill Evans's liner notes to *Kind of Blue*, have contributed to a focus on scalar organization.[19]

---

17. Yuri Broze and Daniel Shanahan, "Diachronic Changes in Jazz Harmony: A Cognitive Perspective," *Music Perception* 31, no. 1 (September 2013), esp. 36 and 41. The authors question the assumption that 1959 marks the turning point for syntactic change, and their data ultimately points instead to 1956 as the watershed year.

18. Many of the points I make here are treated in further detail in Keith Waters, *The Studio Recordings of the Miles Davis Quintet 1965–68* (New York: Oxford University Press, 2011), 41–52. See also Jack Chambers, *Milestones: The Music and Times of Miles Davis* (New York: Da Capo, 1998), orig. publ. University of Toronto Press 1983 and 1985; James Lincoln Collier, *The Making of Jazz: A Comprehensive History* (Boston: Houghton Mifflin, 1978); Ekkehard Jost, *Free Jazz* (New York: Da Capo Press, 1994), orig. publ. Universal Editions, 1974; Ashley Kahn, *Kind of Blue: The Making of the Miles Davis Masterpiece* (New York: Da Capo, 2000); Andrea Pejrolo, "The Origins of Modal Jazz in the Music of Miles Davis: A Complete Transcription and a Linear/Harmonic Analysis of *Ascenseur pour l'échafaud (Lift to the Scaffold)*–1957" (PhD diss., New York University, 2001); Frank Tirro, *Jazz: A History*, 2nd ed. (New York: W. W. Norton, 1993).

19. Davis: "All chords, after all, are relative to scales and certain chords make certain scales. When you go on this way, you can go on forever. You don't have to worry about

These early characterizations undoubtedly caused some writers and historians to overemphasize the scalar/modal features, treating the music as if it is *purely* horizontal, or somehow devoid of an underlying harmonic framework.[20]

Critics of the term modal jazz have pointed out that slow harmonic rhythm is more crucial to modal jazz than the adherence to the pitches of a mode or scale. Since the improvisers on the Davis and Coltrane recordings do not necessarily limit themselves to the pitches of a particular mode, it is the infrequency of chord changes that more clearly defines that repertory.[21] This view shifts the emphasis away from improvisation and toward

changes and you can do more with the line. It becomes a challenge to see how melodically inventive you are." Hentoff, "An Afternoon with Miles Davis," in *Miles on Miles*, ed. by Paul Maher Jr. and Michael Dorr (Chicago: Lawrence Hill, 2009), 18. Originally published in *The Jazz Review* 1, no. 2 (December 1958): 11–12.

By the time of this interview Davis had enjoyed a decade-long friendship and association with the composer and theorist George Russell, whose treatise *The Lydian Chromatic Concept of Tonal Organization* likely formed the earliest impetus for equating scales with individual chords, and for using these scales as a repository of pitches for improvisation. First published in 1953, its second 1959 edition added musical examples and was more widely distributed. George Russell, *The Lydian Chromatic Concept of Tonal Organization for Improvisation*, 2nd ed. (New York: Concept Publishing, 1959).

Pianist Bill Evans wrote the liner notes for *Kind of Blue* (Columbia/Sony 64935), and his comments emphasize the modal/scalar aspects of two compositions. "So What," he wrote, is "based on 16 measures of one scale, 8 of another and 8 more of the first." Evans wrote about "Flamenco Sketches" that it "is a series of five scales, each to be played as long as the soloist wishes until he has completed the series." Cannonball Adderley's part to "Flamenco Sketches" appears in a photograph taken at the recording session to *Kind of Blue*. Published in 2000, the photograph shows five notated scales with the instructions to "play in the sound of these scales." Not all the five scales are visible in the photograph (Adderley's mouthpiece cap obscures the first and fifth scales). The second scale provides the pitches of E♭ dorian (modes indicated here are transposed from the E♭ key of the alto saxophone), and the third scale the pitches of B♭ major. The notes of the fourth scale are the mode of G harmonic minor that begins on D (D, E♭, F♯, G, A, B♭, C, D). See Kahn, *Kind of Blue*, 70.

20. Writing about "Milestones," James Lincoln Collier states that "it is built not on chord changes but on modes," in Collier, *The Making of Jazz*, 431. Similarly, Jack Chambers on "Milestones": "it is Davis's first completely successful composition based on scales rather than a repeated chord structure." Chambers also writes about *Kind of Blue* that "Davis's major contribution to jazz form, of which *Kind of Blue* stands as the most influential example, involves a principled shift from the constraints of chordal organization to the different constraints of scalar organization." See Chambers, *Milestones* I, 279 and 309. Like Bill Evans's liner notes for "So What" and "Flamenco Sketches," these views downplay the role of harmonic organization (provided by accompanists and potentially interpreted by the soloists) in favor of a distinctly scalar view of the music. They also do not address the manner in which soloists use pitches from outside any underlying scales/modes.

21. Barry Kernfeld, "Adderley, Coltrane, and Davis at the Twilight of Bebop: The Search for Melodic Coherence" (PhD diss., Cornell University, 1981), esp. 160–62. See also Barry Kernfeld, *What to Listen for in Jazz* (New Haven: Yale University Press, 1995), 67–69.

composition and accompaniment, and places the representative Davis and Coltrane modal jazz pieces within a broader jazz compositional tradition, including compositions with vamp-based organization and slow harmonic rhythm (such as Afro-Cuban grooves or "cubop" works such as Dizzy Gillespie's "Manteca," *montunos*, and funky jazz).

Since different listeners and writers consider modal jazz in different ways, it is perhaps most advantageous to consider modal jazz as a network of features that may appear in some combination, no one of which is definitive:

1. Modal scales for improvisation (or as a source for accompaniment)
2. Slow harmonic rhythm (single chord for 4, 8, 16, or more bars)
3. Pedal point harmonies (focal bass pitch or shifting harmonies over a primary bass pitch)
4. Absence or limited use of functional harmonic progressions (such as V-I or ii-V-I) in accompaniment or improvisation
5. Harmonies characteristic of jazz after 1959 (Suspended fourth—"sus"—chords, slash chords, harmonies named for modes: i.e., phrygian, aeolian harmonies)
6. Prominent use of melodic and/or harmonic perfect fourths.

A comparison with the list of postbop features discussed earlier shows a number of correspondences, but with the crucial distinction based upon slower vs. faster harmonic rhythm.[22]

All this makes clear that categories such as tonal, modal, or postbop jazz can be porous and malleable. Certainly many of the harmonic resources developed heard in Davis's *Kind of Blue* (and his collaborations with Gil Evans), and by Coltrane's classic quartet may be heard in postbop works with faster harmonic rhythm. Booker Little blended different rates of harmonic rhythm

22. Not all writers agree. Ron Miller identifies two categories of modal jazz composition: "modal simple" (applying to the modal jazz examplars discussed above: Davis's "So What" and Coltrane's "Impressions") and "modal complex" (applying to compositions with fast harmonic rhythm and freer forms, exemplified by the works of Wayne Shorter). Miller's "modal complex" category thus equates to the compositions described in this book as postbop.

For Miller, the two modal types belong to one of three larger categories of jazz composition: tonal, modal, and avant-garde. The modal designation for compositions of faster harmonic rhythm (Miller's modal complex) is likely due to Miller's equating all harmonies to modes. Ron Miller, *Modal Jazz: Composition and Harmony* (Rottenburg, Germany: Advance Music, 1996), 9.

Chord/scale equivalence provided a broad and successful pedagogical thrust in the wake of George Russell's work, especially through the evangelizing work of David Baker, Jerry Coker, and Jamie Aebersold.

within compositions, alternating between 8- or 16-bar vamp (or single harmony) sections and sections of faster harmonic rhythm. During the 1960s, Joe Henderson and Wayne Shorter continued to compose conventional 12-bar blues compositions along with postbop compositions exhibiting tonal ambiguity. Tonal cadences appear in Woody Shaw compositions that also use m3 axis progressions. It is likely that jazz composers and performers of the 1960s were more interested in exploring new resources in different ways, and less interested in categorical distinctions such as tonal, modal, and postbop. Nevertheless, maintaining a general and flexible sense of these terms provides a useful entry point when considering the music of these, and other, composers.

COLTRANE AND HIS LEGACY

Coltrane's "Giant Steps" is perhaps the most celebrated composition based on axis principles, and it works out M3 transpositional schemes in systematic ways. It is one of a number of Coltrane compositions (and reharmonizations) that explore such axis progressions, alongside "Exotica," "Satellite" (based on "How High the Moon"), "26-2" (based on "Confirmation"), and his arrangements of "Body and Soul" and "But Not For Me."[23] Other compositions, such as "Central Park West," used m3 axis progressions.

In "Giant Steps," the harmonic sequences are systematic and arrive at their stations regularly. This even caused its composer some concern. "I'm worried," stated Coltrane in the liner notes to the album *Giant Steps*, "that sometimes what I'm doing sounds just like academic exercises. . . ."[24] David Baker suggests that "Giant Steps" was "written in the manner of an etude"; Lewis Porter refers to it as a "thorough study, an etude" on major-third relationships.[25] And by all accounts Coltrane's tour de force improvisation emerged out of the result of seemingly countless hours of practicing,

23. For further discussion of Coltrane's axis compositions, along with precedents both in earlier compositions and in Nicolas Slonimsky's *Thesaurus of Scales and Melodic Patterns*, see David Demsey, "Chromatic Third Relations in the Music of John Coltrane," *Annual Review of Jazz Studies* 5 (1991): 145–80. Demsey also states that Coltrane's teacher at the Granoff School, Dennis Sandole, introduced Coltrane to progressions that involved equal subdivision of the octave. See also Masaya Yamaguchi and David Demsey, *John Coltrane Plays "Coltrane Changes"* (Milwaukee: Hal Leonard, 2003), 4–7.
24. *Giant Steps*, Atlantic 1311.
25. David Baker, *The Jazz Style of John Coltrane* (Lebanon, IN: Studio P/R, 1980): 37; Porter, *Coltrane*, 146.

providing a repository of melodic formulas that allowed the tenor saxophonist to skillfully negotiate the rigors of the harmonic progression.

"Giant Steps" investigated the M3 axis relationships in distinct ways. A lead sheet to "Giant Steps" appears as Example 1.4. The 16-bar composition is a single-section composition (i.e., without a bridge or repeated internal sections) in two halves. Measures 1–8 tonicize downward M3 axis points in two passes. The first pass at mm. 1–4 tonicizes B, G, and E♭; the second pass at mm. 5–8 is a sequence of the opening four measures and tonicizes G, E♭, and B. (Asterisks indicate these M3 axis arrival points.) And these tonicizations appear quickly—each pass tonicizes its keys one per measure via an intervening dominant chord. In contrast, the second half of the composition tonicizes its keys upwards. Initiated by the ii-V progression at m. 8, the keys progress E♭, G, B, E♭. The m. 16 turnaround then reverses direction, impelling the motion back to B again at the top of the form. In contrast to the first half of the composition, these tonicizations in the second half appear every two bars via an intervening ii-V progression. Here the ii-V progressions appear on weak measures (i.e., even-numbered measures, mm. 8, 10, 12, 14) and the major seventh harmonies of the M3 axis occur on strong measures (i.e., odd-numbered measures).

Example 1.4. Lead Sheet to "Giant Steps"

Thus, with downward M3 axis progressions of mm. 1–8 and upward progressions of mm. 9–16, the harmonic contour of the two halves contrasts decidedly. Each half completes the octave begun by its first chord. Measure 7 returns to B, which began the downward progressions at m. 1, and m. 15 returns to E♭, which began the upward progressions at m. 9. As many authors have noted, the fleeting ic4 harmonic sequences make the determination of a global key difficult, but the completed M3 axis progressions of B-B (first half) and E♭-E♭ (second half) in either half provide a type of tonal priority that outweighs G, and most concur with Henry Martin, who states "since the E♭M7 chord concludes the piece, it outweighs BM7 in structural significance.[26] But what is crucial to acknowledge is that it relies on symmetrical transposition patterns, patterns that erode more conventional tonal designs. Thus the question of a single-key tonic is here perhaps academic if E♭ is deemed tonic solely due to its position at the end of the composition, rather than to ongoing tonal processes throughout the composition. "Giant Steps" provided a crucial platform for postbop composition. It provided compelling organizational principles whose symmetries bypassed many of the conventions of tonal jazz.

Melodically, the two halves of the composition differ. The melodic sequence of mm. 9–16 (begun in m. 8),[27] shadows the harmonic sequence closely. The initial three-note idea (mm. 8–9, G-F-B♭) becomes duplicated up a major third. (This melodic sequence is foreshadowed in mm. 4–5.) The melody becomes transformed only slightly for the keys of B and E♭ (mm. 12–13 and 14–15). Thus the 2-bar harmonic sequences support the 2-bar melodic sequences.

However, the melody of the first half of "Giant Steps" is not as evidently sequential as the second half. The melody at mm. 1–4 is sequenced down by M3 mm. 5–8. Yet the consecutive M3 axes, supporting major seventh harmonies at mm. 1, 2, and 3 (as well as mm. 5, 6, and 7) do not support a sequential melody that obviously shadows the downward progression in this half of the composition.[28]

26. Henry Martin, "Jazz Harmony: A Syntactic Background," *Annual Review of Jazz Studies* 4 (1986): 25. David Demsey likewise proposes E♭ as the key of the piece.

27. This corresponds to Slonimsky's melody that accompanies the M3 axis progression in Nicolas Slonimsky, *Thesaurus of Scales and Melodic Patterns* (New York: Charles Scribner's Sons, 1947), vi.

28. This question of axis melody along with axis harmonic progressions invites considering the melodies to the antecedents for "Giant Steps" as well as to Coltrane's other M3 axis compositions, in order to evaluate whether those melodies appear as sequential or not. The melody to the bridge of "Have You Met Miss Jones" initially is sequential, with the 2-bar melodic sequence corresponding to the downward harmonic contour

All the above suggests that "Giant Steps" works out its M3 axis routines in a number of different manners: 1) through descending and ascending harmonic contours; 2) through length of harmonic sequence (appearing every bar, every two bars, or—by comparing mm. 1–4 and 5–8—every four bars); and 3) and melodic structure (which does not shadow the consecutive M3 axis sequences during the first half of the composition, but does during the second half). One manner in which the M3 sequences of "Giant Steps" are completely consistent involves chord quality: *each* of the M3 harmonic arrival points supports major seventh harmonies.

One of the ongoing stories of this book is that of the legacy and the transformation of "Giant Steps" and its axis frameworks. But in some compositions under discussion, not all dimensions of harmony, melody, and rhythm necessarily work together as systematically as they do at mm. 8–15 of "Giant Steps." For example, in Hancock's "Dolphin Dance" (mm. 1–17), Corea's "Inner Space" (Introduction and mm. 15–18), and Corea's "Song of the Wind" (mm. 24–36), the melodies involve M3 melodic axis progressions, yet the harmonies are not similarly sequential, and instead relate to systematic M3 transpositions through substitution principles. In some cases, stages along the M3 axis may not appear in metrically regular fashion. These examples show how postbop composers transformed the axis principles heard in "Giant Steps" since harmony, melody, and meter do not necessarily collaborate in similar lockstep fashion. Such adaptations make the axis organizational principles less mechanical and predictable, and provide a window into emerging compositional concerns of the 1960s.

After 1960, Coltrane moved away from those axis principles, and many of his quartet compositions rely on the slow-moving or static harmonic underpinnings associated with modal jazz. For Coltrane, whatever axis solutions "Giant Steps" offered ultimately became improvisational rather than compositional, through superimposing transpositional designs over slower-moving harmonies.[29] Thus while Coltrane stopped writing such

---

of the 2-bar harmonic sequence at mm. 17–20 (establishing the axis points of B♭, G♭, and D). Yet at the arrival of Dmaj7, marking the point where the harmonic contour reverses, the sequence ceases. The melody to Coltrane's "Countdown" is less sequential. As the harmonic contour descends, the melody ascends by M3 at the downbeats of mm. 2–3. The melody to mm. 3–4 shadows the harmonic progression somewhat more closely, with the M7 harmonies at the downbeats of mm. 3–4 elaborating consecutive fifths. The melody to mm. 10–12 further elaborates a melodic sequence based on M3 axis motion. Further, the ii-V progressions appear on weak (even-numbered) measures and the tonicized M7 harmonies on strong (odd-numbered) ones, like mm. 7–16 of "Giant Steps."

29. Lewis Porter describes the transition with pre-quartet compositions such as "Fifth House," during which Coltrane superimposes a M3 axis harmonic progression

harmonic sequences, his improvisations continued them over static harmonic fields, allowing a range of techniques for playing inside and outside the tonal centers.

The legacy of Coltrane's classic quartet also extended into elaborating an improvisational vocabulary for minor pentatonic scales, often with an emphasis on perfect fourths, as well as a harmonic vocabulary for stacked fourth chords.[30] These ideas were not new: minor pentatonic scales featured prominently in minor-mode funky jazz compositions, and arpeggiations of perfect fourths appear in the melody to John Carisi's "Israel" (1949, from Miles Davis, *Birth of the Cool*). But Coltrane's quartet foregrounded those materials, emphasized by the harmonic vocabulary of fourth chords (and their inversions) supplied by Coltrane's pianist McCoy Tyner. (Tyner's own 1962 recording, *Reaching Fourth*, called attention to that aspect of his playing.) Postbop compositions such as Shorter's "E.S.P" and "Witch Hunt," and Woody Shaw's "Beyond All Limits" made perfect fourths a central element of melodic design.

OTHER POSTBOP RESOURCES

All the above suggests that postbop composers tapped into a broad legacy. Other writers may be interested in further exploring points of aesthetic contact between the postbop composers discussed here and other composers. The works of Charles Mingus, Ornette Coleman, Bill Evans, Eric Dolphy, Andrew Hill, Freddie Hubbard, and others are linked to broader overlapping networks and shared aims of the 1960s composers showcased here. Further, that network extends to jazz composers working after the 1960s, including current ones. Although I don't examine those networks here, they would provide potent avenues of inquiry, both for composers prior to and during the 1960s (such as Mingus, Coleman, Dolphy, Hill, Hubbard, etc.) and composers during and after the 1960s (such as McCoy

over the static pedal point of the A sections during his solo. About using sequential cycles in his improvisations above the freer and more open underpinnings of his quartet, Coltrane stated, "At first I wasn't sure, because I was delving into sequences, and I felt that I should have the rhythm play the sequences right along with me, and we all go down this winding road. But after several tries and failures and failures at this, it seemed better to have them free to go—as free as possible. And then you superimpose whatever sequences you want to over them." See Porter, *John Coltrane*, 166.

30. See Porter, *John Coltrane*, 237–44 for a discussion of pentatonics and fourths in Coltrane's "Acknowledgement." Elsewhere in the book he discusses Coltrane's use of penatonics, at 151–52, 233–37, 242, and 295.

Tyner, Keith Jarrett, Richie Beirach, Dave Liebman, Steve Coleman, Maria Schneider, and many others). And undoubtedly some postbop strategies were retained by Shorter, Hancock, and Corea in their jazz-rock (or jazz-funk) fusion work of the 1970s.

The postbop solutions described in this book provided a working language for later jazz composers in flexible ways. Many blended tonal, modal, and postbop syntaxes, using them as creative prompts within and among compositions, without significant regard for syntactic purity. Thus, we may classify and clarify distinctions between syntaxes, which emerged through evolutionary processes. But evolution in no way should not be regarded as linear and one-dimensional. Instead it is fluid, branching, and with potential to move chronologically forward and backward—less conveyor belt and more garden of forking (and re-intersecting) paths.[31]

Beginning with Wayne Shorter, and following with Herbie Hancock, Chick Corea, and additional postbop composers (Booker Little, Joe Henderson, Woody Shaw), the following chapters chronicle postbop approaches that arose during a time of intense artistic ferment

31. For more on evolutionary perspectives, see chapter 6.

CHAPTER 2
Wayne Shorter

Wayne Shorter was one of the most prolific jazz composers of the 1960s, and his compositional career continued another half century. Between 1959 and 1964 he recorded as a leader, with Art Blakey and the Jazz Messengers, Lee Morgan and Thad Jones, and Wynton Kelly, and copyrighted fifty-three compositions (now contained at the Library of Congress).[1]) In many ways, Shorter's sixteen compositions recorded by Miles Davis's Second Classic Quintet from 1965 to 1968 helped engender the quintet's open sound on their studio recordings. In addition, he wrote most of the compositions for a series of eleven significant *Blue Note* albums made under his own name from 1964 to 1970.

Regarding Shorter's compositional predecessors:

Finally, while it is difficult to itemize specific compositional influences on Shorter, it is possible to speak of shared compositional priorities with other jazz composers. Certainly a motivic focus and nonstandard harmonic progressions also apply generally to the compositions of Thelonious Monk. The use of blues-based or minor pentatonic melodic motives recalls the compositions of Charles Mingus and John Coltrane. In addition, Booker Little's compositions, written between 1958 and 1961, show a similar interest in forms outside AABA and ABAC frameworks, unusual section lengths, and a harmonic language that

1. See Patricia Julien, "The Structural Function of Harmonic Relations in Wayne Shorter's Early Compositions: 1959–63," PhD diss., University of Maryland, 2003.

makes use of hard bop progressions alongside more unusual and ambiguous progressions.[2]

Shorter's compositions are intriguing, elusive, and often harmonically ambiguous. The earlier works often rely on strong, memorable melodic motives supported by harmonic progressions that, while rooted in the hard bop tradition, nevertheless frequently move in unconventional ways that defy cliché. For example, "Sakeena's Vision" (Art Blakey and the Jazz Messengers, *The Big Beat*; see Discography for more information) resolves to its final G minor harmony through Fm7 to E7; "Sincerely Diana" (Blakey, *A Night in Tunisia*) moves to its final B♭ minor harmony via a ii-V progression, D♭m7 to G♭7, a half-step above the usual cadential progression to B♭. Many of Shorter's early works make use of ii-V (or ii-V′) progressions that resolve unusually. Often, Shorter uses pedal point harmonies or slower harmonic rhythm to distinguish sections of AABA compositions: "One by One" (Blakey, *Ugetsu*), "This Is For Albert" (Blakey, *Caravan*), and "Yes and No" (Shorter, *JuJu*) rely on pedal point (and slower moving) harmonies during the A sections, while the B sections provide a release with more active harmonic and melodic motion.

There are ways in which Shorter's compositions after 1964 differ from the 1959–1963 compositions. Some ("Masqualero," from Miles Davis, *Sorcerer*) rely on the slower harmonic rhythm typically associated with modal jazz. Others ("Witch Hunt," Shorter, *Speak No Evil*) contrast sections of slower harmonic rhythm with sections that offer a more consistent and regular harmonic rhythm. Most, however, rely on a more regular harmonic rhythm similar to other postbop compositions discussed in this book. Like the earlier works, the works recorded after 1964 still rely on clear evident melodic motives, either using one primary motive ("Infant Eyes," from Shorter, *Speak No Evil*; "Footprints," Shorter, *Adam's Apple*; "Fall," Miles Davis, *Nefertiti*; "Dolores," Davis, *Miles Smiles*) or two ("Deluge," "House of Jade," "Mahjong," all three from Shorter, *JuJu*; "Limbo" and "Prince of Darkness," both from Davis, *Sorcerer*; "Pinocchio," Davis, *Nefertiti*). These later works continue Shorter's trend of writing single-section compositions, either with 16-bar or with less regular formal sections. Nearly all Shorter's compositions written for the Miles Davis Quintet are single-section compositions: "Pinocchio" is 18 bars, "Dolores" is 22 bars, "Vonetta" (Davis,

---

2. Keith Waters, *The Studio Recordings of the Miles Davis Quintet, 1965–68* (New York: Oxford University Press, 2011), 29–30. This chapter compresses some of the same points made in the Davis book about Shorter's earlier compositions, and revisits Shorter's "Pinocchio."

Nefertiti) is 15 bars and includes a 5/4 measure. Some conventional song forms (AABA, ABA, AA′BA) use sections that do not always adhere to 8-bar groupings.[3] Stylistically, they range between standard walking bass 4/4 feels at different tempos, ballads, jazz waltzes, funky jazz tunes, and more freely conceived compositions (such as those heard on *The All Seeing Eye*).

The chapter begins with a consideration of features of some of Shorter's earlier works, in particular the use of axis progressions in "Children of the Night" (Blakey, *Mosaic*) and "El Toro" (Blakey, *The Freedom Rider*), as well as elasticized phrases in "Virgo" (from *Night Dreamer*, Shorter's first Blue Note recording). A discussion of "Penelope" (Shorter, *Etcetera*) and "El Gaucho" (Shorter, *Adam's Apple*) follows: harmonically, formally, and stylistically those two compositions diverge, but they nevertheless both begin with the same melodic phrase, offering a window into Shorter's reharmonizations of similar melodic materal. Shorter recorded "Pinocchio," an 18-bar single-section composition, with the Davis Quintet (*Nefertiti*). The final composition discussed in the chapter is "Face of the Deep" (*The All-Seeing Eye*), written for four horns and rhythm section, which uses an extended harmonic language largely based on upper structure triads above bass pitches.

SOME PRELIMINARIES: EARLIER WORKS

"Children of the Night." Ultimately it is difficult to summarize or condense Shorter's rich and varied compositional output.[4] Certainly even Shorter's early works reflect a deep fascination with principles that were to shape many of his 1960s compositions. His "Children of the Night," recorded with Blakey (*Mosaic*, 1961), involves both pedal point progressions as well as a m3 axis progression. It begins by alternating F♯m7/B (or Bsus11) with GM7(♯11)/B in mm. 1–8. The use of the latter harmony creates an Aeolian progression (since GM7(♯11)/B inflects the pitches of B Aeolian), a progression that also appears in a number of Hancock compositions. (See chapter 3.) Following, mm. 9–13 move along a m3 axis with intervening

---

3. Waters, *The Studio Recordings of the Miles Davis Quintet*, 28, identifies nineteen single-section Shorter compositions written between 1959 and 1964. The book also discusses a number of Shorter compositions recorded with Davis.

4. Patricia Julien and Steven Strunk have focused on harmonic progression in Shorter's works, especially unusual progressions, unexpected chord qualities with functional progressions (such as the use of minor dominant chords), and the use of progressions that create stepwise motion in the bass. Patricia Julien, "The Structural Function of Harmonic Relations in Wayne Shorter's Early Compositions: 1959–1963," PhD diss., University of Maryland, 2003; and Steven Strunk, "Notes on Harmony in Wayne Shorter's Compositions," *Journal of Music Theory* 49, no. 2 (2005): 301–32.

ii-V progresssions (EbM7/ Dm7 G7/ CM7/ Bm7 E7/ AM7). The melody is sequential, transposed down by m3 in accord with the harmony. The composition's closing progression (DM7 C#m7 F#7 BM7) recalls the m3 axis progression. Here the melody is not sequential, but relies on a common tone (F#, decorated with G) to link the m3-related harmonies. Shorter often relies on both melodic techniques—sequential melody or common-tone melodic connections—for axis progressions. In other cases, chromatic voice-leading (a half-step melodic shift that coincides with a change of harmony) supports such harmonic progressions.

"El Toro." Shorter's most thorough exploration of axis progressions appears in "El Toro" (Art Blakey and the Jazz Messengers, *Freedom Rider*), which systematically takes up the M3 axis principles of Coltrane's "Giant Steps." The relationship to Coltrane's "Giant Steps" is unmistakable.[5] Like "Giant Steps," it is a 16-bar composition, and—characteristic of many Shorter compositions—it is a single-section composition (without repeated internal sections or a bridge).[6] In "El Toro," however, the M3 processes operate alongside others, particularly those at mm. 1–4 that establish D minor, and set up a large scale tonal motion from D minor (expressed with a functional harmonic progression) to Db major (maintained through downward motion along a M3 axis).

Despite the relationship to "Giant Steps," there are nevertheless aspects of its design that challenge an evident 8 + 8 design and create formal wrinkles that provide some ambiguity. The result creates a sense of metric elasticity, a hallmark of many Shorter compositions, including both those with 4- and 8-bar groupings, as well as those with less-regular phrase groupings.

A lead sheet for "El Toro" appears as Example 2.1.[7] The opening 4-bar phrase in D minor is answered by a harmonic shift to Db major in mm. 5–7. The second half of the composition tonicizes a series of M3-related major seventh chords (shown by asterisks in the example), moving from A (m. 9), to F (m. 11), and to Db (m. 13). Measure 15 returns to A. Like mm. 8–15 of "Giant Steps," the mm. 8–15 harmonic sequences of "El Toro" appear every two bars. Also like mm. 8–15 of "Giant Steps," the tonicized M3-related chords occur on strong measures (i.e., the odd-numbered

---

5. Shorter himself described visits to Coltrane in late 1958 or early 1959 and hearing Coltrane practice "Giant Steps" progressions. See Lewis Porter, *John Coltrane: His Life and Music* (Ann Arbor: University of Michigan Press, 1999), 151.

6. For more on Shorter and single-section compositions, see Waters, *The Studio Recordings*, 27–28.

7. Patricia Julien discusses "El Toro" in "The Structural Function of Harmonic Relations in Wayne Shorter's Early Compositions," 175–86. The lead sheet and some of my points are indebted to her very fine analysis.

measures), and the intervening ii-V progressions on weak measures (i.e., the even-numbered measures). Unlike mm. 8–15 of "Giant Steps," the harmonic contour of the 2-bar sequences descends rather than ascends.[8]

Example 2.1. Lead Sheet to "El Toro"

Along with the M3 axis harmonic progression, there is a 2-bar melodic sequence also transposed downward by M3, beginning at m. 8 and continuing until m. 13 (the melodic sequence is varied in m. 12), with #4-5 melodic motion above the M7 harmonies (D#-E, m. 9, B-C, m. 11, G-G#, m. 13). Further, while m. 13 advances the melodic #4-5 motion (against the bass) heard in mm. 9 and 11, it does so more leisurely, as the G# holds across mm. 14–15, becoming the common tone with the AM7 harmony at m. 15.

By foreclosing the melodic sequence at mm. 14–15, Shorter abandons the patent 8 + 8 measure design heard in "Giant Steps" in those same

8. Further, the final turnaround is one that appears in a number of Shorter compositions, with a ii-V progression appearing a half-step higher than a typical turnaround. The final harmony here, a ♭VI7 (B♭7), operates as a V'/V harmony (in European classical music, this would be described as an augmented sixth harmony) leading directly—without an intervening structural dominant chord—to the opening D minor harmony at the top of the composition.

measures. Further, this points to a wrinkle that projects a decided degree of formal ambiguity. The melodic cadence to G♯ anticipates the sixth bar of the 8-bar subsection, appearing just before m. 14. Its placement works against song-form traditions, which typically locate the melodic cadence at the point of tonic arrival, usually two bars before the end of the composition (or in the final bar of the composition if the return to tonic appears there, as with 32-bar compositions based on rhythm changes). Thus the harmonic cadence to AM7 in bar 15 resonates with tonal jazz practice (occurring two bars before the end of the composition), but the melodic cadence is not coordinated with it, and appears one bar earlier than where the melodic cadence normally occurs in song forms. As a result, the melodic arrival (to G♯, anticipating m. 14) is out of phase with the harmonic arrival (to AM7, m. 15).[9] (Shorter used a similar effect in his later 16-bar composition "Nefertiti," whose melodic cadence occurs in the same location, anticipating m. 14 by an eighth note.) Further, the shift to walking bass occurs in m. 8, skewing the sense of 8 + 8 measure regularity. The underlined harmonies in Example 2.2 are intended to show how those features crosscut the 8 + 8 design, beginning with the shift to walking bass (m. 8) and ending with the melodic cadence arriving one bar early (anticipating m. 14).

Example 2.2. Harmonic Progression to "El Toro" (Walking bass begins m. 8, melodic cadence anticipates m. 14)

Dm7	F7	Em7(♭5)	A7	E♭m7	A♭7	D♭M7	Bm7 E7
m. 1	2	3	4	5	6	7	8*

AM7	Gm7 C7	FM7	E♭m7 A♭7	D♭M	E7	AM7	Fm7 B♭7
9	10	11	12	13	14**	15	16

*= Begins walking bass
** = Melodic cadence (anticipated by eighth note; appears one bar earlier than harmonic cadence)

This provides much of the intrigue and ambiguity of the composition, particularly in its second half. Gone is the systematic etude-like 8 + 8 regularity of "Giant Steps." Hearing the composition this way highlights the manner in which Shorter weaves formal asymmetry into the regular 16-bar form during the head statements.

Metric Elasticity in "Virgo." The technique described above shows an elasticity, even within consistent 16-bar forms such as that of "El Toro."

9. The melodic cadence leading to m. 14 sounds far more definitive than the G heard in the final measure 16, since G♯ lasts significantly longer than does G.

Elsewhere, elasticity is provided by irregular phrase lengths. "Infant Eyes," for example, is an ABA form consisting of three 9-bar sections. It is dominated by a single 2-bar rhythmic motive (stated four times in each section). The ninth bar provides a link between the A and B sections, and between the B and A sections. In both cases, that ninth-bar link uses a functional dominant harmony (mm. 9–10, B♭7-E♭M7; mm. 18–19, D7-Gm7). This points to a significant postbop practice of departing from conventions in one dimension (in this case by avoiding 8-bar metrical regularity) while realizing them in another (by using V-I cadences to link the 9-bar segments).

"Virgo" (*Night Dreamer*) likewise shares irregular phrase groupings. An ABAC composition, it is 29 bars. While its first A and B sections are 16 bars, the following A and C sections together consist only of 13 bars. Example 2.3 is not a lead sheet, but includes framing melody and harmonic progressions in order to show some significant details. Note the first two phrases (mm. 1–4, 5–8) are roughly parallel. Both begin with the same motive (transposed at m. 5; consisting of a downward P5 leap, followed by stepwise motion upward by m3). Both 4-bar phrases close with a similar m3 descent (G-E, mm. 3–4; C-A, mm. 7–8) that in both cases announces an arrival on a M7 harmony (AM7 m. 4, DM7 m. 8).

Example 2.3. Phrase Groupings in Shorter's "Virgo" (mm. 1–20 = 4-bar groupings)

Mm. 9–16 differ. M. 9 uses a different opening and closing motive. The arrival on G minor (m. 12) includes a phrase overlap in the melody that pushes the melodic phrase into the next four bars (mm. 13–16). There the m. 1 opening motive recurs in varied form (m. 13), and the phrase concludes with a D♭m7 G♭7 (ii′7 V′7) that returns the phrase to the opening FM7 harmony.

It is in the A′ portion of "Virgo" that the phrase groupings vary. This becomes evident at mm. 21–29, during the second ending. There is a rhetorical and dramatic effect brought about the repetition of the m. 23 motive, heard above a series of ii-V′ (mm. 23 and 24) or ii-V (m. 25) sequences. The repetition of the motive creates a static pitch field (A-D-F-A-C) above the active progressions. These sequences resolve at m. 26 to B♭M7, which recalls the descending m3 melodic cadence shown by the brackets, heard at mm. 4 (G cadences to E) and 8 (C cadences to A). Those melodic cadences began as "bar 4" events during the first two 4-bar phrases, but now return through repetition at mm. 24, 25, and 26 (shown by brackets). The repeated motive creates a 6-bar phrase, emphasized by the stop time played by the rhythm section during head statements at mm. 24 and 25.

Finally, the composition ends with a 3-bar phrase. A more conventional close might even out the phrase to occupy four bars, most likely by slowing the harmonic rhythm of mm. 27 to two bars, and decelerating the melodic pace. (Virtually all of the "bar 1" events in "Virgo" have one harmony rather than two.) Example 2.4 compares "Virgo" with that more hypothetical harmonization. The comparison suggests that the 3-bar phrase contracts what would be a more conventional 4-bar harmonization.[10]

Example 2.4. Comparison of mm. 27–29 Harmonies of "Virgo" with Hypothetical 4-bar Harmonization

"Virgo" (3 bars)	E7alt A7alt	Dm7	Gm7 C7	
Hypothetical (4 bars)	E7alt	A7alt	Dm7	Gm7 C7
m.	27	28	29	(Hypothetical m. 30)

The above is meant to show some of Shorter's departures from 4-bar conventions. In "Virgo," the 6-bar phrase at mm. 21–26 is an expanded phrase that arises through motivic repetition; the 3-bar phrase may be considered a condensed phrase against the backdrop of a more-conventional 4-bar treatment. Odd-numbered bar groupings (such as the 9-bar

10. The final four bars of "Black Nile" (from the same recording as "Virgo," Shorter's *Night Dreamer*) provide a comparison with regular 4-bar groupings. In its closing progression (B♭M7/E♭7/Dm7/E♭7) the arrival harmony (Dm7) appears in the third bar of a 4-bar progression, as it does in the hypothetical 4-bar closing harmonization to "Virgo" shown in Example 2.4.

phrases of "Infant Eyes" and the 3-bar closing phrase of "Virgo") seem to appear more frequently in Shorter's slower compositions. In faster compositions, departures from 4-bar conventions often appear as 6-bar phrases (as in "El Gaucho" and "Pinocchio," discussed below).

ANALYSIS 1: "PENELOPE" AND "EL GAUCHO"

There would seem to be drastic differences between "Penelope," Shorter's slow jazz waltz featuring a dense harmonic vocabulary and a winding chromatic melodic line (recorded in 1965 and eventually released on *Etcetera*), and "El Gaucho," a straight-eighth jazz composition, consisting solely of M7, m7, and dominant-type harmonies, and whose melody largely expresses minor pentatonic collections (recorded in 1966 and released on *Adam's Apple*). Yet both compositions begin with the same 4-bar melodic line. Shorter elected to refit that line to drastically different surroundings in the later version.

Given that, the difference between the two compositions shows an astonishing degree of flexibility in reworking similar opening melodic material. Here, although the melodic material is relatively fixed, its harmonic environment is entirely fluid and malleable. Example 2.5 includes the mm. 1–4 harmonies and melody for each. (In Example 2.5 I transpose the chords of "Penelope" up a step to match the key of "El Gaucho": with the exception of the first two pickup notes, the pitches are the same.)

Example 2.5. Comparison of mm. 1–4 of "Penelope" and "El Gaucho" ("Penelope" transposed)

The opening harmonies for both share the same root, yet their quality differs. "Penelope" begins with a minor-mode chord (with raised seventh) and "El Gaucho" a major-mode harmony. Further, "Penelope" highlights the postbop technique of shifting harmonies above bass pedal points throughout the opening four bars. Its harmony at m. 2

significantly marks the four bars: B♭M7/F creates a color shift to an implied major mode above the bass, flanked between by the mm. 1 and 3 minor
mode harmonies. "El Gaucho," on the other hand, becomes unmoored
from its opening FM7 harmony, as the bass steps downward to the relative harmony Dm7, all before the faster harmonic rhythm establishes a
series of dominant harmonies.

Such harmonic differences between the two compositions indicate the
depth of Shorter's reharmonization capabilities. For Shorter, the same
melodic phrase carries no fixed harmonic obligations, but allows radically
different solutions, tailored for the type of composition (slow jazz waltz
vs. faster straight-eighth 4/4) at hand. What is retained between the two
compositions involves merely the intervals of the phrase, and its fixed location as the opening phrase to both.

A lead sheet for "Penelope," in the key from the recording, appears as
Example 2.6. Although a 32-bar AABA composition, the A sections create an
asymmetry that works against an evident 4 + 4 bar segmentation. The melodic line is written so that the end of the first phrase's melodic line extends
into m. 5. The following melodic idea begins at m. 6. Thus the opening phrases
create a 5 + 3 bar grouping that crosscuts its 4-bar regularity.

Example 2.6. Lead Sheet to "Penelope" (AABA Form)

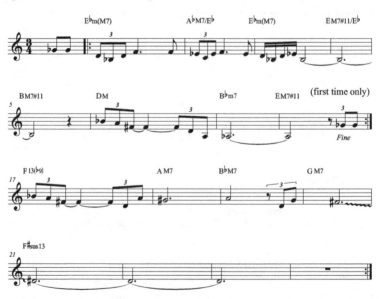

If the use of bass pedal point at mm. 1–4 offers one characteristic postbop technique, the harmonic connection between mm. 4–5 offers another, an upper structure progression. Here the upper structure harmony at m. 4 (EM7♯11) shares the same pitches as that of F♯9(13). Rather than a conventional cadence of F♯9(13) to BM7 at mm. 4–5, the EM7(♯11)/E♭ harmony preserves the upper structure of F♯9(13) but alters the bass pitch. As a result, the progression echoes a more functional cadence, but the bass pitch at m. 4 avoids the more predictable cadential path. The technique, then, suggests how upper structure harmonies fulfill tonal obligations, but the bass pitches avoid evident V-I motion.[11]

The following 3-bar phrase no longer relates to the melody of "El Gaucho." It also makes clear two melodic voice-leading techniques used by Shorter: chromatic motion and common-tone connections. In each instance, they link different harmonies and clarify more-remote harmonic connections. For example, the B♭ that ended the phrase at mm. 4–5 becomes brought up an octave and led down by half-step to A (m. 6). (This B♭-A motion, heard over D major, is a marked detail of the piece and is recalled at the opening to the B section.) That A, through arpeggiation, is brought down an octave and led by half step to A♭ (m.7). The final connection, between mm. 7–8, is a common tone one that sustains the A♭.

These voice-leading techniques are compelling. In some instances, they match the pathway of the upper-structure harmonies, as at mm. 6–7: the A to A♭ melodic motion follows the upper-structure harmonies of D major to D♭ major (the latter formed by the upper structure of the Bbm7 chord at m. 7). The A♭ melodic common-tone connection between the tritone-related B♭m7 and EM7(♯11) is one that Shorter uses in other compositions with similar progressions.[12] Harmonically, the m. 8 EM7(♯11) links back to the m. 1 E♭m(♯7) as ♭IIM7 (or V′M7).

The B section begins by continuing the chromatic voice-leading connections. M. 17 recalls the melody of m. 6. Here, however, it appears at the beginning of a 4-bar unit (rather than as at m. 6, which begins a 3-bar phrase following a 5-bar one). The melody begins as B♭-A (m. 17), which moves to G♯ (m. 18), and returns to A (m. 19). The upper-structure

11. Some listeners may prefer to hear this not as an altered V-I cadence, but as an altered IV-I cadence. In that case, the EM7♯11/E♭ operates as a third-inversion IV chord. Shorter uses this IV-I cadence (in the same key) at mm. 13–14 of "Infant Eyes," with a direct (root position) EM7♯11 to BM7 progression.

12. For example, "Yes and No" similarly uses a common tone to link tritone-related pairs of M7 and m7 chords at mm. 11–14 (B♭M7-Em7, with common tone D) and mm. 29–32 (at the end of the bridge, E♭M7-Am7, with common tone G). Mm. 9–12 of "JuJu" use a similar progression (FM7-Bm7), but without the common tone melodic link.

harmonies often proceed in similar fashion. For example, mm. 17–18 includes a move from upper structure D major to upper structure C♯ minor (the latter the upper structure of the AM7 chord at m. 18). The melodic motion at mm. 18–19 is mirrored precisely, as the G♯-A follows the AM7-B♭M7 progression.

The melody at mm. 19–21 does not continue the same chromatic path. Instead, it moves along the m3 axis, from A-F♯-D♯. The harmonies at mm. 19–20 likewise proceed along that axis, from B♭M7 to GM7. While the bass at the m. 21 harmony (F♯sus13) does not continue along that axis to EM7, the upper structure harmony of the F♯sus13 (or EM7/F♯, heard mm. 21–24) does supply that EM7. The bass (F♯) then avoids the more predictable pathway, while the upper structure EM7 takes it, creating an upper structure progression that participates in the m3 harmonic axis of B♭M7-GM7-EM7.

Downward motion along the m3 axis clearly had some appeal for postbop composers. In "Children of the Night," Shorter used a progression that tonicized E♭M7, CM7, and AM7 via intervening ii-V pairs (see above). And a similar pathway becomes the opening premise for Chick Corea's "Litha." (See chapter 6.) Direct downward m3 progressions of M7 harmonies, such as at mm. 19–21 of "Penelope," have a particular tonal effect that we might describe as a Picardy effect (in eighteenth-century European music, the Picardy third transformed a minor triad into a major triad, often at the end of a composition). The Picardy effect here can be understood by way of a substitution relation. For example, in "Penelope" the first chord of the B♭M7-GM7 progression may be understood as equivalent to the upper structure of a rootless Gm9 chord. The subsequent move to GM7 provides a brightening effect, a discharge brought about from the implied minor to major alteration, as shown in Example 2.7.

Example 2.7. Picardy Effect from Descending m3 Motion

Actual Harmony	B♭M7	GM7
Actual Harmony is Rootless version of:	Gm9	GM7

The motion from GM7 to F♯sus13 has a similar effect. Although the bass does not move down by m3, the upper structure does (i.e., via the progression GM7 to EM7/F♯): again the Picardy effect comes about through the brightening that arises from the same relationship—GM7 forms the upper structure of a rootless Em9 harmony that transforms into EM7 (above the bass F♯): the pitches G and D of GM7 become raised to G♯ and D♯ of EM7/F♯.

The m3 orientation of the melody underscores the m3 axis progression of B♭M7 to GM7 to F♯sus13 (or EM7/F♯) at mm. 19–24, with the last two chords involving an upper structure progression. Yet another type of upper structure progression leads from the upper structure of that chord back to the E♭m(♯7) chord at the beginning of the A section—EM7 links to E♭m(♯7) as ♭II-i, while the EM7 contains F♯ in the bass at mm. 21–24.

"El Gaucho" reuses the opening 4-bar phrase of "Penelope" but offers a radically different attitude in tempo, meter, feel, harmonic strategy, and form. "El Gaucho" is an 18-bar single section composition. It does without the slash chord harmonic vocabulary of "Penelope." Once the opening four bars are stated, it relies on minor pentatonic fragments to link the harmonies.

Both, however, rely on asymmetrical groupings that work to undermine an underlying 4-bar regularity. "Penelope" does so through its 5 + 3 phrase melodic grouping of the A section. As shown by the lead sheet in Example 2.8, "El Gaucho" organizes into 4 + 6 + 8 bars, whose elasticity is heightened by the mid-bar harmonic arrivals at mm. 8 and 14.

Example 2.8. Lead Sheet to "El Gaucho"

"El Gaucho" does not return to the m. 1 harmony at m. 3 (as did "Penelope") but instead creates a stepwise progression to the relative minor harmony of D minor, before launching a sequence of dominant harmonies that twice feature upward chromatic motion (B♭7-B♭9 and E7alt-Fm7).[13] The first relies on the melodic common tone (C, mm. 3–4), and the second begins as a pickup that introduces the pentatonic fragment that inhabits the second phrase at mm. 5–10.

This second phrase melody relies solely on the pitches F-A♭-B♭, with the characteristic Shorter harmonic maneuver of alternating a minor harmony with a major seventh a half-step above. Locally this creates a i-♭IIM7-i tonal move then undermined by the G♭M7-E♭M7 progression (mm. 8–10), supported by the melodic F common tone.[14] This downward m3 transposition of parallel structure chords creates the Picardy effect described above in relation to mm. 19–20 of "Penelope." (That is, the G♭M7 may be heard as a rootless E♭m9 harmony, with the Picardy discharge coming from the progression to E♭M7.)

The final phrase transposes the pentatonic fragment heard at mm. 5–10, but its relation to the underlying harmony differs from the previous phrase. The A-C-D pitches support at first a Cm7 harmony, as sixth, root, and ninth (the previous phrase began by supporting Fm7 with F-A♭-B♭ melody as root, third, and fourth).[15] That Cm7 harmony is cognate to its preceding relative major harmony (E♭M7), and alternates with Dm7, a stepwise parallel structure transposition that likewise supports the pentatonic fragment (with A-C-D melody as 5th, 7th, and root). As in the previous phrase, a melodic common tone (A) reorients the tonal center through further stepwise motion in the bass, which has now progressed C-D-E in a series of parallel structure m7 chords.

Unlike the harmonic vocabulary of "Penelope," "El Gaucho" relies almost entirely upon M7 and m7 harmonies (save for the series of dominant chords at mm. 3–4). The stepwise progressions in the bass, if characteristic

13. This provides a departure from what might be a more conventional progression of B♭7-B7-C7alt-Fm7.

14. The lead sheet does not include the bass figure that accompanies mm. 9–10 and 15–16.

15. Shorter's copyright deposit lead sheet differs drastically from the realization on the recording at the final phrase. The final phrase of his lead sheet is an exact P5 upward transposition of mm. 5–10. The pentatonic subset of the melody is C-E♭-F, and the three harmonies alternate Cm7 and D♭M7 before progressing to B♭maj7. Further, like the second phrase, the lead sheet's final phrase is six bars: the lead sheet indicates therefore a 16-bar composition of 4 + 6 + 6. It is perhaps characteristic of Shorter to ultimately avoid that exact and mechanical transposition during the final phrase. Further, that transposition would have completed the same pentatonic collection begun in the melody at mm. 5–10 (F-A♭-B♭ mm. 5–10, C-E♭-F mm. 11–16). Shorter's melody on the recorded version moves to a different collection (A-C-D, mm. 11–18). Library of Congress Copyright Deposit Eu 62581, dated July 10, 1968.

for Shorter, support both close and distant harmonic moves. For example, at mm. 1–3, FM7-E♭M7-Dm7 moves the opening harmony to its relative harmony, creating a close relationship. But at mm. 11–14, the Cm7-Dm7-Em7 creates a distant relationship between the outer members, and we may understand the surprise harmonic arrival on Em7 as another Picardy effect: Em7 as rootless CM9 brightens the Cm7 orientation of the final phrase. The return to the opening FM7 harmony relies on an upward half-step resolution (Em7-FM7).

While both "Penelope" and "El Gaucho" use the same melodic idea as an opening gambit, the differences between the two compositions show a fertile ability to inventively rework similar material. Not only do the meter, tempo, form, and feel of the two compositions differ, but the overall harmonic and melodic orientation heightens the difference in sound worlds.

ANALYSIS 2: "PINOCCHIO"

Wayne Shorter's "Pinocchio," like "El Toro," is a single-section composition. "Pinocchio," however, is an 18-bar composition. It initially appeared on the 1967 Miles Davis Quintet recording *Nefertiti*, performed with Shorter, Davis, Herbie Hancock, Ron Carter, and Tony Williams.[16] Its head comprises an 18-bar form, with a 6-bar phrase at the end (mm. 13–18). This aspect of the design makes "Pinocchio" circular, since the 6-bar phrase cuts against the 4-bar hypermetric regularity of many standard jazz compositions. The expectation set up by an "absent" two measures at the end of the form allows the return to the top of the form to sound as a continuation. This irregularity of hypermetric design may have been one of the catalysts for the two horn soloists (trumpeter Davis and saxophonist Shorter) to abandon the underlying 18-bar form during their solos, moving instead to a "time, no changes" format, during which the rhythm section maintains a walking bass and swing time feel without preserving an underlying re-peated chorus structure.[17] The circularity of "Pinocchio" may also have been a catalyst for the quintet's alternate take strategy, during which the group

---

16. Shorter also recorded "Pinocchio" with the group Weather Report on the 1978 album *Mr. Gone*, as well as on the *Tribute to Miles* recording made with Herbie Hancock, Ron Carter, Tony Williams, and Wallace Roney, released in 1994.

17. Hancock, in contrast, does preserve the form of the composition, although the horn players may have been unaware of this: the horns' return to the final head statements creates a clash as they begin the melody three bars into Hancock's third chorus.

plays "Pinocchio" merely as repeated statements of the melody, without standard improvisations by horns and piano.[18]

Example 2.9 provides a lead sheet for "Pinocchio." (A lead sheet for "Pinocchio" appears in the *Real Book*, although the harmonies there frequently differ from the ones used by the quintet during head statements.) The opening harmony of E♭ minor reappears at mm. 11–12, prior to the 6-bar closing phrase. That 6-bar phrase ends with B13(♯11), and this ♭VI7 harmony links back to the opening E♭ minor harmony.

Example 2.9. Lead Sheet to "Pinocchio"

The motivic structure of the melody of "Pinocchio" is remarkable. It marks something of an advance for Shorter, many of whose earlier compositions relied on motives that appear more regularly, often at 2-bar

18. This technique duplicates the one that takes place with the quintet's celebrated performance of "Nefertiti," another circular tune which the group likewise plays only as repeated melody statements, without standard horn and piano improvisations. For more on "Pinocchio" and "Nefertiti," see chapter 6 of Waters, *The Studio Recordings*.

intervals.[19] Here notice the opening 1-bar motive appears expanded mm. 2–3, and is expanded further mm. 4–8, creating a 1 + 2 + 5 bar motivic design. The melody in mm. 9–12 creates a 1 + 3 design, before the appearance of the final 6-bar phrase. The expanding motives at mm. 1–8 frequently crosscut underlying 2- and 4-bar groupings, for example at m. 3 (2-bar groupings) and m. 5 (4-bar groupings).

Unlike the melodic design of "El Toro," that of "Pinocchio" does not participate in or support an underlying M3 axis. But it is the harmonic structure that loosely alludes to that axis, here expressed largely through minor-type harmonies. In "Pinocchio" this M3 axis is less overt (to some, perhaps, more hypothetical) than in "El Toro" because of the intervening harmonies that embellish it. Example 2.10 summarizes the M3 axis harmonies, which provide an overall skeletal framework. The figure includes an additional stepwise passing harmony at m. 3, shown in parentheses.

Example 2.10. M3 Axis Harmonies of "Pinocchio" (Large-scale Organization)

Harmony	E♭m6/9	(D♭min6/9)	Bm(M7)	Gm6/9	E♭m6/9	Bsus13
m.	1	3	5	7	11	17–18

The figure shows the harmonies moving from E♭ (m. 1) through D♭ to B (m. 5), to G (m. 7), and returning to E♭ (mm. 11–12). Each of those steps along the M3 axis support minor-type harmonies, but they do not all share the identical quality: unlike the 6/9 chord types at mm. 1, 7, and 11–12, the m. 5 B minor harmony includes a major seventh above the root.

Thus mm. 1–12 depart from the opening E♭ minor harmony and return to it while moving through the M3 axis. The last step along the axis (to B) occurs at mm. 17–18. Here, however, that Bsus13 harmony (sometimes played by the quintet with the cognate harmony G♭m9) does not share the same minor quality as the E♭-B-G-E♭ axis members heard in mm. 1–12. Instead, its quality is heard as ♭VI7 upon the return to the m. 1 E♭m6/9 harmony. Without an intervening V chord (B♭7), this last chord-first chord progression (B13(♯11)-E♭m6/9) avoids a more characteristic and predictable tonal cadence.[20]

19. Shorter's "Infant Eyes," for example, relies exclusively on a single 2-bar rhythmic motive. As in "Pinocchio," Shorter also uses expandable and collapsible motives in "Nefertiti," released on the same album as "Pinocchio."

20. "El Toro" similarly relies on a ♭VI7 chord (B♭7) to link to the opening chord (D minor). This ♭VI7-i motion between the last chord and first chord occurs in a number of other Shorter compositions, including "Sincerely Diana" (G♭7 to B♭min7) and "Iris" (heard during the head as D♭7♯11 to Fmin7, from Davis, *E.S.P.*).

Thus the M3 axis interpretation is provisional for several reasons. One is that the final step (B) houses a different quality harmony than the minor-type harmonies at mm. 1, 5, 7, and 11. It therefore abandons the axis principles of "Giant Steps" and "El Toro," which rely on a strict sequence of same-type harmonies.

Further, unlike "Giant Steps" and "El Toro," the intermediary harmonies do not explicitly tonicize those M3 steps through ii-V (or V) chords. Like many of Shorter's other compositions written during the mid-1960s, "Pinocchio" often suppresses overt V-I and ii-V-I progressions. Yet it is possible to consider the additional harmonies (those omitted in Example 2.10) as operating functionally, but in a way in which their function is at-tenuated. For example, the harmonies that appear mid-bar at mm. 2 and 10 operate analogously. A-9 is followed by D♭-6/9 (mm. 2–3), and B-9 is followed by E♭-6/9 (mm. 10–11). Example 2.11 shows the ways in which Am9 and Bm9 operate as ii′ chords (rather than more-conventional V or V′ chords).

Example 2.11. Use of ii′ (Substituting for V′) in "Pinocchio," mm. 2 and 10

Harmony	E♭m6/9	Am9 (ii′)	D♭m6/9
Substitutes for:		D13 (V′)	
Substitution Strategy:		ii′ substitutes for V′	
m.	1	2	3

Harmony	C9	F9	Bm9 (ii′)	E♭m6/9
Substitutes for:			E13 (V′)	
Substitution Strategy:			ii′ substitutes for V′	
m.	9	10		11

Thus, A-9 at m. 2 substitutes for D13, and the B-9 at m. 10 substitutes for E13. The use of a ii′ chord rather than a V′ chord may be considered as arising from a "sus chord" imperative that emerged during the 1960s, one that suppressed the active and directed chordal thirds or sevenths of harmonies. Such substitutions retain functional vestiges but curtail the tonal direction.[21]

In addition, as the above figure shows, there is a broader chain of dominant chords operating in mm. 9–11, linking C7 (m. 9), F7 (m. 10), and Bm9

---

21. We might understand the absence of the leading tone in these progressions as suppressing unqualified dominant function and invoking subdominant function. See Daniel Harrison, *Harmonic Function in Tonal Music* (Chicago: University of Chicago, 1994), and James McGowan, "Dynamic Consonance in Selected Piano Performances of Tonal Jazz" (PhD diss., University of Rochester, 2005), esp. chapters 4 and 5.

(ii′ substitute for E7, m. 10) en route to E♭m6/9 (mm. 11–12). This chain of dominant-type chords (along with the Bm9 substitute) forms the pathway from Gm6/9 (mm. 7–8) to E♭m6/9 (mm. 11–12).

The Am9 harmony (second half of m. 4) recalls the same chord at m. 2, but now has a different resolution, to Bm(M7).[22] As with that harmony at m. 2, it is possible to hear this Am9 harmony as substituting for a more functional one. Again, this relies on a view of substitution, as shown in Example 2.12. The example shows the substitution requiring two steps. The first step considers A-9 as substitute for its relative harmony, the third-related CM7. The second considers this CM7 as a tritone substitution (V′) harmony leading to the Bm(M7). This forms V′M7 rather than the more common V′7 (i.e., CM7 rather than C7; with CM7 as ♭IIM7 of the destination harmony Bm(M7)). With CM7 rather than C7, the leading tone to B minor (A♯/B♭) is suppressed and appears at the arrival to B minor. All these features show how the progression derives from, yet makes significantly more ambiguous, a more familiar sounding tonal context.

Example 2.12. Substitution Techniques at m. 4

Harmony	Am9	Bmin(♯7)
Substitutes for:	CM7	
Substitution Strategies:	1) Am9 is Relative of CM7;	
	2) CM7 is V′M7 (or ♭IIM7) of	
	Destination Harmony Bm(M7)	
m.	4	5

The final Bsus13 harmony (mm. 17–18), the last step along the M3 axis, follows G♭13. That m. 16 G♭13 harmony operates as V7 of B. It is the last of a four-chord sequence that begins with G♭sus13 (m. 13) and ends with G♭13 (m. 16). The intervening harmonies (Em9-F13(♯11), mm. 14–15) therefore delay the resolution of the G♭sus13 to G♭13 through stepwise linear motion in the bass (E-F-G♭),[23] as shown in Example 2.13.

22. The melodic pathway is similar between mm. 2–3 and 4–5. Certainly the focus on the B♭ common tone in the melody at mm. 1, 3, and 5 helps motivate the stepwise progression from E♭m6/9-D♭m6/9-Bm(♯7).

23. These upward-moving chromatic harmonies, retrogressive in comparison with the more-typical downward-moving chromatic progressions, appear elsewhere in Shorter's compositions, such as in mm. 9–12 of "E.S.P."

Example 2.13. Harmonies at mm. 14–15 Elaborate Vsus13/B to V13/B

Harmony	G♭sus13	Em9		F13(♯11)	G♭13	Bsus13
Function	Vsus/B	(chromatic stepwise elaboration delays resolution of sus chord)			V/B	
m.	13	14		15	16	17–18

The above proposes a M3 axis of "Pinocchio," but one that is provisional due to the intervening harmonies, which link the steps along the axis. Although many of these intervening harmonies are not explicitly functional, Examples 2.12 and 2.13 relate them to more-functional progressions through principles of harmonic substitution. The overall M3 axis bass motion of "Pinocchio" (E♭-B-G-E♭-B) is similar to that in "El Toro" (which moved D♭-A-F-D♭-A): it completes the octave and moves one giant step further. Yet the axis steps of "El Toro" appear regularly every two bars, while they appear in "Pinocchio" irregularly and unsupported by similar sequential designs in the melody.

"Pinocchio" shows just how far jazz composition had moved since Coltrane's "Giant Steps." It shows the earlier model receding further into the background, and an ongoing commitment to harmonic and formal ambiguity in the hands of particular composers. Many of the harmonic substitution strategies suppress the more-directed and active chordal thirds or sevenths (mm. 2–3, 4–5, 10–11) or use retrogressions (the chromatically ascending progressions of mm. 14–16). Further, its formal circularity avoids the formal orientation provided by compositions of consistent 4-, 8-, and 16-bar segments.

Shorter's Lead Sheet. Shorter's lead sheet copyright deposit[24] is unusual in several regards. A transcription of it appears as Example 2.14. It includes written-out harmonies in the bass clef at mm. 1, 3, 11, 13, and 15–18, which in most cases are used in place of chord symbols. This practice appears in earlier Shorter lead sheets, such as for the introduction to "Night Dreamer" (Shorter, *Night Dreamer*), as well as in the contemporary "Nefertiti," and later works such as "Paraphernalia" (Davis, *Miles in the Sky*), but is most apparent in the lead sheets for Shorter's 1965 recording *The All-Seeing Eye*, which provide written parts with no chord symbols whatsoever.[25] The latter provide the specific voicings played by the horns during the head statements, along with a bass part, providing only a rough guide for the path taken during the improvisations by soloists and rhythm section. On the individual lead sheets for "Night Dreamer," "Pinocchio," "Nefertiti," and

24. Shorter's lead sheet copyright deposit (Eu 42286, dated March 13, 1968) is contained at the Library of Congress.
25. "Genesis" (Copyright deposit Eu 916674), "Chaos" (Eu 916675), "The All-Seeing Eye" (Eu 916676), and "Face of the Deep" (Eu 916677). All four deposits dated December 3, 1965.

"Paraphernalia," the intent seems to be to indicate (or regulate) the type of voicings played by the pianist.

Example 2.14. Recreation of Shorter's Copyright Deposit Lead Sheet to "Pinocchio"

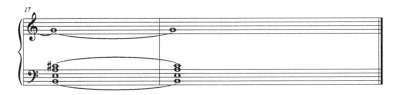

In the case of the "Pinocchio" lead sheet, there are instances in which the notated harmony accords with the harmony played on the recording: m. 1 includes an inversion of Cm7(♭5) (related to the E♭m6/9 played by the quintet); m. 13, a G♭/D♭ dyad (related to the G♭sus13 chord); mm. 15–16, A diminished and A♯ diminished triads in inversion (related to F13(♯11) and G♭13♯11); and m. 18, an A triad above a B bass (roughly akin to the B13(♯11) harmony). However, mm. 3 and 11 include harmonies (an inversion of Dm7(♭5) and a whole-tone sonority), which in neither instance accords with the D♭m6/9 (m. 3) nor the E♭m6/9 (m. 11) harmony heard on the recording. The notated harmony at m. 3 appears as a whole-step upward transposition of m. 1, seemingly suggesting Fm6/9. The notated whole-tone harmony at m. 11 (A♭-C-D-G♭) might suggest a dominant-type chord, perhaps B♭9(♭13).

Similarly, the chord symbols by greater and lesser degrees conform to the harmonies heard on the recording. This suggests either that the group made deliberate changes to the lead sheet, or that Shorter intended his symbols to indicate upper structure harmonies (without including bass note). For example, mm. 5–6 are performed on the recording as Bm(♯7). That harmony does appear at m. 6 of the lead sheet. However, the previous measure includes D+7, which, given the melody, I take to indicate DM7♯5, a rootless upper structure harmony of Bm9(♯7). The lead sheet's G-13 chord symbol (mm. 7–8) accurately depicts the bass pitch, although Gm6/9 perhaps more accurately describes the harmony heard on the recording (Hancock does sometimes interpret this by moving between Gm9 to Gm6/9).

The B♭maj7b5 chord at m. 9 forms a rootless upper structure of the C13 harmony played by the quintet on the recording. The following m. 10 chord symbol (E♭maj7) is less relatable to the F13 chord heard on the recording, but it does form a rootless upper structure of Fsus13. M. 13 is unique, since it includes both written pitches and chord symbol. The written pitches (G♭ and D♭) there do accord with the G♭sus13 harmony from the recording, while the chord symbol of C♭-7 is peculiar, given the E♭ of the melody. The final chord symbol of the lead sheet, E-7 (m. 14) accurately describes the harmony heard on the recording.

Melodically, too, there are a few differences in rhythm and pitch between the lead sheet and recorded performance. The second beats of mm. 1 and 9 are performed using eighth-note triplets, the first of which is the sustained pitch from the previous beat. And in m. 5 (third beat), the lower pitch of the arpeggiation begins with D, rather than C♯.

What does this all this tell us about Shorter's postbop compositions? First, there is a definite fluidity in the way these compositions are realized on the recording. The alternatives posed to the lead sheet (which, after all, Shorter considered definitive enough to submit as a copyright deposit) show a high degree of compositional flexibility. Second, Shorter's practice of including at times notated harmonies (instead of chord symbols) implies that chord symbols are no longer sufficient at all times to convey the intended harmonic messages. The idea of notating pitches suggests not that symbols are too limited, but perhaps are not specific enough to capture a desired sonority.[26] Finally, the lead sheet shows 1960s postbop composers shaping and molding an emerging language.

ANALYSIS 3: "FACE OF THE DEEP"

Shorter's recording *The All-Seeing Eye* is perhaps the most ambitious of his *Blue Note* recordings, both in terms of its commitment to the jazz avant garde, as well as in its compositional designs and four-horn writing. It was recorded in 1965, the same year as the sessions that produced Shorter's *The Soothsayer* (only released in 1979) and *Et Cetera* (released in 1980), as well as the celebrated Plugged Nickel recordings of the Miles Davis Quintet. As mentioned above, all of Shorter's lead sheets for the recording dispense with conventional chord symbols and instead include only the written horn parts along with those for bass.

The album provided Shorter with the opportunity to depart from a number of other conventions as well. The compositions feature mixed meter ("Chaos" includes a notated bar of 9/4 within the 4/4 bars; "The All-Seeing Eye" alternates 7/4 and 6/4; the opening of "Genesis" twice alternates one bar of 24/4 with five bars of 3/4 before moving to a more consistent 4/4). They use upper-structure triads above bass pitches ("The All-Seeing Eye") or other dissonant sonorities, such as diminished triads with ♯7 ("Genesis"), and triadic planing above a fixed bass pitch ("The All-Seeing Eye"). The use of upper structure triads above the bass to create M7♯5, dim(♯7), and other sonorities ("Face of the Deep," see below) expanded Shorter's harmonic vocabulary, providing ways to fruitfully break out of the standard harmonic vocabulary of major, minor, dominant, and half-diminished sonorities and their extensions. Such slash chord sonorities became an important technique of postbop composition.

Following the introduction, "Face of the Deep" is written as a 13-bar composition in 4/4. A transcription of Shorter's lead sheet appears as Example 2.15, and I have provided my own lead sheet interpretation with annotations in the following Example 2.16.[27] The group performs "Face of the Deep"

26. Naturally, Hancock does not adhere precisely to these notated harmonies. He is more careful in adhering to Shorter's notated harmonies in the performance of "Paraphernalia." See Waters, *The Studio Recordings*, 247–50.

27. I made two changes to Shorter's lead sheet in Example 2.15 in order to accord with the recording. The final chord of the introduction is played as C♯ (Shorter's lead sheet indicates it as C♮); the pickup upper pitch to m. 7 is played as D♯ (Shorter's lead sheet indicates it as E♭).

slowly and freely. Despite the irregular number of bars, however, the composition unfolds as a series of four related phrases, at mm. 1–2, 3–4, 5–8, and 9–13.[28] Each proceeds differently, but each relies on the minor third melodic kernel of A♭-G-F, stated directly (mm. 1–2), with a melodic lead-in and elaborated (mm. 3–4), as an expanded phrase with motion upward to a melodic high point (mm. 5–8),[29] and a phrase preceded by and followed by similar overlapping minor third descents (B-B♭-A♭ m. 9, A♭-G-F m. 10, F-E-D mm. 11–13), ending on the melodic low point of the composition.

Example 2.15. Recreation of Shorter's Score to "Face of the Deep"

28. This four-phrase organization is similar to other Shorter compositions such as "Fall" and "Vonetta." For further discussion of "Vonetta," see Waters, *The Studio Recordings*, 175–79.

29. I refer to the m. 7 D♯ as the melodic high point, even though E♭ is heard in m. 2. Its expanded treatment in mm. 6–7 makes it a marked event in the melody.

Example 2.15. Continued

D.C. al Fine

Example 2.16. Lead Sheet Rendition of Shorter's Score to "Face of the Deep"

Intervals above chord names represent distance between bass pitch and upper structure triads ("4ths" represent fourth chords)

Like the mm. 9–13 phrase, the introduction is similarly designed as a series of three overlapping stepwise descents, although the intervallic organization of the introduction is not as consistent. Like the final phrase, the introduction begins as half then whole step (D-C♯-B). It then moves to whole step (B-A-G), then half step (G-F♯-E♯). Harmonically, the introduction relies primarily upon parallel motion of similar upper structures for each of the three stepwise third descents. The introduction's first stepwise descent uses tritone plus perfect fourth sonorities (E♭-A-D for chord 1; D-G♯-C♯ for chord 2; chord 3 changes to perfect fourths). The second stepwise descent uses perfect fourth plus tritone sonorities (C-F-B for

vertical

chord 4, B♭-E♭-A for chord 5; A♭-D♭-G for chord 6). The third stepwise descent uses augmented triads (B-D♯-G for chord 7; B♭-D-F♯ for chord 8; A-C♯-E♯ for chord 9).

The lead sheet interpretation at Example 2.16 begins after the introduction. It interprets upper-structure triads above bass pitches when those triads are major or minor: the first four harmonies are E/B♭ (indicating E major triad above B♭ bass), A♭m/B♭ (A♭ minor triad above B♭ bass), B♭/G♭, and C♯/A. While it is possible to indicate these harmonies with more-conventional chord symbols (for example, E/B♭ may be indicated as B♭7♭9/♯11), the slash chord notation more carefully indicates Shorter's voicings in most cases. The example also indicates the relationship of upper structure triad to bass pitch, helping reveal the slash chord vocabulary used here. For example, the first chord (E/B♭) involves a major triad a tritone above the bass, the second chord (A♭m/B♭) a minor triad a m7th above the bass, and the third and fourth chords a major triad a M3 above the bass (these latter two chords might also be considered as M7♯5).

I make a brief digression here in order to compare this first phrase with part of Shorter's earlier introduction to "Night Dreamer" (the introduction appears on Shorter's lead sheet,[30] but not on the recording) in order to show the development of Shorter's use of upper structure triads above bass. It is possible that Shorter reworked the "Night Dreamer" introduction as "Face of the Deep": there are instances of phrases from earlier works that return in later ones (as discussed above, the first melodic phrase of "Penelope," from *Et Cetera*, returns as the first phrase of "El Gaucho," from *Adam's Apple*). A transcription of the "Night Dreamer" introduction from Shorter's lead sheet appears as Example 2.17. The A♭-G-F melodic kernel of "Face of the Deep" (down a half step, then whole step) appears here twice, transposed up by step (B♭-A-G). I have also included the slash chords used to harmonize both statements of that melody: E♭/F—Bm7/C—C/D and F♯/A—F/E♭—C/D. Above those chords the example shows the distance of the upper structure triad from the bass pitch (for example, E♭/F is shown as m7).

30. Library of Congress Copyright Deposit Eu 827262, dated May 25, 1964.

Example 2.17. Recreation of Shorter's Copyright Deposit Lead Sheet to Introduction of "Night Dreamer" (Chord Labels added to Shorter's Original Lead Sheet)

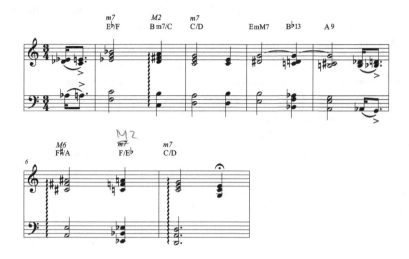

For the first phrase (mm. 1-4), the parallel harmonization of upper structure triads, E♭-D-C matches the melodic pathway (although the second chord is a Bm7 chord, rather than a D triad, the parallel motion is evident). In that case, the first and third chords are major triads a m7 above the bass (indicated as m7), while the second includes a major triad a M2 above the bass. For the second phrase (mm. 5-6), the first two upper structure triads (F#-F) move in parallel motion, before returning to the C triad that likewise closed the first phrase. In that case, the first chord (F#/A) involves a major triad a M6 above the bass, the second chord (F/Eb) a M2 above the bass, and the third a m7 above the bass.

All of this shows an interest in slash chords formed by triads over bass pitches. In the introduction to "Night Dreamer" the slash chord harmonies are limited to m7, M2, and M6 triads above the bass. They comport with three types of harmonies. For example, major triads a m7 above the bass (E♭/F, C/D) supply sus chord harmonies. Major triads a M2 above the bass (D/C and F/E♭) include 6/9/#11 harmonies (the Bm7/C also includes a M7 along with 6/9/#11). Major triads a M6 above the bass (F#/A) involve ♭9/#13 harmonies.

"Face of the Deep" expands this vocabulary. For those instances of major triads above bass pitches, the majority involve M3, such as B♭/G♭, C#/A (m. 2), E/C (m. 5), C/A♭, G/E♭ (m. 6). They form M7#5 harmonies, which became an important postbop resource as the decade continued. In addition to those, additional slash chord harmonies include distances (between bass and upper structure triad root) as tritone, m2, m6, m7, m3, and M7 (the latter, such as B/C at m. 6 and B♭/B at mm. 12 and 13, form a diminished triad with #7).

Shorter does not limit himself strictly to triadic upper structure harmonies. There are less-standard harmonies, such as the DM7(#9) chord heard in m. 4. Elsewhere, Shorter relies on other upper-structure harmonies, such as perfect fourths (F6/9, m. 3, GM7(#11), m. 9), as well as perfect fourth plus tritone (E♭-A-D, mm. 11–13).

"Face of the Deep" may be heard as an exercise in creative reharmonization of recurring (and elaborated) melodic material,[31] with an expanded harmonic vocabulary and an emphasis on relationships between bass and upper structure harmonies that are more dissonant than conventional jazz harmonies. Certainly some of the inner voice activity is motivated by half-step motion (see the inner voice path of E-E♭-D-C# mm. 1–2, and the B♭/E♭-A/D-A♭-D♭ path of m. 3, for example). In most instances, the bass provides a counterpoint that does not operate in parallel to the upper structure harmonies (as it did frequently, for example, in the introduction to "Night Dreamer").

And while there are emphasized and extended harmonic points of arrival (such as the BM7(#11) at mm. 7–8, and the two-chord vamp mm. 12–13), there is little else harmonically that provides a tonal mooring. What recurrence there is occurs during the final phrase, as the harmonization of the A♭-G-F melodic kernel at mm. 9–10 recalls the harmonies E/B (m. 1), E♭/F (m. 3), and C#/A (m. 2), blending some phrase 1 and phrase 2 harmonies that earlier supported the A♭-G-F motive.

It may be fruitless to posit an underlying harmonic framework for "Face of the Deep." Instead, the scaffolding is primarily provided by recurring elements of the four-phrase melody, which is then richly treated to a series of colorful reharmonizations, ones that activate a harmonic vocabulary that departs significantly from Shorter's earlier compositions. The use of fourth-based structures and melodic common tones over shifting harmonies (such as A-D-G to A♭-D♭-G at m. 3, beat 2) provide a technique that reappears in some of Chick Corea's works such as "Song of the Wind" (discussed in chapter 4).

Shorter's earlier works such as "Children of the Night" and "El Toro" use axis progressions in evident manners. If similar to those in Coltrane's "Giant

31. This is similar to the technique heard in Shorter's "Vonetta," which also emphasizes M7#5 harmonies. See Waters, *The Studio Recordings*, 175–79.

Steps," Shorter's axis progressions appear alongside other compositional designs that often enhance formal ambiguity. That ambiguity is present in works such as "Virgo," which elasticizes some of the melodic phrases, relative to more-typical 4-bar paradigms. Although "Penelope" and "El Gaucho" use the same opening melodic idea, the overall differences between the two show a fertile compositional imagination, one that allows distinctly different harmonization paths through similar material. The M3 harmonic axis of minor chords in "Pinocchio" is fleshed out by harmonies that relate to more-conventional tonal harmonies through substitution principles, all within an 18-bar circular form. And "Face of the Deep" relies on a slash-chord harmonic vocabulary that supports a series of four related phrases.

The question of primacy of melody vs. harmony is perhaps a chicken-or-egg one. Herbie Hancock stated that he often composed works by coming up with the harmonic progression first, to which he then composed a melody.[32] Shorter's imaginative reharmonizations of similar melodic material, such as described above with "Penelope," "El Gaucho," and "Face of the Deep" might argue for a different strategy, one that offers shifting harmonic perspectives on fixed (or similar) melodic shapes. Shorter's compositions often bypass conventional or predictable harmonic pathways, making them challenging for performers to negotiate, but the strongly arched melodies permit varied harmonic strategies, such as extended pedal points ("Penelope"), triads over bass pitches ("Face of the Deep"), as well as more conventional M7, m7, and dominant seventh harmonies ("El Gaucho" and "Pinocchio"). The chronology of compositions discussed here is not intended to advance an evolutionary view (of simple to complex or traditional to avant-garde). It instead suggests a composer with an astonishingly vast and malleable range of techniques and solutions.

32. Gil Goldstein, *Jazz Composer's Companion* (Rottenburg: Advance Music, 1993), 114.

CHAPTER 3
Herbie Hancock

Hancock's compositions provided some of the signature sounds of the 1960s, especially his funky jazz hit "Watermelon Man" (from Hancock's *Takin' Off*, covered by Mongo Santamaria and others) and his jazz standard "Maiden Voyage" (*Maiden Voyage*). He composed virtually all the compositions on his seven Blue Note recordings, as well as on a 1969 Warner Brothers release.[1] His first two recordings, *Takin' Off* (1962) and *My Point of View* (1963), were remarkable hard bop recordings. During his time in Miles Davis's second quintet (1963–1968), his compositional language and treatment of harmony and harmonic color expanded. *Empyrean Isles* (1964, for quartet) and *Maiden Voyage* (1965, for quintet) combined disparate influences such as Bill Evans, John Coltrane, and (arranger) Gil Evans. These compositional aesthetics remained in his final two recordings for Blue Note, *Speak Like a Child* (1968, for sextet) and *The Prisoner* (1969, for nonet), both of which offset the improvisations with sculpted arrangements for larger instrumental groupings.[2] By 1969, Hancock signed with Warner Bros. Much of *Fat Albert Rotunda*, written for a television special (*Hey, Hey, It's Fat Albert*), relied on funky/soul jazz, presaging his move to jazz-rock

---

1. His recording *Inventions and Dimensions* (1963) was largely improvised in the studio. Ron Carter composed "First Trip," heard on *Speak Like a Child*.

2. Hancock acknowledged the influence of Gil Evans on *Speak Like a Child*, stating, "*Speak Like a Child* was directly from Gil Evans. . . . When I planned *Speak Like a Child* I tried to get a sound that approached Gil's textures with the least number of instruments." Quoted in Gil Goldstein, *Jazz Composer's Companion* (Rottenburg, Germany: Advance Music, 1993), 115.

fusion in the 1970s. Nevertheless, two of its compositions maintained a postbop orientation, "Jessica" and "Tell Me a Bedtime Story."[3]

Hancock's postbop compositions maintain a decided openness that arises from different sources. Harmonic rhythm at times plays a role: individual chords may span four bars, sometimes in sequences of suspended fourth chords ("One Finger Snap," from *Empyrean Isles*; and "Maiden Voyage"). Pedal point harmonies arrange chords of shifting loyalty above stable bass pitches ("Little One" and "Dolphin Dance," both from *Maiden Voyage*). Aeolian progressions and harmonies derived from subsets of the ascending melodic minor collection (both discussed below) provide dense, colorful, and richly complex sonorities. Some of the compositions are single-section, without the repeating sections of song forms. The harmonic progressions offer different strategies in either fulfilling or avoiding expectations, sometimes in combination. For example, suspended fourth chords used as tonic or dominant harmonies allow harmonies to progress tonally but provide a degree of ambiguity, since the suspended fourth bleaches out the more active and goal-directed chordal thirds. Bass motions descend conventionally by half step or fifth, but in sequences of suspended fourth or other harmonies ("One Finger Snap" and "Speak Like a Child").[4] Evident melodic cadences are at times undermined by substitute harmonic resolutions. At the same time, the motivic structures of the compositions are compelling and lyrical. All of these factors contribute to the tantalizing combination of inevitability and ambiguity that characterize Hancock's compositions of the decade.

Hancock studied music composition while an undergraduate at Grinnell College. He acknowledged his fascination for "chord color in music," and described how Clare Fischer's arrangements for the vocal group the Hi-Los and Robert Farnon's orchestrations of popular songs had an early influence on his harmonic thinking.[5] He offered in an interview a brief glimpse into his compositional craft, stating "Compositionally, from a structural point of view, 'Watermelon Man' and 'Maiden Voyage' are probably

---

3. Hancock recorded several of his original compositions with the Miles Davis Quintet. With one exception ("Madness," from *Nefertiti*, 1967), Hancock also recorded these same compositions as a leader. For details on the Davis Quintet versions of "Little One," "Riot," and "Madness," see Keith Waters, *The Studio Recordings of the Miles Davis Quintet 1965–68* (New York: Oxford University Press, 2011).

4. For more on those processes in the two compositions, see chapter 6.

5. Hancock's comment on "chord color" taken from liner notes to *My Point of View*, reprinted in the liner notes to *Herbie Hancock: The Complete Blue Note Sessions* (B2BN 7243 4 95569 2 8), 10. His comments on Fischer and Farnon are from Len Lyons, *The Great Jazz Pianists: Speaking of Their Lives and Music* (New York: Da Capo Press, 1983), 272.

my two strongest pieces. I'm talking strictly about craft—the balance, the relationships that are working throughout the piece. They're almost mathematical."[6]

Hancock also described his working methods as often proceeding first from harmony, before turning to melody:

Harmony before melody

> One way I used to write, which was a suggestion from Donald Byrd when I first came on the scene in New York, was to start with some chords or a bass line. My harmonic senses are more readily available than anything I think. It's easier for me to find a series of chords that sparks my interest than it is to find a melody that will do the same. For me it's never just the melody—it's the harmonic environment that it's in. But once I get started, working from the harmony, the ball may bounce between the melody leading the chords or the chords leading the melody.[7]

In this chapter I examine three Hancock compositions: "King Cobra" (*My Point of View*, 1963), "Dolphin Dance" (*Maiden Voyage*, 1965), and "Jessica" (*Fat Albert Rotunda*, 1969). Like those of Shorter, Corea, and others, Hancock's compositions, particularly those after 1963, transformed and challenged the traditions of hard bop, and offered postbop solutions for harmonic progression, harmonic vocabulary, form, and melodic and motivic structure.

ANALYSIS 1: "KING COBRA"

If it is useful to distinguish between Hancock's 1962–1963 hard bop compositions—which largely relied on tonal jazz procedures—and his later postbop ones, in some cases shared harmonic and compositional details blur the distinctions. For example, "Empty Pockets" (*Takin' Off*) and "King Cobra" (*My Point of View*) use tonic suspended fourth chords; "Alone and I" (*Takin' Off*) begins with a series of shifting harmonies over a bass pedal point. Yet in some of these earlier instances these ideas are put to more conventional use: "Empty Pockets" is a 12-bar blues, and "Alone and I" uses its extended pedal point as an introductory dominant, one that resolves to a tonic harmony when the song's melody begins.

6. Lyons, *Great Jazz Pianists*, 275.
7. Gil Goldstein, *Jazz Composer's Companion* (Rottenburg: Advance Music, 1993), 114.

Another—perhaps less obvious—connection between the earlier 1962–1963 recordings and the later ones involves the use of M3 axes. Hancock explores that axis in two compositions from *My Point of View*, before returning to it again in "Dolphin Dance." As shown in Example 3.1, "The Pleasure Is Mine" begins with a 2-bar phrase that moves from C to E major. Here the composition moves along only two stages of the axis and does not continue to A♭, but the C-E stages connect directly and evidently in both the harmonic and melodic dimensions. The example includes the trumpet, tenor saxophone, and trombone parts, Hancock's chord symbols from his lead sheet, and I have provided chord symbols that reflect the horn and bass parts for mm. 1–4.[8]

Example 3.1. M3 Axis Progression (C-E) in "The Pleasure is Mine," mm. 1–4 (voicings played by trumpet, tenor saxophone, trumpet)

"King Cobra" represents even a more committed progressive design, one intentionally designed to avoid harmonic clichés. "The chords in most jazz tunes flow in a certain way," Hancock acknowledged in the liner notes. "I wanted to expand the flow so that it would go in directions beyond the usual."[9] Its A section uses a M3 axis within broader pedal point regions. Further, that axis participates in a larger compositional design, one that yields to a m3 axis later in the composition.[10] The M3 organization is clearest at the beginnings of the first two phrases in mm. 1–16. Example 3.2 contains an explanatory diagram. Example 3.3 indicates the larger dimensions of the M3 axis in the A and A′ sections.

8. Library of Congress Copyright Deposit Ep 190686, dated April 14, 1964.

9. Reprinted in the liner notes to *Herbie Hancock: The Complete Blue Note Sixties Sessions* (B2BN 7243 4 95569 2 8), 18.

10. I discuss "King Cobra" in Keith Waters, "Modes, Scales, Functional Harmony, and Nonfunctional Harmony in the Compositions of Herbie Hancock," *Journal of Music Theory* 49, no. 2: 333–57.

Example 3.2. Explanatory Diagram with Chords and Accompaniment to "King Cobra" (Melody Omitted)

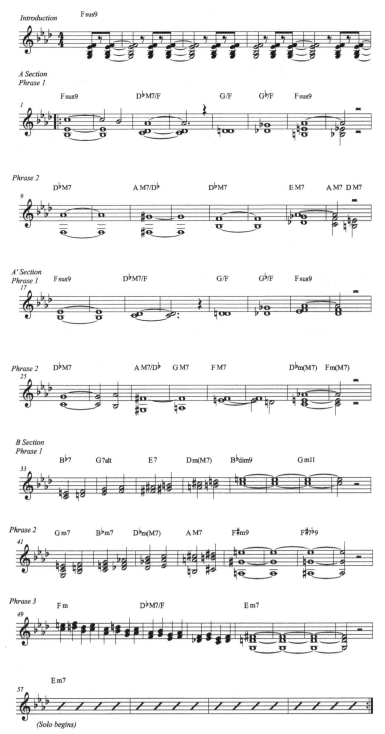

Example 3.3. M3 Axis Organization in the A Sections of "King Cobra"

A Section, Phrase 1
Harmony	Fsus9	D♭M7/F
m.	1	3

A Section, Phrase 2
Harmony	D♭M7(♯11)	AM7/D♭	D♭M7
m.	9	11	13

The opening progression (Fsus9-D♭M7/F) corresponds to an abstracted axis bass progression, but not an axis harmonic progression, since the harmonies are not the same quality. The opening harmony is a suspended fourth chord, while the second harmony is D♭M7/F (mm. 1–4). By themselves, these two harmonies loosely form a tonal progression (i–♭VIM7).[11] This avoids the more obvious harmonic axis shifts heard in "The Pleasure Is Mine" (or Coltrane's "Giant Steps"): their color shifts rely on similar structure harmonies at a distance of four sharps or flats. Mm. 1–3 forms an Aeolian progression, since the second harmony (a first inversion M7 chord) may be heard as a subset of the F Aeolian collection.[12] As a point of comparison, Example 3.4 shows Hancock's progression in relation to two hypothetical stages. The first provides a direct M3 harmonic axis progression of M7 chords. The second alters the first and third harmony to Fsus9. The third is Hancock's progression. It introduces the pedal points that form the first inversion M7 chords.

Example 3.4. Comparison of Direct M3 Axis Progressions with Hancock's "King Cobra"

Direct M3 axis	FM7	D♭M7	FM7	D♭M7	AM7	D♭M7
1st and 3rd chord altered	Fsus9	D♭M7	Fsus9	D♭M7	AM7	D♭M7
Hancock's progression	Fsus9	D♭M7/F	Fsus9	D♭M7(♯11)	AM7/D♭	D♭M7
m.	1	3	7	9	11	13

11. In fact, it is possible to regard all of mm. 1–8 as an expanded tonal progression over the F pedal point, with G/F (m. 7) as V/V and G♭/F (m. 8) as ♭II (or V′, a substitute for V).

12. Hancock uses a similar Aeolian progression (Fsus to D♭M7♯11/F) as the opening progression to the improvisational chords of "Little One" (from *E.S.P* and *Maiden Voyage*); see Keith Waters, *The Studio Recordings of the Miles Davis Quintet, 1965–68* (New York: Oxford University Press, 2011), 95–109. In both "King Cobra" and "Little One" the first—more open sounding—sus chord moves to a denser second harmony. The opening harmonies to "Cantaloupe Island" (Fm7 to D♭9) are similar, but adhere more to hard bop practice—there is no extended pedal point, and the D♭9 acts as a conventional elaboration of the F minor tonic.

The example shows that the continuation into Phrase 2 (at mm. 9–16) marks a more evident commitment to the harmonic axis, as the harmonies move DbM7(#11)-AM7/Db-DbM7. (In Hancock's 1964 lead sheet for trumpet, he omits the pedal point for the second chord in that progression, indicating merely DbM7-AM7-DbM7.)[13] Again this forms an Aeolian progression, with the AM7/Db a subset of the Db (or C#) Aeolian collection.

The use of F and Db pedal points (as shown in Example 3.4) in Hancock's progression moves the bass through two steps of the axis (F and Db), while the upper structure harmonies move through all three (F-Db-A).Thus the characterization of the overall progression as based on a M3 axis is a broad one, given the reliance on pedal points, as well as the initial progression (Fsus9-DbM7/F), which does not preserve the same quality harmonies.

Example 3.5 shows how mm. 17–32 (the A′ section) provide a varied repetition of mm. 1–16. Harmonically the first two phrases (mm. 1–8 and 17–24) are nearly identical. Yet the progression of second phrase of A′ (mm. 25–32) differs from mm. 9–16. The axis movement is most explicit at mm. 25, 27, and 29, as all harmonies are heard as root position (or first inversion) M7 harmonies along the Db-A-F axis. The intermediate harmony of GM7 (m. 28), heard in a weak measure relative to its surrounding harmonies, fills in and passes between the upper structure chords AM7 (over Db bass, m. 27) and FM7(#11, mm. 29–30).

Example 3.5. Elaboration of Axis Progression in Phrases 1 and 2 of A′ Section, mm. 17–32

A′ Section, Phrase 1

Harmony	Fsus9	DbM7/F
m.	17	19

A′ Section, Phrase 2

Harmony	DbM7(#11)	AM7/Db	GM7	FM7(#11)	Dbm(M7)	Fm(M7)
m.	25	27	28	29	31	32

At the end of the A′ section (mm. 31–32) the final two harmonies return to Db and F, but now those axis bass pitches use different upper structure

13. Library of Congress Copyright Deposit Eu 190686, April 14, 1964. Since Hancock's lead sheet is for Bb trumpet, I have transposed his chords up a step to concert key here.

harmonies, D♭min(M7) to Fmin(M7). The section therefore closes with the same M3 axis, but with the harmonic climate altered. These two harmonies provide a cadence to the A′ section. The lead sheet shows that the horn voicings in mm. 31–32 create an upper structure pedal point above the shifting bass. That is, the two chords preserve the same augmented triad above the changing bass pitch, as shown in Example 3.6.

Example 3.6. Cadential Progression at mm. 31–32 Share Similar Upper Structure

Harmony	D♭m(M7)	Fm(M7)
Upper structure triad	C, E, A♭	C, E, A♭
Bass	D♭	F
m.	31	32

Overall, M3 axis progressions provide a frame for the A and A′ sections. But "King Cobra" offers compelling and broader alternatives to more systematic uses of that axis. Further, intervening progressions elaborate and expand that frame through the use of different axes. Such designs appear at the ends of phrases, and provide alternative cadences. For example, mm. 5–6 (and 21–22) return to the tonic Fsus9 chord through GM/F and G♭M/F. Thus the upper structures move along a m2 axis.[14] Even less tied to conventional practice is the mm. 15–16 progression that closes the first A section. Here the harmonies progress through a P4 axis of common structure harmonies of EM7 AM7 DM7(♯11), with each including as a common tone the G♯/A♭ heard in the melody that ends the phrase.[15]

The B Section: m3 Axis and conclusion. In contrast to the A and A′ sections, the B section moves along a different axis. It appears most clearly at the two phrases at mm. 33–48, which express a m3 axis in the melody and bass. On the recorded performance, the move away from the rhythmic ostinato accompaniment and the use of bowed bass and cymbals further set into relief these two phrases. Example 3.7 provides the melodic and harmonic progression there, indicated as Phrase 1 and Phrase 2. In Phrase 1 (mm. 33–40), the melody moves through the octatonic (diminished) scale, filling

14. This progression is similar to that heard mm. 5–6 of the jazz standard "On Green Dolphin Street."
15. Notice that the AM7 corresponds to the chords heard during improvisation: the horn writing during the head features a chromatic passing fourth (C–F) that links D♭–G♭ to B–E there.

out the m3 axis motion (that m3 axis motion appears on downbeats of each measure).

Example 3.7. B section, m3 Axis in Melody and Bass

C/Gm   C/B♭m

B Section Phrase 1	m3 axis in melody						
Melody	E (F)	G (A♭)	B♭ (B)	C♯ (D)		E	
Harmony	B♭7	G7alt	E7	Dm(M7)		B♭dim9	Gm13
	m3 axis in bass			break in bass axis		return to bass axis	
m.	33	34	35	36		37	39

B♭ D♭ E G C   G B♭ D F A C♯

B Section Phrase 2	m3 axis in melody		Same m3 axis, new octatonic collection			
Melody	E (F)	G (A♭)	B♭ (C)	C♯ (D♯)	E	
Harmony	Gm7	B♭m7	D♭m(M7)	AM7	F♯m9	F♯7(♭9, ♯11)
	m3 axis in bass			new m3 axis in bass		
m.	41	42	43	44	45	47

Yet the descending bass motion at mm. 33–40 does not move exclusively through the m3 axis. It begins systematically by cycling downward through the m3 axis via dominant harmonies (B♭7, G7alt, E7), inverting the ascent in the melody. At m. 36 the bass motion abandons the axis, but regains it at mm. 37–40 with the motion from B♭ to G. The departure at m. 36 avoids a more predictable D♭7 harmony, although the replacement Dm(M7) harmony may be heard as sharing a similar upper structure (the upper structures are virtually identical in the case of Dm13(M7) and D♭7♯9/b13). The use of Dm(M7) evokes the D♭7 axis harmony while avoiding the more-predictable move in the bass. The result forms an upper-structure progression.[16]

Hancock's 1964 lead sheet indicates the harmonies at mm. 37 and 39 as slash chords, C/Gm and C/B♭m.[17] This creates a type of upper struc- ture pedal point: the upper triad holds while the harmony beneath shifts. I hear the m. 39 harmony as Gm13 (more or less consistent with Hancock's slash chord notation), but the m. 37 harmony as B♭°7 with added ninth, C (differing from Hancock's CM/B♭m notation since it excludes the F of the lower structure B♭m). Nevertheless, the two harmonies still preserve C major within their upper structures, retaining C major as an upper struc- ture pedal point.

upper structure pedal point

16. And from a chord/scale perspective, both Dm(M7) and D♭7alt may be said to rely on the same underlying scalar collection: an ascending D minor melodic scale.

17. Perhaps the more accurate term is "polychord," since Hancock represents the lower structures (below the slash) as minor triads—B♭m and Gm in each case—and uses a triangle following C to represent the common upper structure C major triad. In contrast to the term "polychord," "slash chord" typically refers to a chord over a single bass pitch, rather than over a triad.

Example 3.7 further shows that second phrase of the B section also relies on the m3 axis in the melody and bass. As in mm. 33–40, the melodic pathway at mm. 41–48 creates an octave ascent that begins and ends on E, with m3 axis pitches occurring on the downbeat. However, note the path changes at mm. 43: there the melodic line migrates to another octatonic (diminished) collection, one that preserves the same axis pitches on downbeats, as shown by the figure. Meanwhile, the bass motion also migrates from one axis to another. Mm. 41–43 progress G-B♭-D♭, preserving minor mode harmonies moving in parallel motion to the melody. At mm. 44–48 the axis shifts in the bass to A-F♯, now in contrary motion to the melody.[18]

The harmony at mm. 47–48 (F♯7♭9♯11) resolves to Fm(M7) at m. 49–51, providing the composition's first and only functional dominant harmony (as V'): that is, it is the only dominant harmony whose bass resolves directly down by fifth or half step. The infrequency of functional dominant harmonies illuminates an evident postbop strategy. Yet the harmonic endpoints of Phrases 1 and 2 of the B section (see Example 3.7) animate a broader turnaround strategy (Gm13 at mm. 39–40 and F♯7(♭9, ♯11) at mm. 47–48). If camouflaged through the chord-to-chord motion, the goals of both phrases suggest a functional progression in F, with Gm13 standing in for ii7, and F♯7(♭9, ♯11) substituting for V.[19]

Heard in terms of their final chords, then, the B section Phrases 1 and 2 participate in the resolution to Fm(M7) at mm. 49–51, with the mm. 47–48 F♯7(♭9, ♯11) effecting the resolution directly. The Fm(M7) recalls the same harmony heard at the end of the A' section (m. 32). Its return here contributes to the F centricity of the composition, with F appearing in two guises: Fsus9 at the beginnings of Phrases 1 and 2 in the A and A' sections, and Fm(M7) at mm. 32 and 49–51.

As shown in Example 3.8, Phrase 3 includes a 4-bar segment (mm. 49–52) notable for its melodic design, which reverses the E to E octave ascent heard twice before in the B Section's Phrases 1 and 2. It forms a melodic descent that initially elaborates the F melodic minor collection. Further, the Fm(M7) harmony yields to one more Aeolian progression at m. 51, as the harmony moves to D♭M7/F.

18. To be clear, the axis motions described here are bass axis progressions rather than harmonic axis progressions, since the harmonies are not all the same quality.

19. The octatonic melody in both phrases also contributes, more abstractly, to a functional harmonic design. The octatonic melody of Phrase 1 (E-F-G-A♭-B♭-B-D♭-D-E) may be heard to imply G7 (V7/V), and the final pitches of Phrase 2 (B♭-C-C♯-D♯-E) to imply C7 (V7). Such a technique appears in some of Hancock's improvisations. See Keith Waters, "Blurring the Barline: Metric Displacement in the Piano Solos of Herbie Hancock," *Annual Review of Jazz Studies* 8 (1996): 19–37: it shows how mm. 9–12 of Hancock's first F minor blues chorus in "The Eye of the Hurricane" relies on those two octatonic collections to imply V7/V and V.

Example 3.8. B Section, Melody and Harmony to Phrase 3

Melody	E (F) D (E) C (D) B♭ (C)	A♭ (B♭) G (A♭) ⟋ F♯ F (G) E♭ F		Solos begin	Top of Form
Harmony	Fm(M7)	D♭M7/F ⟶ Em9	Em9	Fsus9
m.	49	51	53	57–60	1

Yet the tonicized return to F at m. 49 participates in the composition's final twist, one that challenges its sense of tonal arrival. Rather than returning to the top of the form at m. 53 and providing tonal continuity, there is a downshift that undermines the F tonal center. The half-step motion down to Em9 at mm. 53–60 provides the flash point for the piece's harmonic and formal ambiguity. The downward motion to Emin9—and its expanded harmonic rhythm of 8 bars—sound as a new point of resolution, aided by the melodic overlap as the melody continues into the downbeat of m. 53 (there the chromatic motion F-F♯ in the melody sounds in contrary motion to the F-E in the bass). In addition, the solos begin midway (at m. 57) through this 8-bar E minor section. By consistently beginning at m. 57, the solos overlap with the beginning of the form, creating a sense of formal circularity. And the end of the form avoids any turnaround progression. There is merely a tonal upshift back to F at m. 1. It works against the gravitational pull heard at the downward E arrival at m. 53. The upward half-step resolution back into m. 1 creates a dizzying and curious tonal effect, one that seems to defy gravity.[20]

"King Cobra" provides ambitious alternative compositional designs. At a broad level, a M3 axis frames the A and A′ sections, while the m3 axis frames Phrases 1 and 2 of the B section. Additionally, ends of phrases in the A and A′ sections use m2 and P5 axes to create alternative turnarounds. Finally, the end of the form closes with a half-step resolution to E minor that compromises the F centricity and launches the solos, enhancing the harmonic and formal ambiguity. Throughout, there is a determined avoidance of functional dominants, with only one dominant harmony, which resolves by half step (at mm. 47–48). Certainly there are clear hard bop references, such as the blues scale melodic opening heard in Phrase 1 of

---

20. In a broader sense, the bass/melody counterpoint throughout this section seems to play an important role as well. The contrary motion leading into m. 53 (bass F-E and melody F-F♯) reverses at the top of the form via Hancock's comping: the Em9 to Fsus9 harmonic progression is supported by F♯-F motion in the upper voice of the piano.

the A and A′ sections. Yet the formal ambiguity, pedal point constructions, Aeolian progressions, and use of axes in place of more-conventional tonal progressions offered Hancock multiple postbop techniques, ones that his later compositions continued to explore.

ANALYSIS 2: "DOLPHIN DANCE"

The compositional ideas of "King Cobra"—the M3 axis, shifting pedal point harmonies, and Aeolian progressions—form an important point of departure for "Dolphin Dance." And, more generally, ideas of formal circularity, those that worked to erase the formal boundaries at the top of the form, became worked out even more thoroughly in "Dolphin Dance." It begins as a 38-bar composition, yet once initially stated the final four bars (mm. 35–38) return not to mm. 1–4, but link each time to m. 5. Therefore the initial head statement lasts 38 bars, but the improvised sections last 34 bars. In a sense mm. 35–38 provide an alternative to mm. 1–4, but they offer different harmonies and severely challenge the sense of formal return. The result is a circular flow, enhanced by the tonal flow that suspends the effect of a single underlying tonic. If "King Cobra" provides enough cues to support its F centricity, "Dolphin Dance" in contrast consistently migrates without alighting long enough anywhere to support the same type of tonal centricity. The result is a composition that is richly ambiguous, both formally and tonally. But the evidently lyrical and motivic melody, and the use of locally functional harmonic progressions along with other harmonic designs, all contribute handily to an unruffled ambience that masks the composition's deeper ambiguities.

An explanatory diagram for "Dolphin Dance" appears as Example 3.9. It is a single-section composition with three broad subsections: mm. 1–17 (with active harmonic motion and two main melodic motives); mm. 17–24 (a descending series of expanded bass pedal points beneath a return to the opening motive), and mm. 25–34 (an ascending sequence to a qualified cadence). The additional four measures at mm. 35–38 replace mm. 1–4. They restate versions of the opening motive, and provide a 3-bar pedal point along with (at m. 38) a harmonic link to m. 5. Therefore mm. 35–38 are formally ambiguous: they can be heard both ending the head and as beginning a new chorus. (The original recorded performance ends with a vamp on the mm. 30–34 progression.)

Example 3.9. Explanatory Diagram for "Dolphin Dance"

Mm. 1–17, Melody. The opening motive—a four-note melody—is one of Hancock's most compact, lyrical, and memorable. It returns throughout the composition, preserving generally the original shape and rhythm while altering the pitches (and frequently the intervals). Its use as a melodic reference point possibly explains some of the allure of replacing song forms with single-section compositions: they allow an ongoing sense of motivic

continuity and development and avoid the evident repetition of the 8-bar sections of AABA and ABAC forms.

During mm. 1–17 we hear two different lyrical motives. The opening 2-bar motive and its three varied restatements (mm. 1–9) link to a different 4-bar motive at mm. 9–16. That motive is heard twice, with its repetition keeping the rhythm and shape of the original. As Example 3.10 shows, the skeletal melody for both segments elaborates largely stepwise motion. The first 8-bar segment moves downward, and the second 8-bar segment progresses upward. Beneath the lyricism of mm. 1–9 the skeletal melody creates the descending stepwise melodic progression of G-F-Eb-D-C-B. And the motives at mm. 9–16 elaborate an ascending stepwise progression, beginning with F#/Gb, and through G#/Ab, Bb (elaborated by G), C, to D.

Example 3.10. Stepwise Skeletal Melody and Key Regions in "Dolphin Dance," mm. 1–17

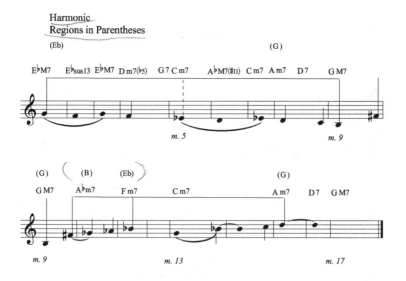

Both stepwise motions share the same boundary interval of a m6, although the intervallic construction of each differs. (Mm. 9–16 form a whole tone ascent.) Additionally, they share another feature. Each stepwise m6th clearly marks its M3rd midpoint. At a 4-bar level the opening pitches of mm. 1, 5, and 9 descend through G-Eb-B. During mm. 9–16 the primary pitches link F#/Gb (mm. 9–10), Bb (mm. 11–14), and D (mm. 15–16). We can appreciate the melodic balance between the two 8-bar segments: the first progresses downward a m6th and the second progresses upward a m6th, and both emphasize the M3 midpoint. As a result of that midpoint, the

melody [handwritten]

melody expresses two different M3 axes (G-E♭-B, mm. 1–9, F♯-B♭-D, mm. 9–16), axes that are filled out through stepwise motion.

Mm. 1–17, Harmony. If the melodic structure of these 8-bar segments expresses these axes, in what ways does the harmonic progression participate? At mm. 1–9, the melody outlines three steps of the axis (G, E♭, and B), but the larger harmonic outline only progresses through two—mm. 1–9 begin with E♭ major (corresponding to the G of the melody) and end with G major (corresponding with B of the melody). At mm. 9–17, the melody moves to a different axis, with three giant steps (F♯, B♭, and D). There the harmony merely begins and returns to G major, without intervening B major or E♭ major harmonies. Throughout the opening 17 bars, then, the harmonies only inconsistently support the M3 melodic axes through appearances of E♭ and G major at significant arrival points of mm. 1, 9, and 17.

But it is possible to hear the overall harmonic progressions at mm. 1–17 as cooperating in an E♭ major-G major-B major harmonic axis. To do this requires a view of substitute and elaborative harmonies, ones that replace a more evident and obvious M3 harmonic cycle. Such a view leads to harmonic regions rather than a direct successions of M3 progressions. For "Dolphin Dance," regions extend to 1) *substitutions*: relative minor harmonies that stand in for major harmonies, and 2) *elaborations*: harmonies that embellish major harmonies and their relative minor substitutions. [handwritten margin note: *Harmonic Regions not progressions*]

My argument here is that harmonic regions of a M3 axis (the major keys of E♭, G, B, E♭, and G) in mm. 1–17 guide the underlying harmonic organization. In some instances the major keys are replaced entirely by their relative minor *substitutions*. In some instances the primary harmonies (and their minor key substitutes) use *elaborations*. Further, the harmonic regions do not circulate in rhythmically regular fashion (that is, they do not necessarily appear every two or four bars). As a result—and in contrast to regularly circulating and direct M3 axis progressions—the M3 harmonic axis of mm. 1–17 of "Dolphin Dance" is subterranean. [handwritten: *underground*] While the melodic dimension more explicitly reflects two M3 axes, the harmonic progressions explore a single M3 axis in a less explicit way. The following discussion will suggest how, beginning with mm. 1–9.

Example 3.11 indicates the individual harmonies, the axis motion of the melody, and the two harmonic regions heard in mm. 1–9. The opening seven measures use both substitutions and elaborations work to express its E♭ major region. In addition to E♭M7 at mm. 1 and 3, the relative substitute, C minor, appears tonicized in mm. 5, and reappears at m. 7. Further, both E♭ major and its substitute C minor use elaborations. In each case, the elaborating harmonies (indicated by the chords in parentheses) are flanked by the primary harmonies. At m. 2, E♭sus13 (or D♭M7/E♭) elaborates E♭M7. Similarly, in m. 6, A♭M7(♯11) elaborates C minor. The role for both those elaborating harmonies is the same: in each case, they provide a harmony for a melodic neighboring tone—E♭sus13 supports the melodic pitch F (a neighboring tone to the G in mm. 1 and 3), and A♭M7(♯11) supports the melodic pitch D (a neighboring tone to the E♭ of mm. 5 and 7).

This E♭ major region of mm. 1–7 then progresses to a new region of G major through a ii-V cadence (m. 8).[21]

Example 3.11. Harmony, Melody, and M3-related Harmonic Regions in mm. 1–9

Chord	E♭M7 (E♭sus13) E♭M7 D-7♭5 G7	Cmin (AbM7♯11) Cmin	Am7 D7 GM7
Skeletal Melody	G	E♭	B
Harmonic Region	E♭ major (mm. 1—4)	E♭ major (mm. 5—7)	G major (m.8—9)

Example 3.12 indicates the harmonic regions of mm. 9–17. Those measures both begin and end in G major. Through substitutions and elaborations, the intervening progressions support harmonic regions of B major and E♭ major. Here those substitute minor harmonies replace and fully stand in for those major keys. The progress of those harmonic regions corresponds to the progress of the F♯-B♭-D melodic axis pitches. At mm. 9–10 the melodic move to F♯ serves as a common tone link between G major and to A♭ minor. That A♭ minor harmony substitutes for B major, whose region is served only by that harmony.

As the melody proceeds upwards to B♭ the harmony shifts to F-9 and C-9. Within is a slight echo of mm. 7–8, with A♭ minor to F minor (mm. 10–12) a transposition of the Cm7 Am7 progression at mm. 7–8. Yet the outcome is different: a direct transposition of mm. 7–9 would have yielded A♭m7-Fm7-B♭7-E♭M7. Rather than take that pathway, the A♭m7-Fm7 progression at mm. 10–12 instead moves to C minor at mm. 13–14, the relative minor substitute of E♭. Thus the E♭ major region uses the C minor harmony as well as the preceding F minor harmony (mm. 11–12), which acts as a prefix elaboration of C minor, much as the A♭M7(♯11) harmony at m. 6 elaborated C minor at m. 7. Finally, as the melodic activity steps from B♭ to D (mm. 13–16), the harmonic activity moves from the E♭ region to another G major region, which is tonicized conventionally. Thus the intervening harmonic

---

21. The overall progression at mm. 1–9 has some structural similarities to "The Pleasure Is Mine" described above—the bass progression moves through vi en route to a cadence to the new key a major third above.

regions of B major and E♭ major are served only through relative minor substitutions and their elaborations.

Example 3.12. Harmony, Melody, and M3-related Harmonic Regions in mm. 9–17

Chord	Gmaj	A♭ minor	(F minor)	C minor	A-7 D7	GM7
Melody	F♯		B♭		D	
Region	G major	B major	E♭ major		G major	
m.	9	10	11	13	15—16	17

In summary, mm. 1–17 use two broader melodic axes: G-E♭-B (mm. 1–9) and F♯-B♭-D (mm. 9–17), with the first descending and the second ascending. The first occurs regularly, every four bars, while the second occurs less regularly, appearing 2 + 4 + 2 bars. At the same time, those melodic axis pitches appear with a single (E♭-G-B-E♭-G) harmonic axis. That harmonic axis is significantly less evident than the melodic axes: it progresses through those key regions with the aid of substitutions and elaborations. The pacing of harmonic regions is less systematic than that of the melodic axis.

These measures make clear how Hancock very broadly interprets M3-related melodic and harmonic motions by avoiding overly predictable (or rhythmically systematic) axis progressions. Thus although the composition explores some symmetries of the M3 axes, the pacing of those events is neither symmetrical nor regular. Yet the main effect of the harmonic regions is clear. The upward direction of the axis harmonic regions, each moving four steps sharpward in tonal space, helps motivate the composition's ever-brightening effect as it progresses through these measures.

Mm. 17–25. Mm. 17–25 return to the opening melodic motive, even including a rhythmic and pitch rhyme between m. 5 and m. 21. Yet in comparison to mm. 1–9, the stepwise downward progress of the skeletal melody moves more quickly, progressing B-A-G-F-E♭-D each measure between mm. 17–22. Further, mm. 17–25 relies on longer bass pedal points beneath shifting harmonies. These pedal points descend stepwise downward from G (m. 17) to F (m. 21) en route to E♭ (m. 25, interrupted by an intervening motion at m. 24).

The melody at mm. 17–18 transposes that of mm. 1–2. Similarly, the mm. 17–18 harmonies (GM7 and Gsus13) transpose the mm. 1–2 harmonies. But the exact transposition of melody and harmony ceases afterwards. The G pedal continues and the following harmonies create movement in the inner voice. The suspended fourth of m. 18 moves upwards by half-step to form a ♯11 above the bass at m. 19. These two harmonies (FM7/G and

FM7♯5/G) provide a variation on a more traditionally functional progression. Example 3.13 indicates how Hancock's upper structure harmonies might relate to a more functional progression, as an expanded ii chord in a C major context.

Example 3.13. Comparison of Hancock's mm. 18–19 Progression with More Conventional Progression

Hancock's progression mm. 18–19	FM7/G (Gsus13)	FM7♯5/G		
More conventional progression	Dm9 (ii)	Dm9(♯7)	Dm9	G7 (V)

Rather than realizing this tonal context, however, "Dolphin Dance" instead maintains the G pedal point, establishing a sound world of a sus chord (m. 18) along with its half-step displacement (m. 19). The upper structure of the following harmony (E♭M7♯5/G, m. 20) transposes downward by whole-step the upper structure of the FM7♯5/G of the previous measure. Yet since the bass does not move similarly down by step, the resultant chord with bass provides a dense and colorful harmony.[22]

If unusual, the m. 20 E♭M7♯5/G nevertheless participates in the sound world of sus chords and half-step displacements. That m. 20 harmony links to the following chord, E♭M7/F. But rather than the progression E♭M7♯5/F to E♭M7/F, the inner voice half-step motion of ♯5-5 (B to B♭) takes place while the bass shifts from G to F. This provides another layer of displacement, now in the bass, which delays the arrival of F, as shown by the comparison between Hancock's progression and a hypothetical one more in line with mm. 18–19 (Example 3.14).

Example 3.14. Comparison of Hancock's mm. 20–21 Progression with Hypothetical Progression

Hancock's progression mm. 20–21	E♭M7♯5/G	Fsus13 (= E♭M7/F)
Hypothetical progression	E♭M7♯5/F	Fsus13 (= E♭M7/F)

The Fsus13 harmony at mm. 21 and 23 is itself embellished with F13(♭9) at m. 22. That harmonization participates with the melody, with the embellishing melodic D as a neighboring pitch to the E♭ that appears at

---

22. It is possible to hear both the FM7♯5/G and E♭M7/♯5/G as subsets of a melodic minor mode, with the first chord referring to D melodic minor, and the second chord to C melodic minor.

mm. 21 and 23. In comparison with more conventional tonal progressions, there is a reversal of roles here. In that conventional tonal context, Fsus9 embellishes (by delaying) an F7 harmony, which often results in a resolution of that F7 harmony to B♭. Here, however, it is the dominant harmony (F13♭9) that embellishes the Fsus9 harmony. Thus while some of the chord-to-chord activity maintains ties to tonal progressions, there is a shift in orientation. The result here makes the sus chord primary and the dominant harmony secondary and elaborating. And any tonal obligations of those progressions (such as a resolution to B♭ following Fsus9 and F13b9) remain deliberately unmet.

Mm. 25–38. The arrival on E♭ in the bass at m. 25 might suggest the opening path of the skeletal melody at mm. 1–5, since the entire section moves the bass from from G (mm. 17–20), through F (mm. 21–23) to that E♭. It might also suggest a M3 axis, but that view skews the overall tonal orientation of the section. It also ignores the Em7 A7 progression at m. 24, which participates in that orientation. As the following diagram shows, mm. 24–26 supports G major, using a secondary progression (E-7 A7), a tritone substitution harmony of the preceding A7 harmony (E♭7(♯11), the V′/V indicating the tritone substitution), and a direct ii-V progression (A-7 D7, m. 26). The E♭ in m. 25 does not form a bass arrival point for G-F-E♭: instead it participates (as a secondary V′ chord) in a G major tonality.

And certainly a longer-range view of mm. 17–26 could suggest that the entire passage from mm. 17–26 elaborates G major. Following the opening GM7 sonority and expanded G pedal (mm. 17–20), the F pedal at mm. 21–24 elaborates ♭VII7 (as V′/vi in G). That F pedal point then yields to the harmonies at mm. 24–26 that further set up the promise of G major, as Example 3.15 shows.

Example 3.15. G Major Tonal Orientation of mm. 24–26

	E-7 A7	E♭7(♯11)	A-7 D7
G major	ii/V V/V	V′/V	ii-V
m.	24	25	26

Yet G major does not return as the form continues to unfold. Instead, a series of ascending ii-V motions progress upward by step, with the melody initially following upward by sequence. Following m. 26 (implying G), the harmony sequences up by step twice. The first sequence provides a standard cadential ploy by suggesting ii-V of ii (B-7 E7, mm. 27–28): jazz standard compositions typically return that progression back to ii-V en route to the tonic harmony (Am7 D7 Bm7 E7 Am7 D7 G). An upward sequenced step-wise ii-V progression (mm. 29–30, C♯-7 F♯7, following the passing harmony of D-7) is less common in jazz standard compositions, but in those instances suggest ii-V of iii. In those compositions (as in Lee Morgan's "Ceora," mm. 13–15, which moves to iii or in Neil Hefti's "Shiny Stockings," mm. 13–15, which moves to III) that sequence delays the ultimate cadence to I.

But in contrast to those standard-tune examples, "Dolphin Dance" does not move downward and fulfill those tonal obligations by returning to G major. Instead the three ii-V sequences now settle on a cadence at the last of them. This cadence (mm. 29–31) illustrates a postbop aesthetic choice. In this case, an evi-dent or conventional move in one dimension is paired with a less-conventional move in another. At mm. 29–30, the melody executes a familiar melodic ca-dence, one that implies B major (with the melodic D♯ at m. 30) capped by a conventional 5-1 melodic close. At the same time, the C♯m7 F♯7 progression also implies an arrival on B. However, the bass pitch works against the grain of that convention by resolving to E rather than an expected B.

If the bass does not cooperate by realizing those conventions, there is yet a sense in which the upper structure of the harmony more closely realizes them. The result is an upper structure progression. That is, the upper structure of Esus13 includes the pitches of Bm9, fulfilling the ex-pected pathway (although consistent with B minor rather than B major). At the same time, the bass thwarts the expectation of B. The upper structure progression provides a degree of familiarity to the unusual cadence, but operates at one level of remove from the more predictable B arrival in the bass. Thus melody and upper structure harmony operate in a more conven-tional tonal manner, but the bass pitch does not.

That cadence launches a 4-bar segment at mm. 31–34, and the result creates a metrical reorientation. Mm. 25–30 retrospectively form a 6-bar phrase, the only portion of the composition that departs from 4- and 8-bar sections. Mm. 31–34 then provide another 4-bar pedal point plateau that alternates Esus13 and CM7/E. This Aeolian progression (due to the use of the first inversion M7 harmony) sounds as an ending gesture here. If a familiar progression heard in other Hancock compositions (compare with mm. 1–4 of "King Cobra" discussed above),[23] it appears in those other compositions more typically as an opening, rather than closing, gesture.

The final four bars (mm. 35–38) precede the opening solo and subse-quently replace mm. 1–4 once the opening head is stated. Prior to the

---

23. The improvisational harmonies for Hancock's composition "Little One" use a sim-ilar opening progression by beginning with Fsus7 and D♭M7♯11/F.

functional ii-V cadence at mm. 38 (Dm7♭5 G7, connecting to C minor at m. 5), the bass downshifts from E to an E♭ pedal point as the melody provides two variations on the opening 4-note motive. At mm. 34–35 this creates motivates contrary motion between bass (E-E♭) and melody (B-C). (This is similar to the contrary motion heard in "King Cobra" at mm. 52–53: there the bass also progresses down and the melody up by half step: see the discussion earlier in the chapter.)

Although these four bars serve as a substitute for the opening four bars, the harmonies here are decidedly less conventional. For example, at m. 2 E♭sus13 was an elaborative harmony (for E♭M7 at mm. 1 and 3), but at m. 35 the E♭sus13 chord is the opening harmony, one that provides the point of departure for the following harmonies of EM7♯5/E♭ and Bmaj7♯5/E♭ (mm. 36 and 37).[24] These pedal point harmonies are subsets of the melodic minor collection: EM7♯5/E♭ is a subset of a mode of D♭ melodic minor, Bmaj♯7/E♭ of A♭ melodic minor. Their appearance in "Dolphin Dance" shows Hancock's expansion of harmonic resources by mid-decade that now includes these additional pedal point harmonies related to the ascending minor mode collection. While Hancock's vocabulary had already expressed more-conventional uses of modes of melodic minor harmonies—particularly with altered dominant chords[25]—the melodic minor-related sonorities of "Dolphin Dance" evoke that familiar collectional sound, but one detached from a more functional tonal context.

The harmonic progress at mm. 30–38 (with E pedal point, E♭ pedal point, then Dm7♭5 G7, which connects to the m. 5 C minor) coincides with the harmonic progressions of some other Hancock compositions that similarly alternate downward bass motion by half step and by fifth. In these situations the bass proceeds as it would in more-conventional tonal contexts, but often with less conventional upper structure harmonies.[26]

In sum, mm. 1–17 explore M3 axes through both melody and harmony. This is more evident and systematic in the melodic dimension. It is less so in the harmonic dimension, given the use of harmonic regions that involve substitute and elaborating harmonies. Mm. 17–24 explore pedal point harmonies over G and F as the opening motive returns. Mm. 25–30 set up a qualified cadence (to Esus13) through a sequence of ascending ii-V

24. Hancock also uses the same pair of harmonies in mm. 7–8 of "Little One." See Waters, "Modes, Scales," 348–50.

25. For example, one way to express that collection involves the right hand alternation of E♭ and D♭ triads above a G7altered chord stated in the left hand.

26. See Chapter 6 for discussion of this technique in Hancock's "One Finger Snap" and "Speak Like a Child," as well as in Wayne Shorter's "Nerfertiti.

motions, and mm. 30–38 stage two pedal points (progressing E to E♭), the second using harmonies related to modes of the ascending melodic minor collection. Following the ii-V motion at m. 38, the form then bypasses the original mm. 1–4 and connects to m. 5.

The memorable and lyrical compact melodic motives of "Dolphin Dance" serve longer, ongoing, and largely stepwise melodic lines during much of the composition. Each are subsets of scalar collections: the skeletal pitches of mm. 1–9 (these are the downbeat pitches, and include the passing C of m. 8) progress G-F-E♭-D-C-B (subset of C melodic minor), those of mm. 9–16 progress F♯/G♭-A♭-B♭-C-D (a subset of the whole-tone collection), and mm. 17–24 consists of the line B-A-G-F-E♭-D, which then returns upwards to A via the same collection (a subset of C melodic minor). The ascending ii-V sequences of mm. 25–30 do not participate in a scalar collection, but the melody of the final four bars (mm. 34–38) rely on the pitches of an A♭ diatonic collection.

More significantly, these longer melodic contours shape the composition's overall balance. Melodically, the first two 8-bar segments are balanced: downward motion of a m6th (mm. 1–9) precedes upward motion of a m6th (m. 9–16). Less exact, but still complementary, is the largely downward melodic motion of mm. 17–22 followed by the upward sequential motion of mm. 25–30.[27] That upward sequential motion places the melodic high point of the composition at F♯ at m. 29.

If "King Cobra" challenged established principles of jazz composition through formal circularity and harmonic ambiguity, "Dolphin Dance" extended those challenges. Since the four bars at mm. 35–38 replace the opening bars, the opening mm. 1–4 harmonies never return, creating circularity by eroding the sense of return to the top of the form.[28] The 6-bar phrase at mm. 25–30 also offsets the clear 4- and 8-bar sections throughout the rest of the composition, enhancing that circularity.

27. These ideas of balance return to the Hancock quotation presented earlier in the chapter: "Compositionally, from a structural point of view, 'Watermelon Man' and 'Maiden Voyage' are probably my two strongest pieces. I'm talking strictly about craft—the balance, the relationships that are working throughout the piece. They're almost mathematical." Quoted in Lyons (1983), 275.

28. The question of where the form "begins," then, is ambiguous after the opening head statement. During the recorded performance, the saxophone and piano solos begin m. 35 (over the E♭ pedal point). But Carter's accompaniment frequently continues the texture of the previous measures by breaking up the time at mm. 35–38, and moves to walking bass accompaniment at m. 5. Harmonically, too, the E♭ pedal point is part of a larger downward process begun by the E pedal (mm. 30–34) and continued through the cadence to C minor at m. 5—in that sense, m. 5 sounds as a clearer "top of the form" arrival point.

Further, despite a number of conventional harmonic progressions, there is no overall sense of a global tonic to the composition. Instead, there are merely successions of harmonic regions and pedal point plateaus, creating stations that are tonicized to greater or lesser degrees. The opening E♭ major harmony never returns. (During the out head on the recorded performance, the horns play the mm. 1–4 melody against the mm. 35–38 chords.) The recorded performance ends with a vamp over the two E pedal point harmonies at mm. 31–34. Thus the composition avoids a single and unequivocal tonic.

In addition to its formal and harmonic ambiguity, "Dolphin Dance" is significant for other reasons. It is one of several Hancock compositions to explore a M3 axis in subtle ways. Further, during the pedal points in the bass the shifting harmonies are formed through sus chords, Aeolian progressions, and non-standard harmonies derived from melodic minor collections. In addition, it combines those pedal point harmonies with more standard tonal progressions. Its appearance in fake books has virtually guaranteed its ongoing use by jazz players. In many ways "Dolphin Dance" is one of Hancock's most compelling compositions of the 1960s, due to its slowly unfolding lyrical melody supported by a richly diverse palette of harmonic colors.

ANALYSIS 3: "JESSICA"

"Jessica" appeared on Hancock's 1969 recording *Fat Albert Rotunda*.[29] If less formally ambitious than "King Cobra" or "Dolphin Dance"—it consists of a repeated 8-bar form—"Jessica" still maintains a strongly lyrical and harmonically adventurous profile. It also is systematically grounded in an intervallic axis, here the perfect fourth. Some of Hancock's earlier compositions worked out that P4 axis in the harmonic dimension, either with direct P4 motion (the A sections of "Theme From Blow Up," recorded with Bobby Hutcherson, progress Emaj-A7alt-Dsus), or more indirectly ("Little One" is based primarily on pedal point harmonies over the bass motion of F-E♭-B♭).[30] Instead, "Jessica" explores the P4 axis in the melodic dimension. The axis does not appear as foregrounded on the note-to-note level as in compositions such as Wayne Shorter's "E.S.P.," "Witch Hunt,"

29. Hancock recorded "Jessica" again in 1977 in a live performance with the V.S.O.P. Quintet (Columbia 34976).
30. See Waters, *The Studio Recordings*, 96–97.

or "Speak No Evil." But clearly that intervallic axis was of deep interest to postbop composers,[31] and Hancock subtly embeds it into the composition in sophisticated fashion.

An explanatory diagram, including the Introduction, appears as Example 3.16. Even the repeated two-measure introduction is given over to the P4 axis. The first measure of the introduction (over G minor) begins with an arpeggiated triad on the first beat, which then yields to an arpeggiated P4 chord (A-D-G) on the second beat. This harmony is then transposed by a P4 on the final beat of the measure (to D-G-C). This first measure of the introduction is then *itself* transposed by a P4 during the second introductory measure (as is the harmony, which moves from G minor to C minor). The introduction therefore pursues the P4 relation on several levels: the first measure contains a P4 chord and its P4 transposition, the following measure then transposes the previous measure by P4.

Example 3.16. Explanatory Diagram for "Jessica" Showing P4 Axis Melody

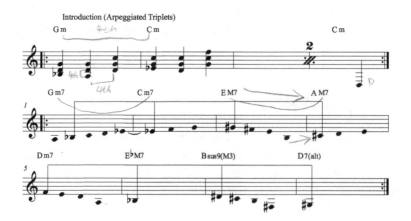

The melodic structure of the entire composition further explores this axis. As the beaming in Example 3.16 suggests, the melody embellishes an ongoing ascending P4 (or descending P5) motion, with axis pitches occurring once per measure. The axis is expressed in two lines (mm. 1–4 and 5–8). The first line, occurring between mm. 1–4, connects B♭, E♭, G♯, and C♯. (All of these pitches begin on the downbeat with the exception

31. And earlier, of course: Carisi's "Israel" uses it melodically in mm. 9–12.

of the first pitch B♭, which is delayed by A.) At the same time, the chord qualities shift. Since the first two harmonies are minor and the second are major, the progression avoids a mechanical sequence of common structure harmonies. Example 3.17 includes the axis melodic pitches, two hypothetical progressions (the first consisting of a consistent sequence of minor harmonies, the second a consistent sequence of major harmonies), and Hancock's progression. Hancock's progression moves from the first hypothetical line to the other (as shown by the harmonies in bold in the example). As a result, each pair of chords (mm. 1–2 and 3–4) involves a P4 axis motion (G to C, mm. 1–2; E to A, mm. 3–4). Thus the melody proceeds consistently through the axis while the progression avoids a systematic harmonization. The contrapuntal foundation between melody and bass is consistent, however, with the bass and melodic axis pitch preserving parallel tenths during the entire 4-bar passage.

Example 3.17. Comparison of Hancock's Progression with Two Hypothetical P4 Axis Progressions

Melodic Axis	B♭	E♭	A♭/G♯	D♭/C♯
Hypothetical Progression 1	**Gm7**	**Cm7**	Fm7	B♭m7
Hypothetical Progression 2	G♭M7	C♭M7	**EM7**	**AM7**
Hancock's Progression	Gm7	Cm7	EM7	AM7
m.	1	2	3	4

Mm. 5–8 provide two variations on the melodic motive heard mm. 3–4. Further, these measures again express a P4 axis of F, B♭, E♭, and A♭, as shown in Example 3.18. Its beginning pitch (F) does not continue where the mm. 1–4 axis left off (C♯), but its following pitches (B♭-E♭-G♯) echo the first three pitches of the mm. 1–4 axis. The bass itself continues its own P4 axis that began in m. 3 and continues until m. 5, linking E, A, and D.

Example 3.18. Melodic Axis and Harmonic Progression of mm. 5–8

Melodic Axis	F	B♭	D♯	G♯
Hancock's Progression	Dm7	E♭M7	Bsus13 (with 3rd)	D7(alt)
m.	5	6	7	8

The harmonic progression at mm. 5–8 moves more freely than at mm. 1–4. While mm. 5–6 offer the same chord qualities (m7 and M7) heard in mm. 1–4, the m. 7 harmony involves a sus chord with a major third in the melody.[32] The final D7alt offers a functional dominant (and another P4 axis motion in the bass) back to the G minor harmony at the top of the form. Despite the flexible harmonic progression, the bass/melody counterpoint alternates 3rds (m3 between D/F at m. 5, M3 between B/D♯ m. 7) and 5ths (P5 between E♭/B♭ m. 6, dim5 between D/G♯ m. 8).

The contrapuntal organization has an effect on the varied motives heard at mm. 3–4, 5–6, and 7–8, each of which begins with a M3 or m3 between bass and melody. Those motives that begin with bass/melody M3 use a whole step between their first two pitches (m. 3 G♯-F♯-E-B; m. 7, D♯-C♯-B-F♯), and the motive that begins with bass/melody m3 uses a half step between its first two pitches (m. 5, F-E-D-C). In each case, this allows the motive to accord with the harmonic environment.

For "Jessica," the skeletal melody provides a P4 axis in two linear strands, at mm. 1–4 and 5–8. That melodic axis is worked largely through metric downbeats. The harmonies progress more freely. Perhaps another way to hear the dimensions of bass and melody is through a role reversal: if P4 axis motion (i.e., descending fifth motion) enacts characteristic tonal moves in the bass, here those moves are transplanted from the bass to the melodic dimension. Regardless, the composition, like others of the decade, explores the P4 axis, with that axis woven subtly into the fabric of the composition.

Yet considering "Jessica" simply as an 8-bar composition does little to address the details of the 4-horn arranging heard on the *Fat Albert Rotunda* recording. Example 3.19 is an explanatory diagram that includes the harmonizations of the opening two head choruses (which also return at the end), as well as the following four measures that set up the trumpet solo. The scoring, for trumpet, alto flute, trombone, and baritone saxophone, is harmonically rich, and contains a number of subtle harmonic movements, characteristic harmonies, and reharmonization techniques not evident from the explanatory diagram of Example 3.16.

32. This is a similar chord to the one heard in "Theme from Blow Up" described earlier, which included a Dsus13 chord with F♯ in the melody. The chord is voiced sometimes as simply B13: see the discussion below of the four-horn arrangement.

Example 3.19. Explanatory Diagram with Chords and Accompaniment to "Jessica" (Melody Omitted)

* D in baritone saxophone 8ve lower than notated (m. 6, second chorus)

The trombone plays the melody during the first chorus, accompanied by the arpeggiating figure in the piano. The alto flute's countermelody at mm. 4–8 is stated initially below, then above the trombone. During the second chorus, the trumpet provides the melody, at first accompanied by flute and trombone, with the baritone saxophone added to the texture during mm. 4–8. The third chorus launches the trumpet solo. (The horn writing continues through a fourth and beginning of the fifth chorus, in dialogue with the piano solo. Those portions are not included in Example 3.19.)

The explanatory diagram of Example 3.19 at times assigns more than one harmonic label to each measure to account for inner voice pathways. M. 4 of the first chorus notes the F-E motion (played by the piano) by AM7(♯5) to AM7. The same harmony in m. 4 of the second chorus likewise includes an E♯, which then moves upward to F♯. Measure 7 of the first chorus accounts for the F♯-E♯ pathway (in both the piano and flute) by the addition of ♯11 to the B13 label. Additionally, the character of the D7 harmony in the following measure (m. 8, first chorus) changes, from D13(♯11) to D7 altered by the addition of ♯9 (F) and ♭13 (B♭) in the piano.

One notable characteristic of the harmonic color arises from frequent use of ♭6 (particularly shifts between ♭6 and 5) on minor-chord harmonies. For example, in m. 5, first chorus, the alto flute line moves from B♭-A over the D minor harmony. At mm. 1–2 of the second chorus, the effect intensifies, as flute oscillates between D-E♭ over the G minor harmony. At the same time, the chromatic motion in the trombone alights on A♭ over the following C minor harmony. The A♭ is again strongly present in the C minor harmony in the following chorus (m. 2, third chorus), enhanced by the minor ninth D-E♭ played by piano and flute. Hancock's piano improvisation is often flecked by this ♭6 Aeolian color over the minor-chord harmonies.

The examples discussed above maintain bass pitch and overall chord quality in each chorus despite the shadings of harmonic color. Additionally, the diagram reflects particular tactics for reharmonization, by transforming either the bass or chord quality. At m. 6, second chorus, the bass moves from root (E♭) to the major seventh (D). In m. 3 of the third chorus, the chord quality shifts: rather than E6/9 (as heard in the earlier choruses), the horn voicings reflect Esus13. The shift to a dominant-type harmony (with suspended fourth) effects more-directed motion to the following A major harmony. Finally, m. 5, third chorus, the harmony is heard as Gsus13, replacing the D minor harmonies heard earlier in that measure. The replacement Gsus13 harmony is cognate to D minor, since it preserves an upper structure of Dm9.[33]

Overall, the recorded version is harmonically sumptuous. A comparison with the three-horn writing of his earlier "King Cobra" shows some similar traits, particularly the contrasts between open and closed voicings. However, the writing in "Jessica" offers freer independent lines, and significant voice-crossings among the four horns. Even if the large 60-bar framework of "King Cobra" is distilled to miniature size with the 8-bar one

33. During the piano improvisation, bassist Buster Williams uses some of the same reharmonizations, keeping D in the bass over the E♭M7 harmony (at 2:06), and using G against the D minor harmony (at 2:45).

of "Jessica," the written choruses of "Jessica" are significantly and fluidly reworked, showcasing a remarkable palette of harmonic colors.

"King Cobra" marked for Hancock an important compositional advance, with designs that deliberately challenged more traditional ones. M3 and m3 axes broadly structure a composition with formal ambiguities toward the end of the form, provided by the E minor harmonic arrival (mm. 53–60) that undermines the overall centricity of F. In "Dolphin Dance" formal ambiguities are amplified, given that the progression at mm. 34–38 replaces the opening progression at mm. 1–4, and the composition unfolds without articulating a global sense of tonic. Both are extended single-section compositions. "Jessica," an 8-bar single-section composition, uses a smaller compositional frame and uses a P4 axis to shape the melodic lines, with an arrangement that offers shifting perspectives on the harmonic progression.

The melodic language in these (and other Hancock) compositions is expansive. This is no doubt due to many features, not least of which involve longer melodic skeletal lines that lie beneath the compelling melodic motives. In mm. 1–17 of "Dolphin Dance," two motives create skeletal step-wise melodic lines, ones that fill in the M3 axes; in "Jessica," the P4 melodic axes provides a thread through the composition. Hancock's harmonic language is equally expansive, arising through many sources: expanded pedal point harmonies (creating Aeolian and other progressions), use of sus chords, and progressions that at different times access, transform, or avoid the successions of tonal jazz. These offer just a few of Hancock's significant contributions to postbop composition in the 1960s.

CHAPTER 4
Chick Corea

Chick Corea's compositional output is among the largest and most diverse of any jazz composer. As a result, his 1960s compositions provide only a small sample. After that decade, his work included Brazilian and jazz-rock fusion with the group Return to Forever (and the later Elektric Band), solo piano works and improvisations, and more-composed works (Concerto for Piano, *Children's Songs*, *Lyric Suite* for Sextet, String Quartet, and *The Continents*). Likely his most well-known are those compositions recorded with Return to Forever in the early 1970s, such as "Spain" (*Light as a Feather*), "La Fiesta," and "Crystal Silence" (*Return to Forever*).

Nevertheless, his 1960s compositions figure prominently in the music of the decade, although his recording career began later than that of Shorter or Hancock. Corea's postbop works appear on several recordings he made as a leader: *Tones for Joan's Bones* (1966, later released as *Inner Space* in 1973 with additional compositions), the piano trio recording *Now He Sings, Now He Sobs* (1968; the CD version contains additional tracks from the same session), *Sundance* (1969), and *Is* (1969). (The latter two recordings, along with alternate takes, were later combined on the CD *The Complete "Is" Sessions*.) He also recorded some of his compositions as a sideman with Willie Bobo (*Do That Thing/Guajira*, 1963), Blue Mitchell (*The Thing to Do*, 1964, and *Boss Horn*, 1966), Hubert Laws (*Laws' Cause*, recorded 1966 and 1968), and Stan Getz (*Sweet Rain*, 1967). Among his 1960s works include imaginative 12-bar blues works ("Matrix" and "Steps," both from *Now He Sings, Now He Sobs*), and reworkings of standard tunes.[1]

---

1. "Chick's Tune," from Blue Mitchell's *The Thing to Do*, uses an original melody over the chords to "You Stepped Out of a Dream"; "Now He Beats the Drums, Now He Stops," from *Now He Sings, Now He Sobs*, provides a postbop remake of Irving Berlin's "How Deep Is the Ocean."

Corea's compositional (and pianistic) influences stemmed from many sources. Perhaps most significant were John Coltrane, McCoy Tyner, Thelonious Monk, and Bill Evans. Some are evident homages: "Samba Yantra," from the *Now He Sings* sessions, reworks the accompaniment to Eric Dolphy's "India." Yet it is incorrect to describe his 1960s compositions as derivative, and they easily transcended those influences. Many (but not all) of Corea's 1960s compositions are single-section compositions.[2] The "Trio for Flute, Bassoon, and Piano" (from Hubert Laws' *Laws' Cause*, rereleased on Corea's *Inner Space*) was a more-composed chamber work in line with his later composed works for string quartet or orchestra.

Corea's melodic language is compelling. It owes something to the pentatonic language cultivated by Coltrane's classic quartet, but that description does little to address its richness and variety. There is also a special interplay between harmony and melody: a systematic or sequential move in one dimension may go unmatched in the other, for example. Further, there is a deep rhythmic dimension to the music, and Corea frequently uses melodic rhythm as a way to set up then depart from musical expectations—the compositions often avoid predictability by rhythmically varying their melodic sequences.[3]

The harmonic sound world of his 1960s compositions is unique and individual. In part it emerges from individual chords based on P4ths and P5ths, M7#11 harmonies, ♭II (as M7, sus7, or Dominant 7th) in place of structural V chords, varied or transformed turnarounds (used at the end of the form to return to the opening harmony), and Phrygian bass motions (described below with "Inner Space"). Axis progressions figure prominently in "Windows" (which uses a P5 harmonic axis), and "Inner Space" (part of which uses a M3 melodic axis). Although not as well known as those two works, his later "Song of the Wind" (recorded in 1969) shows a broadening of harmonic resources, especially through an increased use of slash chords, polychords, and harmonies derived from the augmented (or hexatonic) scale.

This chapter discusses those three Corea compositions from the decade: "Windows," "Inner Space," and "Song of the Wind."

ANALYSIS 1: "WINDOWS"

Corea originally recorded "Windows" in 1966 with Hubert Laws (*Laws' Cause*, rereleased on Corea's *Inner Space*). He rerecorded it with Stan Getz (*Sweet Rain*, 1967), and again with piano trio during the *Now He Sings, Now He Sobs*

2. Corea's "Tones for Joan's Bones" has an ABAC form.
3. For example, compare the m3 (–m2, –M2) double-axis progression at bars 1, 3, 5, 7 of "Litha" (DM7-C#m7-BM7-B♭m7-A♭M7-Gm7-FM7) with the rhythmically altered m3 melodic sequence in mm. 1–7. For more on "Litha," see chapter 6.

session (1968). He later described it as an early-career compositional exercise, one that he subjected to consistent reworking.[4] It is likely his most well-known 1960s composition. It has an ongoing 48-bar form that unfolds as a series of 8-bar segments. As a jazz waltz, "Windows" owes something to Bill Evans. Further, it works out in extended fashion a significant detail of Evans's harmonic procedures, as the following analysis is meant to show.

As the composition proceeds, the opening B minor harmony recedes further into the distance, replaced by an ascending P5 harmonic axis that takes place via a series of tonicized keys. Yet this axis framework by no means occurs in predictable or mechanical fashion. Instead, it takes some detours. During the final 8-bar segment (mm. 41–48), the progression derails the P5 axis motion in order to return the tonality back to B. (Like several of the Corea compositions discussed here, the form ends with an expanded turnaround that links back to the opening harmony at the top of the form.) Since the form ends with the turnaround back to m. 1 (rather than an end-of-form harmonic arrival), the original performance concludes with a coda, using a vamp that alternates BM7 and C#m7.

Harmony and the P5 Axis. In the opening to Bill Evans's "Blue in Green"[5] a minor key harmony becomes reframed as iv of a new key a perfect fifth higher. This effects one movement along the P5 axis. The first three chords of "Blue in Green" (transposed here) appear as Example 4.1.

Example 4.1. Opening Progression to "Blue in Green" (Transposed)

	Bm13	C#7alt.	F#m7
B minor	i		
F# minor	iv	V	i

Example 4.2 shows a more elaborated version of this progression.

Example 4.2. More Elaborated Version of P5 Harmonic Axis Progression

	Bm	G#m7(b5)	C#7	F#m
B minor	i			
F# minor	iv	ii	V	i

In Evans's "34 Skidoo" (shown as Example 4.3 and transposed; from Evans, *How My Heart Sings*), he activates this P5 axis progression using additional bass motion, which now includes a passing chord (P) in m. 1.

4. Gil Goldstein, *The Jazz Composer's Companion* (Rottenburg, Germany: Advance Music, 1993), 90.
5. "Blue in Green" is also credited to Miles Davis.

Example 4.3. Evans's P5 Axis Progression to "34 Skidoo" (Transposed)

	Bm	Am7	G#m7(♭5)	C#7	F#m
B minor	i				
F# minor	iv	(P)	ii	V	i
m.	1		2	3	4

Both "Blue in Green" and "34 Skidoo" open with this axis progression. Each creates only a single move along the P5 axis.[6] With Corea's "Windows," however, virtually the entire composition moves through the P5 axis, forming an upward spiral of tonicized keys, moving from B minor through F# minor, C# minor, and onward to A♭ minor. Example 4.4 includes the lead sheet. Example 4.5 analyzes the overall progression.

Example 4.4. Lead Sheet to "Windows"

6. The A section to Benny Golson's "Whisper Not" (1956) moves through two stages of that minor key axis, linking C minor to G minor then D minor.

Example 4.5. P5 Axis Pathways through "Windows"

Stage 1
B minor to F♯ minor

Chord	Bm7	A♭m7(♭5)	D♭7	F♯m
B minor	i			
F♯ minor	iv	ii	V	i
m.	1	5	8	9

Stage 2
F♯ minor to C♯ minor

Backdoor Dom

Chord	F♯m7	Am7/D	EM7(♯11)	A♭7 (A7 A♭7)	EM7	D♯m7	C♯m7
F♯ minor	i	bVIsus7					
C♯ minor	iv	bVIIsus7/III	III	V	III		i
m.	9	13	17	25	33		35

Stage 3
C♯ minor to A♭ minor

Chord	C♯m7	/B	B♭m7(b5)	/A♭	E♭7/G	E♭7	A♭m7
C♯ minor	i						
G♯/A♭ minor	iv		ii		V		i
m.	35		37		39		41

Stage 4

	A♭m7	A♭m7/G♭	D♭7/F	D♭7	EM7	D♯m7	C♯m7	C7	Bm7
A♭ minor:	i								
B major/minor:	vi		V7 of V		IV	iii	ii	V'7	i
m.	41	42	43	44	45	46	47	48	1

Example 4.5 presents "Windows" as a series of four overlapping tonal stages. The last harmony of each stage becomes the first harmony of the next one, so that tonicized harmonies at mm. 1, 9, and 35 become enlisted as iv chords en route to a new tonal destination. Stage 4 ends the ascending fifth series. This final stage reinterprets A♭ minor as vi of the opening key and effects an elaborated turnaround, ultimately returning to B minor at the top of the ensuing chorus.

Each stage differs. During Stage 1 (mm. 1–9) the motion to B minor to F♯ minor occurs directly, with the opening B minor redirected as a iv chord, followed by a ii-V progression that enacts the move to F♯ minor.

The route from F♯ minor to C♯ minor (mm. 9–35) is less evident, given the additional harmonies at mm. 13, 17, and 33. Standing outside of the P5 axis motion is A-7/D (mm. 13–16), which links F♯m7 (Am7/D as a suspended chord version of ♭VI7 in F♯) to EM7 (Am7/D as a suspended chord of ♭VII7 in E). Further, there is a highly expanded role for EM7(♯11) for the entire 8-bar phrase at mm. 17–24 that the above analysis downplays, and EM7 reappears to begin an 8-bar phrase at m. 33.[7] But certainly the expanded A♭7 dominant harmony at mm. 25–32 participates more conventionally with C♯ minor (A♭7 as V7) than with E major (A♭7 as III7), as Example 4.5 suggests. In this sense, A♭7 creates an indirect V7-i relation with C♯ minor (m. 35), one mediated by the EM7 and the passing D♯m7 harmonies (mm. 33–34).

Given the expanded role for E major at mm. 17–24 (and its return at m. 33), an alternative P5 axis view might consider E major as providing a relative key *substitute* for the eventual C♯ minor harmony.[8] Substitutions— such as relative major/minor ones—provided postbop composers with powerful methods to evoke tonal relationships but avoid more conventionally predictable tonal moves.[9] This view acknowledges the close relation between C♯ minor and E major. Example 4.6 is meant to capture that close relation. It provides a series of pitches that alternates m3s and M3s, and therefore models standard jazz minor and major harmonies in a way that allows standard extensions of 7ths, 9ths, 11ths (♯11 in the case of major harmonies), and 13ths.[10] The cycle—as a ladder of thirds—provides the range of standard possibilities in jazz practice for m7 and M7 chords that may but need not include extensions of 9th, 11th (♯11 with M7 chords), and 13th. The lines above and below indicate EM7 included within C♯m9, and EM7(♯11) within C♯m13. In practice, jazz musicians might describe EM7 as a rootless C♯m9, or EM7(♯11) as a rootless C♯m13.

Example 4.6. Relationship between Relative Major/Minor Harmonies

```
C#m9
C#   E  G# B D# F# A# C# E#/F ...
     EM7

C#m13
C#   E  G# B D# F# A# C# E#/F ...
     EM7(#11)
```

7. In his analysis of "Windows," Steve Strunk regards E major as the most significant interior tonal region of the piece, acting as a large-scale plagal destination within the overall B tonality. Steven Strunk, "Tonal and Transformational Approaches to Chick Corea's Compositions of the 1960s," *Music Theory Spectrum* 38, no. 1 (2016): esp. 18–22.

8. Chapter 3 discussed relative minor/major substitutions in Hancock's "Dolphin Dance."

9. Elsewhere Corea similarly juxtaposes III with V7 directly in a manner similar to mm. 17–32 of Example 4.5 above. See "What Was," a work in G♯ minor which moves from BM7 to D♯7 in mm. 9–12 in Chick Corea, *Now He Sings, Now He Sobs* (Rottenburg, Germany: Advance Music, 1988), 22.

10. The cycle does not model specific harmonic voicings in practice, which often are personal and distinct among different players.

In the case of "Windows," hearing E major in a relative relationship with (and temporarily substituting for) C♯ minor addresses the expanded role of E major in Stage 3. Example 4.7 models this view.

Example 4.7. E major as Substitute for C♯ minor

Corea's Progression	EM7(♯11)	G♯7 (A7 G♯7)	EM7	D♯m7	C♯m7
Substitutes for:	C♯m13		C♯m9		
Substitution Technique:	Relative		Relative		
m.	17	25	33	34	35

It may be possible to generalize further, and include the passing D♯m7 chord at m. 34 as participating in this expanded C♯ minor harmony. Thus the mm. 33–35 progression EM7-D♯m7-C♯m7 stands for C♯ minor, with "stand for" describing a progression that meaningfully relates to and meaningfully delays the more-expected C♯ minor. (A similar transformation of C♯ minor also comes into play during Stage 4 of "Windows.")

And a view of EM7 as a substitute for C♯m9 aids in understanding a significant aspect of the 8-bar phrase begun with the EM7 at m. 33. That measure inaugurates a stepwise bass line. The m. 35 C♯m7 is part of that broader passing motion in the bass. Hearing mm. 33–35 as part of an expanded C♯ minor harmony shows how E major participates in the ongoing P5 axis motion (F♯ minor to C♯ minor) en route to Stage 3.

Stage 3's axis motion is more evident than is that of Stage 2. It uses passing motion in the bass (C♯-B-B♭-A♭-G) that allows the tonicized C♯ minor to operate as a iv chord, then move through ii (B♭m7(b5)) and V (E♭7) chords en route to A♭ minor.

Stage 3 is the last step through the P5 axis, which so far has moved from B minor-F♯ minor-C♯ minor-A♭ minor. Stage 4 begins by making a feint toward yet another P5 axis move. Stage 4 begins similarly to Stage 3, suggesting yet another instance of that axis progression. Example 4.8 compares that hypothetical with Corea's progression.

Example 4.8. Comparison of Hypothetical Progression (P5 Axis Continued) with Cormea's mm. 41–48 (Stage 4)

Hypothetical	A♭m7	A♭m7/Gb	Fm7(b5)	B♭7	E♭m7				
A♭ minor	i								
E♭ minor	iv		ii	V7	i				

A♭-7

Corea's Progression	Abm7	Abm7/G♭	D♭7/F	D♭7	EM7	D♯m7	C♯m7	C7	Bm7
A♭ minor	i								
B Major/Minor	vi		V7/V		"ii"			V'7	
m.	41	42	43	44	45	46	47	48	1

33   34   35

A comparison of the two versions shows that mm. 41–42 begin as if continuing the axis motion to E♭ minor (with A♭m7 and A♭m7/G♭). But instead the tonicized A♭ minor acts as a hinge. It is the last stage along the P5 axis, and then serves as vi (or ii of V) en route to V7 of V at mm. 43–44. Mm. 45–47 provide an example of the EM7-D♯m7-C♯m7 progression, the identical progression discussed at the end of Stage 2 above, one described as standing for the C♯ minor harmony. Ultimately these harmonies at mm. 45–47 cede to C7 (the tritone substitute harmony for F♯7, indicated as V′7), then to B minor at the top of the form. Since the progression at mm. 45–48 implies B major, rather than B minor, the harmonic movement back to B minor at the top of the form has a reverse Picardy effect, shifting the implied major mode of the final four bars into minor.

These final eight bars create an elaborated turnaround progression, fulfilling a role similar to that heard in the final twelve bars of "Inner Space" (described below). A more conventional turnaround might move directly to F♯ at mm. 45–48, housing either a 4-bar dominant, or a iii-vi-ii-V progression over an F♯ pedal point. Thus Corea's mm. 45–48, with its stepwise bass, may be heard as a variation of such a turnaround. We also might understand the variation to be one that exchanges the role of bass for melody, since the only melodic pitch heard during mm. 45–48 is F♯, the dominant of the ensuing B minor.

This interpretation of "Windows" proposes that Corea turns an ascending fifth sequence of tonicized minor harmonies into the harmonic premise of virtually the entire composition. Each of the four stages arises via functional progressions (i.e., that include iv, ii, and V7 harmonies), although the particular paths vary by means of harmonic rhythm, use of passing motion, harmonic inversions, etc. (The underlying axis progression is most fully elaborated in the move from F♯ minor to C♯ minor, given the enhanced role of E major as a substitute for C♯ minor.) Only in Stage 4 (mm. 41–48) does the cyclic activity cease. Its turnaround performs a tonal intervention, motivating a return to the beginning B harmony at the top of the form. The interpretation suggests the centrifugal forces created by the outward-moving P5 axis motion (in mm. 1–40) become interrupted during that final turnaround, as more conventional (and centripetal) tonal processes prevail. The reliance upon a turnaround at the end of the form also suggests that boundaries between postbop processes (via axis progressions of same-quality harmonies) and tonal processes (via a turnaround that links to the opening harmony) are, in many cases, porous.[11]

---

11. This point is especially true with this early work of Corea's. Steven Strunk prefers a single-key interpretation of "Windows" with a significant motion to E major (as IV)

I return to Corea's end-of-form turnarounds at the end of the discussion of "Windows."

Melody: Motives and Paths. Along with the harmonic scheme, the melodic dimension is equally compelling. The opening melodic motive of the piece dominates mm. 1–8, returning as a 2-bar motive throughout mm. 1–8. It returns again mm. 17–24, now augmented to a 4-bar motive. The motive begins as upper structure arpeggiation (3rd-5th-7th-9th), with the ninth brought down an octave before moving stepwise to the root (C♯-B, m. 2). The second statement in mm. 3–4 then paraphrases the motive. Transposed downward by third to accommodate the second harmony of G♯m7(b5), the motives in mm. 5–8 work similarly through the arpeggiation and use the ♮ninth (A♯).

The compact and memorable lyricism of the opening motive recalls that of the opening motive of Hancock's "Dolphin Dance," and—as in mm. 1–17 of "Dolphin Dance"—the skeletal melody throughout creates longer underlying stepwise lines.[12] Example 4.9 shows that there are three primary stepwise skeletal melodies, indicated as Stepwise Descents 1–3. During the opening 8 bars the downbeat pitches frame ongoing stepwise motion of D-C♯-B through A♯-G♯, and ending with a skip downwards to C♯. Further, there is a varied echo effect between mm. 8–9 and 13–14, with the final principal pitches of the motive (A♯-G♯-C♯) transposed up by half step and rhythmically compressed (B-A-D; the final note moves upwards by fourth rather than downward by fifth.) The return of the motive at mm. 17–24 outlines m6 stepwise motion through B-A♯-F♯-E that links to D♯/E♭ at the beginning of the next 8-bar section.

Example 4.9. Skeletal Melodic Pathways of "Windows"

mm. 1–9	Stepwise Descent 1: D-C♯-B-A♯-G♯-C♯ (leap to last pitch)
mm. 13–16	Transition: B-A-D (half-step transposition of A♯-G♯-C♯ of previous descent), C provides melodic link to Stepwise Descent 2
mm. 17–25	Stepwise Descent 2: B-A♯-G♯-F♯-E-E♭
mm. 25–33	Melodic Pivot around E♭ (G♭-F♭) E♭
mm. 33–48	Stepwise Descent 3: D♯-C♯-C♭-B♭-A♭-F♯

in "Tonal and Transformational Approaches to Chick Corea's Compositions of the 1960s." In addition, some may argue that the melody to "Windows" largely effects a move from B minor (mm. 1–9), to B major (mm. 17–24 and mm. 33–48), similarly offering a single-key interpretation to "Windows" (with merely a modal shift from minor to major). One way to reconcile a single-key interpretation with the axis interpretation offered here relies on a tonal interpretation of the P5 pathway, moving i-v-ii-vi, with the latter two stages making an implied shift from B minor to B major.

12. In addition to the skeletal downward stepwise melody, there are further structural similarities between the melody of mm. 1–9 of "Dolphin Dance" and mm. 1–9 of "Windows." Both involve in mm. 1–4 two statements of the opening 4-note motive (a varied restatement occurs in "Windows"), and another twofold statement of the motive down a third (mm. 5–9).

Rather than continuing a melodic stepwise descent, this F♯-E-E♭ melodic cadence at mm. 24–25 becomes the point of departure for the next 8-bar phrase. There, in mm. 25–32, the melody pivots around E♭, largely via the F♯-E (notated as G♭-F♭ in mm. 25–32) pitches that formed the mm. 24–25 melodic cadence. Those three pitches (E♭-G♭-F♭-E♭) become increasingly elaborated throughout the section. During the final 16 bars a melodic descent resumes, with Stepwise Descent 3 framing a M6, from D♯-C♯-C♭-B♭-A♭-F♯.

The example shows that the skeletal melody throughout creates longer lines. These longer stepwise lines create an ongoing melodic continuity, a likely motivation for a composer to use an ongoing single-section (rather than a repeated-section) form. With "Windows" it is possible to hear that continuity extending from m. 17 until the end of the form, linking B-E♭ (mm. 17–25), departing from and returning to E♭ (mm. 25–33), and continuing from E♭/D♯ until F♯ (mm. 33–40).[13] The result creates a melodic continuity that unfurls over 32 bars.

Corea's Lead Sheet to "Windows." About "Windows," Corea wrote, "At that time, I wasn't very fluid with my writing. I thought a lot about it and would go over and over it, changing and deliberating over it."[14] A comparison between Corea's 1966 copyright deposit lead sheet and the version on the recording is instructive.[15] Since the harmonies at mm. 33–48 differ between the 1966 lead sheet and the recorded performance, it is likely Corea was referring to those final 16 bars. Example 4.10 compares the two.

13. Viewed in another manner, the melody largely travels through diatonic and melodic minor collections. These collections are in some cases incomplete, but the progress of those collections involves the addition or subtraction of one sharp, as shown here:

> Mm. 1–5: B-C♯-D-F♯-A (three sharp diatonic collection)
> Mm. 5–12: B-C♯-D-F♯-G♯-A♯ (four sharp melodic minor mode)
> Mm. 16–24: B-D♯-E-F♯-G♯-A♯ (five sharp diatonic)
> Mm. 25–32: A♭-C-E♭-E-G♭ (same as five sharp melodic minor)
> Mm. 33–42: B-C♯-D♯-E-F♯-A♯ (five sharp diatonic)
> Mm. 39–48: B-C♯-D-F♯-A♯ (four sharp melodic minor)

The above omits mm. 13–16 (which does not participate similarly), and the final two stages are overlapping. Arguably, the first stage (without G♯ or G ♮) could imply either a two-sharp or three-sharp collection.

14. Quoted in Gil Goldstein, *Jazz Composers Companion* (Rottenburg, Germany: Advance Music, 1993), 90.

15. Corea's copyright deposit lead sheet (EU 921706) is dated January 24, 1966. It differs from the recorded performance between mm. 33–48. Corea provided a lead sheet that more closely corresponds to the recorded performance in *Chick Corea Collection* (Milwaukee: Hal Leonard, 1994).

Example 4.10. Comparison of mm. 33–48 Harmonies of Corea's Lead Sheet and Recorded Performance to "Windows"

$A\flat7$

	33	34	35	36	37	38	39	40
Corea's 1966 Lead Sheet	D♭m7				F♯7		G°	
Recorded Performance	EM7	D♯m7	C♯m7	C♯m7/B	B♭m7(♭5)	B♭m7(♭5)/A♭	E♭7/G	E♭7
m.	33	34	35	36	37	38	39	40

	41	42	43	44	45	46	47	48
Corea's Lead Sheet	A♭m7		D♭7		F♯7		C7	
Recorded Performance	A♭m7	A♭m7/G♭D♭7/F	D♭7		EM7	D♯m7	C♯m7	C7
m.	41	42	43	44	45	46	47	48

Evidently absent from the lead sheet are the passing linear bass motions and the resultant harmonic inversions heard on the recording. While the lead sheet shows that they were not part of Corea's original design, that aspect of the composition provides a contrapuntal dimension that is now a distinctive part of its fabric. Certainly the use of chordal inversions motivated by stepwise bass motion was not new. Compositions such as Dizzy Gillespie's "Con Alma" and Benny Golson's "Whisper Not" featured them.[16] In those compositions the inversion (typically third inversions of M7 or m7 harmonies) fills in a bass descent by third. Additionally, works such as Bill Evans's "Waltz for Debby" and John Lewis's "Django" featured dominant harmonies in first and third inversion, possibly as a marker for European eighteenth- and nineteenth-century music. And Steve Swallow's "Falling Grace" (recorded in 1966) integrated first inversion (dominant) and third inversion (M7 and m7) harmonies, creating longer stepwise bass lines. Like "Falling Grace," "Windows" relies on similar inversions, and the final four-chord progression heard on the recording (mm. 45–48: EM7-D♯m7-C♯m7-C7) shows a further commitment to stepwise bass motion through a series of root position harmonies, ones that ultimately replaced the F♯7-C7 progression of the original lead sheet.

In addition, the slower harmonic rhythm of Corea's 1966 lead sheet follows a significantly more conventional tonal pathway. The seven chords of the lead sheet (at mm. 33–48) direct the harmonic motion more evidently to B at m. 1 as ii7-V7-vii°/vi-vi-V7/V-V7-V'7. Further, note that the m. 33 D♭m7 harmony of the lead sheet creates a direct resolution of the embellished A♭7 harmony heard at mm. 25–32.

16. And certainly the progression I-I6 (en route to IV) characterizes standard blues turnarounds at m. 11, as well as in compositions such as Sonny Rollins's "St. Thomas" (m. 13).

However, the resolution to A♭ minor at m. 41 is more definitive in the recorded version, motivated by an embellished ii-V progression at mm. 37–40. In contrast, the lead sheet supplies a 2-bar passing G° chord mm. 39–40. As a result, the lead sheet version suppresses to a degree the final stage along the P5 axis (i.e., of the tonicized minor harmonies progressing B-F♯-C♯-A♭).

Comparisons between the lead sheet and recorded performance call attention to the role of the end-of-form turnarounds. In all the Corea compositions discussed here, the turnaround technique differs from conventional tonal practice.[17] Conventionally, turnarounds are end-of-form (or end-of-section) insertions that *follow* a tonic arrival, taking place while the melody is at rest. In "Windows," "Inner Space," or "Song of the Wind," the m. 1 harmony does not return directly prior to the turnaround, and the turnaround progression is expanded, at times taking place while the melody is still active.[18] Therefore, in most instances they take on an expanded formal role that drives the progression to the m. 1 harmony. Perhaps "cadential progression" is a better label, but I will use the term "turnaround" in order to highlight its position at the end of the form, even if the turnaround progression is extended.

In my discussions of "Windows" above, I described the turnaround as taking place at mm. 41–48, following the tonicized arrival on A♭ minor that coincided with Stage 4. Corea's original lead sheet offers a turnaround design expanded even further, with all 7 chords at mm. 33–48 collaborating in the m. 1 arrival. (And the elaborated A♭7 at mm. 25–32 further participates in that directed motion.)

---

17. In his "Harmony" entry to *The New Grove Dictionary of Jazz*, Steven Strunk defines a turnaround as follows: "The chord pattern at the end of the final phrase is called a 'turnaround' or 'turnback' because it leads back to the beginning of the theme, and prepares for the start of a new chorus. In a theme with the form aaba the first a section may also end with a turnaround. Composed melodies usually rest during a turnaround." See Steven Strunk, "Harmony," in *The New Grove Dictionary of Jazz*, ed. Barry Kernfeld (London: Macmillan, 1988), 490.

18. Corea's "Litha" also has an expanded turnaround that lasts for the final 36 bars of the 62-bar composition. All these Corea compositions are similar to Miles Davis's "Solar," which likewise does not have a tonic arrival directly prior to its m. 12 turnaround, and so requires a resolution to C minor at m. 1. The melody to "Solar" also creates a circular overlap, since it ends on the leading tone (B) in m. 12, and begins with its resolution (C) in m. 1. In all cases, the absence of tonal arrival toward the end of the form departs from 12 of Terefenko's 13 Phrase Models described here in chapter 1. Only his Phrase Model 13 ends on V, but it occurs primarily in bridge sections (as in the bridge to "I Got Rhythm").

In Corea's compositions discussed in this chapter, the turnarounds provide a particular strategy for his single-section compositions. AABA and ABAC song form procedures of tonal jazz typically corroborate a single-key tonality throughout the composition and, especially, at the end of the form. (See Terefenko's Phrase Models in chapter 1.) The tonal processes within Corea's single-section forms discussed here proceed differently. There are no interior and no end-of-form returns to the opening harmony, so the idea of "tonic" depends solely upon the singular appearance of the m. 1 harmony.[19] Corea's turnarounds provide a tonal magnetism, animating the end of the form and leading inexorably into the arrivals at m. 1. They therefore activate tonal processes on a formal level. But while the song forms of tonal jazz include interior and final affirmations of a single-key tonic, Corea's single-section compositions discussed here do not.

ANALYSIS 2: "INNER SPACE"

Recorded in 1966, "Inner Space" was only released in 1973 as the title track to *Inner Space*. It is a single-section composition with a 30-bar form. There are four subsections of 8 + 6 + 4 + 12 bars, labeled here as A, B, C, and D. The 8-bar introduction expands the 4-bar C section (mm. 15–18), and—with an extension—it ultimately serves as a coda. (During the very last head statement on the recording, the coda follows the B section.) The composition strongly evokes Corea's sound world through its parallel structure M7♯11 chords, harmonies voiced as open fifths in the horns and piano (during the introduction, A, and C subsections), and through its Phrygian progression (during the B section). A lead sheet appears as Example 4.11.

19. This is why the recorded performances of all three end not at the end of the form but either use a closing vamp ("Windows") or a return to the introduction ("Inner Space" and "Song of the Wind").

Example 4.11. Lead Sheet to "Inner Space"

Melody continues to G#
at top of form

By Chick Corea. Copyright © 1973 UNIVERSAL MUSIC CORP. Copyright Renewed. This arrangement Copyright © 2018 UNIVERSAL MUSIC CORP. All Rights Reserved. Used by Permission. *Reprinted by permission of Hal Leonard LLC.*

I describe below how the introduction and C subsection use a M3 axis progression in the melody but avoid a parallel harmonization. The A subsection melody uses a pentatonic collection that similarly avoids a parallel harmonization. The B subsection relies on a Phrygian progression. And the final D subsection provides a transformed turnaround. Although it is literally correct to regard many of the progressions as nonfunctional in a tonal sense, the following proposes a view of harmonic substitutions as a window into the progressions of the Introduction, A, C, and D sections.

Introduction and C Section. At the outset, the skeletal melody of the 8-bar introduction elaborates and completes a M3 axis, with downbeat pitches in the upper (trumpet) voice moving D♯-B-G-D♯ during mm. i–vii. The same skeletal melody returns in mm. 15–18, now with a different melodic elaboration. (Both are shown by numbers 1–4 in the lead sheet.) The framework, taken from the trumpet melody, appears in Example 4.12. (Initially the tenor saxophone is voiced a P5th below.) Corea avoids the same systematic move in the harmonic dimension, however. Example 4.13 provides those axis melodic pitches, two hypothetical progressions, and Corea's progression. Each hypothetical progression moves mechanically in parallel motion to the melody. Hypothetical 1 maintains a consistent M7 with the melody; Hypothetical 2 a consistent ♯11 with the melody. Corea's progression toggles back and forth between the two lines (as shown by the chords in bold). Relative to Corea's progression, the first hypothetical swaps out the first and third chord, and the second swaps out the second and fourth. (Measure numbers for the 8-bar introduction are given as lower-case Roman numerals: i = 1st bar of introduction, iii = 3rd bar, etc.)

Example 4.12. M3 Melodic Axis Pathway in "Inner Space" (Introduction and mm. 15–18)

1. Amaj7#11   **2.** Cmaj7#11   **3.** D♭maj7#11   **4.** Emaj7#11   (Ebmaj7#11) (Dmaj7#11)

Example 4.13. Hypothetical and Corea's Harmonization for Introduction and mm. 15–18 of "Inner Space"

Melody	D♯	B	G	D♯
Hypothetical 1 (M7th with melody)	EM7#11	**CM7#11**	A♭M7#11	**EM7#11**
Hypothetical 2 (#11th with melody)	**AM7#11**	FM7#11	**D♭M7#11**	AM7#11
Corea's Progression	AM7#11	CM7#11	D♭M7#11	EM7#11
m.	i and 15	iii and 16	v and 17	vii and 18

The harmonic progression uses the same type harmony (M7#11), but the melodic pitches alternately form two different intervals with the bass, #11 (chords 1 and 3) and M7 (chords 2 and 4). In this case, we may understand these two harmonies as substitutes for one another. The substitution in this case—a "P4 swap"—is constrained by the relationship to melody, preserving either #11 or M7 with the bass.

Example 4.14 shows this relationship, using a dual m3/M3 axis. The figure show that, unlike relative major/minor relationships, these M7#11 chords overlap but are not adjacent.[20] Corea's specific melodic constraint (D#, as either M7 or #11) appears in bold. Note that the figure indicates chord 1 (AM7#11) or its substitute (EM7#11), as well as chord 4 (EM7#11) or its P4 substitute (AM7#11). Corea's resultant bass motion (A-C-Db-E) alternates m3 and m2.[21] Rather than creating parallel motion between the bass and melody (as with either Hypothetical), Corea's progression instead creates contrary motion. The overall harmonic and melodic organization of the 8-bar introduction returns in compressed fashion during the 4-bar C subsection.

Example 4.14. Dual Interval Axis and P4 Swap between M7#11

AM7(#11)

A C# E G# B **D#** F# A#

EM7(#11)

The introduction and C subsection maintain the same M3 axis in the melodic dimension. Although elaborated, that underlying framework is clear. Yet the harmonic progressions avoid that same axis organization, replaced by an alternation of two harmonic possibilities of M7#11 chords related by P4. This technique provides a rich and potent alternative to mm. 8–15 of "Giant Steps," in which the axis motions of both melody and harmony are, by and large, matched. If we describe the parallel melodic/

20. In jazz practice, M7 substitutions whose roots are a fifth apart are more easily considered when the "lower harmony" is specifically M7#11, and the upper harmony is merely M7. Thus FM7#11 includes CM7; such inclusion relations frequently provide pedagogical shortcuts.

21. This m3 and m2 alternation (A-C-Db-E) would form the augmented scale when completed. Completion of that scale in "Inner Space" would require three more bass moves, F-Ab-A, and would therefore require a second melodic statement of the melodic M3 axis. Corea's progression is an example of a M3 (+m3, +m2) double-axis progression. These double-axis progressions are discussed further in chapter 6.

harmonic activity of "Giant Steps" as providing a first-order grammar (or first-order progression) for the M3 axis, Corea's substitutions instead provide a second-order grammar (or second-order progression), activated by the P4 swap substitution strategy.

A Section, mm. 1–8. The introduction concludes by moving to a m2 axis in both harmony and melody: EM7(#11)-E♭M7(#11)-DM7(#11), and that axis leads harmonically into the C# minor harmony at the opening of the A section. The move to C# minor moves the composition out of the sound world of M7#11 harmonies. In the head to the 8-bar A section, the rhythm section plays mm. 1–4, and the horn melody appears mm. 5–8.

Further, the A section begins the metrical principle on which much of the composition is based. The 4-bar sections are organized to sound as two bars of implied 5/4 and one of an implied 6/4: that is, the quarter notes group as 5 + 5 + 6. At the outset the implied 5/4 arises through an ostinato figure that repeats the P5 G#/D#. During the implied 6/4 bar, the melody harmonizes a pentatonic subset voiced in parallel fifths.[22] (The piano part is consistently voiced in parallel fifths, thus the B major/G# minor pentatonic collection appears beneath the F# major/D# minor collection.) The varied repetition m. 5 ff. completes the pentatonic collection with the change of harmony at m. 9.

In one sense, the harmonic design of Subsection A works independently of that pentatonic melodic design. Yet, in another sense, this section works similarly to the introduction and C sections, which used the P4 swap: that is, it alternated between two potential harmonizations of each primary melodic pitch.[23] But mm. 1–8 alternate between three potential harmonizations. Example 4.15 shows (for mm. 1–4 and 5–8) a series of mechanical parallel harmonizations that preserve either M7 between bass and melody (Hypothetical 1), 9th (Hypothetical 2), or #11 (Hypothetical 3), along with the skeletal melody. Beneath those lines is Corea's harmonization. Corea's progression ranges through that menu of hypotheticals, as shown by the harmonies in bold that match Corea's choices. At mm. 1–4

---

22. This D# minor pentatonic collection is built a whole step above the root of the C#m7 chord. For further discussion of pentatonics in improvisational contexts, see Ramon Ricker, *Pentatonic Scales for Jazz Improvisation* (Lebanon, Indiana: Studio P/R, 1975).

23. The M3 axis, as it appears in mm. 9–16 of Coltrane's "Giant Steps," moves systematically in both the melodic and harmonic domains. Pentatonic melodies harmonized in parallel fashion are heard in rock music, discussed by Nicole Biamonte in "Triadic Modal and Pentatonic Patterns in Rock Music," *Music Theory Spectrum* 32 (2010): 95–110, but less so in jazz practice. For Coltrane's use of pentatonic collections in improvisation, see Lewis Porter, *John Coltrane: His Life and Music* (Ann Arbor: University of Michigan Press, 1998), 151–52, 233–37.

and 5–8 the progression begins in the center of the three hypotheticals (melody is 9th, D♯), moves upward (melody is 7th, C♯), returns to the central position, and moves downward (melody is ♯11th, F♯). The technique for harmonizing the fifth pitch between mm. 1–4 and 5–8 varies, with parallel harmonic motion matching the melodic F♯-D♯ (CM7(♯11)-AM7(♯11), m. 4) and a return to the upper position for G♯ (CM7(♯11)-AM7, m. 8).

Example 4.15. Hypothetical and Corea's Harmonization for mm. 1–9 of "Inner Space"

Mm. 1–4

Melody	D♯	C♯	D♯	F♯	D♯
Hypothetical 1 (M7th)	EM7♯11	**DM7♯11**	EM7♯11	GM7♯11	EM7♯11
Hypothetical 2 (m9th)	**C♯m9**	Bm9	**C♯m9**	Em9	C♯m9
Hypothetical 3 (M7/♯11th)	AM7♯11	GM7♯11	AM7♯11	**CM7♯11**	**AM7♯11**
Corea's Harmonization	C♯m9	DM7	C♯m9	CM7♯11	AM7♯11

Mm. 5–9

Melody	D♯	C♯	D♯	F♯	G♯	A♯/B♭
Hypothetical 1 (M7th)	EM7♯11	**DM7♯11**	EM7♯11	GM7♯11	**AM7♯11**	
Hypothetical 2 (9th)	**C♯m9**	Bm9	**C♯m9**	Em9	F♯m9	
Hypothetical 3 (♯11th)	AM7♯11	GM7♯11	AM7♯11	**CM7♯11**	DM7♯11	
Corea's Harmonization	C♯m9	DM7	C♯m9	CM7♯11	AM7♯11	E♭

As with the introduction and C Subsections, these hypothetical harmonizations offer substitutions, whose use inoculates the composition from more systematic harmonization schemes. The result in all cases, with the exception of the parallel harmonic motion linking F♯ to D♯ (m. 4), provides contrary motion between bass and melody. The relationship of the three chords (M7, m9, and M7♯11 chords) is shown below on the dual M3/m3 axis in Example 4.16. It shows the three hypotheticals for the m. 1 chord (which harmonize the melodic D♯, shown in bold in the figure below). The resultant harmonic substitutions not only include the P4 swap (AM7(♯11)-EM7), but also a relative major/minor relation (C♯m9-EM7), and an additional harmonic relation by third (AM7(♯11)-C♯m9).[24]

24. This particular third relation between A major and C♯ minor (or between C♯ minor and A major) provides an example of what is referred to as a "leading-tone" relationship. This term derives from the work of theorist Hugo Riemann; for an introduction (often referred to as neo-Riemannian theory) see Richard Cohn, "An Introduction to Neo-Riemannian Theory: A Survey and Historical Perspective," *Journal of Music Theory* 42, no. 2 (1998): 167–80.

Example 4.16. Dual Interval Axis and Relation Between M7♯11, m9, and M7

```
AM7(♯11) _____
   C♯m9 _____
      EM7 _____
 A   C♯   E   G♯   B   D♯   F♯ A♯
```

B and C Subsections, mm. 9–22. The subsection begins as the melody completes the D♯/E♭ minor pentatonic collection with B♭, beginning the 6-bar B section. The harmonic arrival of E♭ major at m. 9 sounds fresh: it overturns any suggestion of E♭ minor supplied by that (E♭ minor) pentatonic collection during mm. 1–8. The B section melody (mm. 9–14) begins as a sequence of the mm. 5–8 horn melody, transposed up by P5th. The melodic phrase ends as it begins, with a half-step upper neighbor decoration of B♭ (m. 12) that precedes the rhythm section break and the melodic lead-in to C section.

The harmonic progression here is a common one for Corea. It is perhaps best designated as a Phrygian progression, since the bass exhibits the semitone-tone pattern of the first three degrees of the Phrygian mode.[25] Here the bass moves from E♭ up a half step (EM7♯11), and from there a whole step (G♭ 6/9) before retracing the steps downward. The combination of the 4-bar Phrygian progression and the 2-bar rhythm section break with melodic lead-in (mm. 13–14) form the 6-bar phrase here, the composition's only departure from 4-bar organization.

Subsection C returns to the same M3 melodic axis (D♯-B-G-D♯) and harmonic progression heard in the introduction, but now telescoped into four bars (rather than eight bars, as heard in the introduction). Further, that melodic axis is elaborated differently—each of the primary pitches is embellished with pentatonic subsets before the m2 axis progression (EM7(♯11)-E♭M7(♯11)-DM7(♯11), the same progression as in the Introduction) moves to Subsection D.

Subsection D, mm. 19–30. The last subsection forms a varied turnaround, similar to that heard in "Windows." In "Inner Space," this turnaround

---

25. The term Phrygian refers to that ascending m2-M2 pattern in the bass, rather than to the strict adherence to the pitches of the Phrygian mode. Corea's "La Fiesta" (*Return to Forever*, 1972) uses all major-mode harmonies for the 3-chord vamp. In contrast, "What Was" (*Now He Sings, Now He Sobs*, 1968) uses a similar Phrygian progression, but with a minor-mode harmony for the initial chord. "Inner Space" is closer to "La Fiesta" since all three harmonies are major mode. However, in "Inner Space" the piano right hand maintains a P5 pedal point of E♭/B♭ for all three chords, forming root/fifth with the E♭ harmony, M7/♯11 with the E harmony, and 6th/3rd with the G♭ harmony.

occupies 12 bars and consists of three harmonies, Emaj/F, E♭m7, to DM7(♯11), which then link to the C♯m9 at the top of the form. Corea's progression replaces a more conventional turnaround of V7/ii-ii-V7, as suggested below in Example 4.17.

Example 4.17. Comparison of Standard Turnaround Progression with Corea's Progression, mm. 19–30

				F EG♯B → B⁷
Turnaround Progression	B♭7 (V7/ii)	E♭m7 (ii)	A♭7 (V)	*♯11 ♭7 ♯9*
Corea's Progression	Emaj/F	E♭m7	DM7(♯11)	
m.	19	23	27	

both side

The central E♭m7 acts as a ii chord, and the flanking first and third harmonies are substitutes for V/ii and V. The first harmony, Emaj/F (an E major triad above the bass pitch F), is a subset of the diminished (or octatonic) collection, and completes that collection when transposed along the m3 axis. In 1960s practice, such an axis progression (for example, Emaj/F-Gmaj/A♭-B♭maj/B-D♭maj/D) accesses a network of four potential dominant harmonies (B♭7-D♭7-E7-G7). In "Inner Space," Emaj/F substitutes for B♭7, with extensions that include ♭7, ♭9, and ♯11. In a characteristic postbop maneuver, however, Emaj/F omits the chordal third (of B♭7, i.e., D) and it avoids the descending fifth bass (or descending half-step) motion characteristic of dominant-type harmonies. The dissonant slash chord harmony leads to E♭m7, the ii harmony, voiced in open fourths (B♭-E♭-A♭) in the piano right hand.

The third chord of the turnaround, DM7(♯11), operates as a dominant substitute (V'M7). The D bass is in a tritone relationship with A♭7, and it houses a M7, rather than dominant 7, chord. The harmony thus suppresses the active leading tone (C), replacing it with C♯.[26]

Corea's three-chord progression therefore alters a more conventional turnaround of V7/ii-ii-V. An alternative technique would place a pedal point V in the bass beneath that three-chord progression. In "Inner Space," the dominant appears as a pedal point (A♭) during these twelve measures. It appears not in the bass, but in the upper voice of the piano, which maintains A♭ as the upper pitch during the head statements. The technique appears also in the turnaround to "Windows": in both compositions the melodic pedal point of a fifth scale degree provides a subtle tonal cue in their transformed turnarounds.

26. In that sense, it resembles Vsus7 (in this key Absus7), which similarly omits the leading tone (C).

During the turnaround, the horn melody appears only over the final harmony, and the angular bop phrasing uses metric displacement that avoids a more rote sequential treatment. Example 4.18 compares Corea's mm. 27–30 melody with two hypothetical versions in order to show how Corea avoids more mechanical melodic sequences. Hypothetical 1 places the 4-note idea that begins m. 28 in sequence during the following two measures. In it, the C♯ in m. 30 appears in the same metric location as Corea's (indicated by the asterisk in both versions). However, Corea's 3-note motive in m. 30 truncates the more-predictable restatement of Hypothetical 1. In comparison with m. 29 of Hypothetical 1, Hypothetical 2 shifts the first sequence a beat earlier. It resembles more closely Corea's, since the final two pitches (B-F♯) correspond. But Corea's sequence expands the original four-note motive to a five-note motive in mm. 28–29. The two hypotheticals are meant to indicate the subtle motivic and metrical elasticity in these measures.

Example 4.18. Comparison of Melody from mm. 27-30 of "Inner Space" with Two Hypotheticals

"Inner Space" progresses through four subsections. The introduction and Subsection C use the M3 axis melodically, but avoid a parallel axis harmonic progression by using substitute harmonies that maintain either M7 or ♯11 between bass and melody. Subsection A uses a pentatonic melody, with the harmonic progression similarly altered by substitution techniques (that maintain 9, M7, or ♯11 between bass and melody). In those cases, the melody moves through evident pathways, but a second-order grammar activates the harmonic progression and avoids a rote parallel harmonization. Subsection B employs a Phrygian progression, and Subsection D a varied turnaround that uses substitutions in place of a more standard V/ii-ii-V progression.

The role of substitutions offered here is intended to describe the harmonic progressions in ways that move beyond terms such as "ambiguous," or "nonfunctional." They show how Corea's compositions transform more predictable paths in striking ways.

ANALYSIS 3: "SONG OF THE WIND"

Like "Windows," "Song of the Wind" is a jazz waltz. But comparisons between the two show deep differences, and indicate the degree to which Corea's harmonic language broadened toward the end of the 1960s. If "Windows" relied on functional harmonic progressions to advance along the P5 axis (setting up a series of minor keys ascending by fifth), "Song of the Wind" suppresses those functional progressions in favor of pedal point harmonies, polychords, and harmonies derived from the diminished (octatonic) and augmented (hexatonic) collections. In the central portion of the composition, pairs of chords over an expanded bass pedal point evoke first the Phrygian, then the Aeolian mode. And, as with the introduction and C section of "Inner Space," the final section of "Song of the Wind" uses the M3 axis melodically while similarly avoiding a parallel M3 axis harmonization.

Corea recorded "Song of the Wind" on *Sundance* (1969), *Joe Farrell Quartet* (1970), and *Piano Improvisations vol. 1* (1971).[27] The three performances differ not only in instrumentation (quintet, duo, and solo

27. A transcription of the latter (solo piano) performance is contained in *Chick Corea Piano Improvsations*, transcribed by Bill Dobbins (Rottenburg: Advance Music, 1990). Daniel Duke discusses that 1971 version in "The Piano Improvisations of Chick Corea: An Analytical Study," DMA Thesis, Louisiana State University, 1996, 66–80; Jordan Michael Lynch discusses mm. 29–36 of the same performance in "Where Have I Known This Before: An Exploration of Harmony and Voice Leading in the Compositions of Chick Corea," master's thesis, Bowling Green State University, 2012, 34–35. The *Sundance* recording was later re-released on CD along with Corea's 1969 recording *Is*, with the title *The Complete "Is" Sessions*: it also contains an alternate take for "Song of the Wind." The Farrell recording is a duo version with Corea and Farrell on oboe and flute. Later releases of the *Sundance* versions rename the composition as "Waltz for Bill Evans."

piano respectively), but also in some details of melody and harmony. All the performances retain a degree of looseness that make providing a definitive lead sheet difficult, and the lead sheet provided here may be considered a composite of all the versions (including the later released alternate take from the *Sundance* session). It is extremely indebted to Bill Dobbins's meticulous transcription of the solo piano version, although there are some notable differences between that performance and the others.

"Song of the Wind" is a single-section composition with an introduction (notated here as eight bars) that returns to end the performance. (Corea omits the introduction in the solo piano version, using that music only to close the composition.) The introduction appears in Example 4.19a. The lead sheet, provided in Example 4.19b, indicates four subsections, labeled as A (mm. 1–8), B (mm. 9–16), C (mm. 17–24), and D (mm. 25–36). There are two changes of meter, to 2/4 (m. 22), and to 5/4 (m. 24). Because the harmonic vocabulary at times requires chord labels that are not standard, the following Example 4.19c includes a keyboard harmonization providing a characteristic voicing for each harmony.

Example 4.19a. Introduction to "Song of the Wind"

Example 4.19b. Lead Sheet to "Song of the Wind"

Example 4.19c. Harmonic Realization of "Song of the Wind"

By Chick Corea. Copyright © 1970 LITHA MUSIC CORP. Copyright Renewed. This arrangement Copyright © 2018 UNIVERSAL MUSIC CORP. All Rights Administered by UNIVERSAL MUSIC CORP. All Rights Reserved. Used by Permission. *Reprinted by permission of Hal Leonard LLC.*

Introduction. The introduction (Example 4.19a) begins with an out-of-tempo statement of the opening chord (EM13). If the sound world of that harmony is relatively traditional, the following two measures depart immediately from there, with upper structure triads dissonant against the written bass line. In each case, there is a difference of a half step between initial bass pitch and upper structure triad (E♭ bass with E triad above, then E bass with F triad above). The bass line continues in m. 3, where it then outlines a D minor harmony more consonant with the upper structure F triad, before the m. 4 arrival on C♯m9, when the melody is stated. These opening four bars, leading from E major to C♯ minor, is a path taken both in "Windows" (EM7-D♯m7-C♯m7 at mm. 33–35 and 45–47), as well as in the introduction to "Inner Space" (EM7(♯11)-E♭M7(♯11)-DM7(♯11)-C♯m9 at mm. viii–1). But the harmonic climate supplied by the dissonant slash chords in "Song of the Wind" provides a more progressive outlook on that path.

In the *Sundance* and the *Joe Farrell Quartet* versions, the wind instruments begin with the Introduction melody at m. 4, which consists of two shorter gestures that lead to a chromatic ascent at mm. 6–8. Intervalically, the two gestures are transpositionally related (Gesture 2 is a m3 above Gesture 1), as shown in Example 4.20.

Example 4.20. Transpositional Relationship between Gestures 1 and 2, Introduction

m3 axis	Gesture 1 (mm. 4–5)	G♯	A♯ B		G
	Gesture 2 (mm. 5–6)	B	C♯ D	F♯	A♯

Example 4.20 shows how the second of the two melodic gestures includes an additional pitch (F♯). Further, Gesture 1 descends to its final pitch, while Gesture 2 ascends to its final pitch. But most notably, the rhythmic identity of both motives is drastically changed, masking the intervallic similarities.

The notated bass line at m. 5 creates a 9/8 bar here en route to the longer melodic pitches of the chromatic ascent. Hearing that m. 5 bass line in groups of 3 + 2 + 4 (E-B-E, E♭-B♭, D-C♯-B-F♯) shows its chromatic direction, with initial upper pitches of each group progressing E-E♭-D. The melody of Gesture 2 (B-C♯-D-F♯) coordinates with the final bass grouping of four eighth notes (D-C♯-B-F♯) with 1:1 counterpoint in contrary motion.

The bass to the two consecutive chords at mm. 6 and 7 likewise works in direct contrary motion to the melody, descending chromatically (G♯m11 to FM7(♯11)/G) against the chromatic ascent of the melody.[28]

---

28. On the *Piano Improvisations* version (heard only as an outro in the performance), the voicing of the FM7♯11/G chord is different, heard as Am9/G, and so excludes the F heard in the other versions.

The final chord of the introduction is played out of tempo. It also is the final chord of the repeating form (at mm. 35–36). It is indicated here as A♭M7♯5/E. That harmony may be understood as a variant of an E dominant harmony (with extensions of ♯9 and ♭13). Its strength as a dominant is diluted since the chordal seventh (D) is not part of the chord, and this highlights a postbop strategy of transforming dominant-type harmonies in order to suppress evident tonal cues. Three of the four members of that chord (E-G-A♭-C) include the pitches of the bass motion at mm. 6–8 (G♯-G-E), so this final harmony summarizes those bass pitches.

Much of the introduction commits to a harmonic vocabulary that provides alternatives to more standard M7, m7, and dominant chords. In addition to the dissonant slash chords at mm. 2–3, the final M7♯5 chord (above the E bass) participates in this sound world. Further, the contrary motion heard at mm. v–viii show an evident concern with contrapuntal relationships between bass and melody.[29]

Subsection A, mm. 1–8 (Example 4.19b and c). Both Subsections A and B begin with largely stepwise descending gestures in the melody. In that sense, they resemble mm. 1–9 and mm. 17–25 of "Windows," although the melodic stepwise motion of "Windows" is elaborated by its arpeggiating motive (see the discussion of the melodic structure to "Windows" above). The melody heard in mm. 1–4 of "Song of the Wind" (G♯-F♯-E-D-C♯-B-F♯-G♯) may be heard as evoking the F♯ Aeolian mode, but without A♮.

Example 4.21 reveals that the harmonic progression does not simply support a single mode during mm. 1–4, even though those measures (as well as mm. 5–6) consist of shifting chords over an F♯ bass pedal point. The opening harmony, F♯m9(M7), links to the sound world of the final chord of the introduction. Its upper structure (AM7♯5) merely shifts upward by half step the A♭M7♯5 (over the E bass) heard in the prior chord. The following harmony (CM7/F♯) relates to the F♯ Locrian collection, which then resolves to the Aeolian environment of the melody, first with Bm/F♯, then with the fourth chord F♯2/5 (i.e., F♯-G♯-C♯).[30]

29. The above discussion of harmonic substitutions for the introduction, A, and C Subsections in "Inner Space" also described contrary motion relationships between bass and melody. For more on counterpoint, see chapter 6.

30. The shift from F♯ Locrian (one sharp) to F♯ Aeolian (three sharps) is a different one from many of the modal shifts discussed here and elsewhere. That change relies on a difference of two sharps, while many of the other pedal point modal shifts involve merely a change of one sharp or flat.

Example 4.21. Progression and Collections, mm. 1–4

[handwritten: F# - G# - C#]

[handwritten left margin: B D F A♭ B♭ / F#]

Harmony	F#m9(M7)	CM7/F#	Bm/F#	F#2/5 (fourth chord)
Collection	*[handwritten: F# m.m. ?]*	F# Locrian	F# Aeolian	F# Aeolian
m.	1	2	3	4

During mm. 5–8 the progression moves further afield, although the F# pedal point remains at mm. 5–6. The upper structure there may be *[handwritten margin: F# does not belong]* best described as Bdim9(M7), and heard as derived from the diminished (octatonic) collection.[31] As the F# pedal point disappears, the following harmony nevertheless retains an identical structure, now Edim9(M7), again derived from the diminished (octatonic) collection. The final harmony, E♭M7(#5), moves out of that octatonic landscape. It is related to the sound world of the A♭M7#5/E (introduction, m. viii), and F#m9(M7) of m. 1, which likewise contains M7#5 in the upper structure. *[handwritten: melodic minor? Not WT because ♭7]*

Despite the harmonies' progressive orientation in these four bars, we may nevertheless understand a subtle relationship to a more tonal orientation. That is, the three harmonies operate in a substitution relationship with more-standard dominant harmonies. They preserve the upper structures of those harmonies, and they all collectively drive the motion to the E minor arrival point at m. 9. Example 4.22 shows that relationship— the more standard progression offers a descending fifth progression of dominant-type chords (C#7-F#7-B7), which then impels the motion to E minor at the beginning of Subsection B.

Example 4.22. Comparison of Corea's mm. 5–9 Progression with Standard Progression (Corea's progression uses upper structures from the more-standard harmonies)

Corea's Progression	Bdim9(M7)/F#	Edim9(M7)	E♭M7(#5)	Em9
More-Standard Progression	C#13(♭9)	F#13(♭9)	B+/#9	Em9
m.	5	7	8	9

Subsection B, mm. 9–16. Like the first subsection, B begins with a largely stepwise descent in the melody and likewise begins with the ninth above the bass (G# above the F# bass at m. 1; F# above the E bass at m. 9). Also like Subsection A, the melodic phrase ends an octave below where it began: G#-G# at mm. 1–4; F#-F# at mm. 5–15. Further, the two descending melodies begin with a similar rhythmic profile and therefore rhyme at their outset.

31. However, the F# bass pedal point does not belong to that B-C#-D-E-F-G-A♭-B♭ octatonic scale.

But the harmonic organization differs. Instead of the static bass pedal point of Subsection A, mm. 9–12 creates a bass ascent in contrary motion to the melody. Following the Em9 harmony, the bass effects chromatic motion (G-G♯-A-B♭) whose goal is B—that bass pitch then provides the dramatic focal point of the composition, remaining from mm. 13–24.

The entire subsection, then, imaginatively links the E minor harmony of m. 9 to an expanded B harmony. The harmonies of mm. 10–12 are functionally passing chords, forming the chromatic ascent of the bass while harmonizing the descending stepwise melody. The progression uses harmonic inversions and fourth-chord derived harmonies. Since not all these harmonies are standard ones, they are not always reducible to chord notation, and it is useful to examine them in more detail. They are described in Example 4.23.

Example 4.23. Harmonies at mm. 9–16

Melody	F♯ (E)	D (C)	B	B	A (E♭ A)	G
Harmony	Em9	Cm11/G	G♯ fourths	G fourths/A	E♭M7(♯11)/B♭	CM7/B
			G♯-C♯-F♯-B/G♯ bass	G-C-F-B/A bass		
m.	9	10	11		12	13

At mm. 9–10 the M3-related harmonic progression (Em9-Cm11) matches the overall M3 melodic motion (F♯-D). The use of the m. 10 inversion (with G in the bass) then supports the contrary motion strategy between bass and melody, used instead of a parallel progression in which the bass would have moved to C. Such contrary motion techniques become magnified at m. 11. Although the melody pitch of B remains with both fourth chord harmonies, the bass nevertheless moves chromatically upward (G♯ to A), while the fourth chord harmonies descend chromatically downward (G♯-C♯-F♯ to G-C-F).[32] The m. 12 harmony provides another inversion (E♭M7(♯11)/B♭), leading to the B arrival in the bass (and the Phrygian harmony CM7/B) at the beginning of the next four bars.

In addition to the lavish harmonic vocabulary, there are several syncopations and rhythmic devices that enhance the intensity and the flow of this subsection. The obvious ones are the 6/8 syncopations at mm. 11 and 12, with the A bass heard mid-measure at m. 11 held across the barline,

---

32. The technique is similar to that heard during the introduction to Wayne Shorter's "Face of the Deep." The upper structure chords 3 and 4 move C♯-F♯-B to C-F-B, maintaining the melodic common tone while the accompanying fourths move down chromatically. See chapter 2.

followed by the B♭ bass mid-measure at m. 12. But a more subtle rhythmic wrinkle is created by the pacing in the bass and melody, in which the events are moving out of phase. That is, if the bass arrives "on time" at m. 13, the melody has still not finished its course. The G that arrives at m. 13 is consonant with the upper structure harmony, but it nevertheless delays the ultimate melodic goal of F♯, which is postponed until m. 15. (The lead sheet relies on the alternate take of "Song of the Wind" from *The Complete "Is" Sessions*, played in unison by flute and tenor saxophone. Other versions play the melody here more freely.) A glance at the figure above shows that it would have been possible to compose a version in which the F♯ melody arrived simultaneously with the B bass. (To do so, eliminate the repeated B in m. 11 and move directly to A there, to G in m. 12, and to F♯ at m. 13.) The F♯ delayed to m. 15 not only elasticizes the melodic line (against the 4-bar organization), but it calls attention to the modal organization, particularly the G-F♯ half-step heard against the static B bass. That ultimate combination of B (in the bass) with F♯ (melody) at m. 15 foreshadows the events of Subsection C, which uses those outer voices as a consistent point of departure.

Subsection C, mm. 17–24. This subsection forms the dramatic core of the composition, using the B (bass) and F♯ (melody) to begin a series of melodic ideas every two bars. An alternating two-chord progression (Em9/B and F♯m7/B) repeats until the final measure (m. 24). The progression and melody set up a B Aeolian environment until that last bar of the subsection.[33] The melody pivots around F♯, relying on a 3-note motive (F♯-G-A, mm. 17, 19, 21, 23) with two alternate endings: E (mm. 18, 22) and B (mm. 20, 24).[34]

But it is the harmony at m. 24 that creates the dramatic climax. Although the melodic sequences persist, that harmony wrenches this subsection out of B Aeolian. The harmony here maintains the B pedal point, but stratifies a dense polychord above it that combines an F major (below) with an E major triad (above). The chord provides "Song of the Wind" with its highest level of harmonic density. Standard chord labels become cumbersome, although it is possible to identify the harmony as an extended tertian structure

33. Chapter 3 described Aeolian progressions in Hancock's compositions "King Cobra" and "Dolphin Dance." Those used first-inversion M7 harmonies to effect the progression. In "Song of the Wind," Corea's Aeolian environment is created by a second inversion m11 harmony (Em11/B).

34. The mm. 17–18 motive F♯-G-A-E is similar to the opening motive to Hancock's "Dolphin Dance" (G-A♭-B♭-F): see chapter 3. This is not meant to suggest a direct borrowing, merely a shared melodic vocabulary.

(FM7(♯9, ♯11)/B) or as a double polychord above the pedal point (B pedal + Fmaj + Emaj). Despite the difficulties of labeling, in many ways this chord becomes the composition's pivotal or focal harmony.[35]

The metrical shifts at mm. 22 and 24 expand these dramatic aims. The shift to 2/4 at m. 22 not only overturns the metric predictability of the repeated 2-bar melodic and harmonic sequences, it also accelerates the flow into the m. 24 climax. And while the melody at m. 24 arrives at B, as it did at m. 20, the change of harmony overturns the 2-chord pattern that dominated the subsection. The m. 24 FM7(♯9, ♯11)/B climactic harmony (and the syncopated melodic pitch B) creates a ripple effect, expanding the meter to 5/4, allowing the harmony to linger and reverberate.

Subsection D, mm. 25–36. This final subsection is a 12-bar one. It relies on a single melodic sequence whose pacing is elastic. That melodic idea occurs once in the first four bars (mm. 25–28), four times (every measure) during the second four bars (mm. 29–32), and once during the final four bars (mm. 33–36). The melodic sequence initially sets up two levels of axis motion, as shown in Example 4.24. At the measure level, the phrase sets up a M3 axis, progressing from B to G (mm. 25–26). Subsequent downbeats continue that movement along the axis, from G-E♭-B-G (mm. 29–32). The final four bars slow the pace of the motive, which moves to a different M3 axis that links E (m. 33) to C (mm. 35). In the example those M3 axis pitches appear in bold. Meanwhile, those pitches are linked (on a note-to-note level) by motion through a nested P4 axis.

Example 4.24. Large-Scale Melodic M3 Axis (and Nested P4 Axis), mm. 25 to end

mm. 25	**B**	E	A
mm. 26-29	**G**	C	F
m. 30	**D♯**	G♯	C♯
m. 31	**B**	E	A
m. 32	**G**	C	F
mm. 33–34	**E**	A	D
mm. 35–36	**C**		

The M3 melodic axis pitches that begin each of the sequences (appearing in bold) correspond to the changes in harmony. And while mm. 33–36 move

---

35. On the *Piano Improvisations* performance, Corea alters the harmony by placing an F (rather than B) in the bass—the resultant harmony places an F major triad below an E major triad. In all cases, the result is a harmony that uses 6 of the 7 pitches of the A harmonic minor scale.

to a new axis, all the pitches in bold extend through most of an augmented (hexatonic) collection. (G♯/A♭ would have completed that collection.)

Certainly augmented (hexatonic) collections became part of Corea's vocabulary by the latter part of the 1960s. And it is useful to consider how such ideas also become part of his harmonic grammar. For example, the progression at mm. 25–28 moves from FM7(♯11)/A to Em(M7)/G♯. The latter chord also nearly completes the augmented (hexatonic) collection. (And Corea's improvisations over that harmony often rely on that scale.[36])

The harmonic progression at mm. 29–36 harmonizes those melodic axis pathways. Each new harmony corresponds to the M3 axis pitches shown in bold above. The earlier discussion of the Introduction and Subsection C to "Inner Space" described how the M3 melodic axis relies on second-order progressions: harmonic substitutions that bypass a rote parallel harmonization. The same applies here. Example 4.25 includes the melodic axis, a series of hypothetical harmonizations that move in parallel motion to that melody (i.e., first-order progressions), and Corea's progression.

Example 4.25. Hypothetical and Corea's Harmonization for mm. 29–36 of "Song of the Wind"

Melody	G	E♭	B	G	E	C
Hypothetical 1 (sus9)	**Fsus9**	D♭sus9	Asus9	Fsus9	**Dsus9**	
Hypothetical 2 (M7♯11)	D♭M7♯11	**AM7♯11**	FM7♯11	**D♭M7♯11**	B♭M7♯11	
Hypothetical 3 (sus13)	B♭sus13	G♭sus13	**Dsus13**	B♭sus13	Gsus13	
Corea's	Fsus9	AM7♯11/E	Dsus13	D♭M7♯11	Dsus9	A♭M7♯5/E
m.	29	30	31	32	33	35

The three lines (consisting of sus9, M7♯11, sus13 chords) provide an array through which Corea's harmonization systematically moves, as shown by the harmonies in bold. By avoiding a mechanical harmonization, Corea's progression accesses multiple chord types. The three harmonies may be understood to be in a substitution relation with one another. Example 4.26 shows this relationship, using a dual m3/M3 axis to represent the first chord for each of the three hypotheticals shown above. (For convenience of viewing, the figure provides two dual axes, the first for Fsus9 and D♭M7♯11, the second for B♭sus13.) The sus chords

---

36. On the *Piano Improvisations* version, Corea inserts another harmony at m. 28, an A♭M7♯5/G.

appear as gapped on that dual axis (their omitted third is represented by the parentheses).

Example 4.26. Dual Interval Axis and Relation Between sus9, M7#11, sus13

	Fsus9	()					
Db	F	Ab	C		Eb	G	Bb
DbM7#11							

	Bbsus13	()					
Bb	Db	F	Ab	C	Eb	G	

Instead of a first-order parallel harmonic sequence (formed by any one of the hypotheticals), Corea's progression forms a second-order progression for its M3 melodic axis. As shown by the harmonies in bold, Corea's composition activates that grammar in a determined succession. Note that Corea's harmonization at m. 30 places the AM7(#11) in second inversion (AM7(#11)/E). The resulting bass motion (F-E-D-Db-D-E) alternates m2 and M2, forming an incomplete octatonic collection that accompanies the incomplete hexatonic collection formed by the melodic axis pitches (G-Eb-B-G-E-C).

The final harmony (AbM7#5/E) departs from the array of hypothetical possibilities. It is the same harmony that ends the introduction—a variation of an E dominant harmony (with extensions of #9 and b13, but omitting the chordal seventh, D).

That dominant-type harmony (AbM7#5/E), along with the preceding Dsus9 (mm. 33–36), provides a turnaround. It may be heard as a conventional iv-V turnaround in A. Yet the composition avoids those tonal implications. Rather than linking to an A major or minor harmony at the top of the form, the form begins instead with F#m(M7). One mode of hearing this was described above for the end of the Introduction and the beginning of the form: the upper structure AbM7#5 (over E bass) moves up by m2 to AM7#5 (over F# bass). It is also possible to hear this through harmonic substitution techniques described throughout this chapter: if Dsus9-AbM7#5/E implies the key of A, the progression moves instead to F# minor, the relative minor of A major.

"Song of the Wind" and "Windows": Some Similarities. The discussion of Subsections A and B called attention to some melodic similarities between "Song of the Wind" and Corea's earlier "Windows." In particular, those two subsections, along with mm. 1–9 and 17–25 of "Windows," rely on melodic,

largely stepwise, descents (although "Windows" elaborates that descent through its arpeggiating motive). There are a number of notable structural similarities in melodic design, as indicated in the figure below. Both use a transitional section between their first two melodic descents. The second descent ends similarly in both works, by moving downward by M2 then m2 (F♯-E-E♭ in "Windows," A-G-F♯ in "Song of the Wind"). Both use the pitch goal of the second melodic descent as a pivot pitch, becoming the point of departure for the following melodic material. And each involve a descending melodic sequence that ends the form. Example 4.27 compares the two.

Example 4.27. Comparison of Melodic Designs of "Windows" and "Song of the Wind"

"Windows"	"Song of the Wind"
mm. 1–9: arpeggiating motive elaborates primarily stepwise descent	mm. 1–4: primarily stepwise descent
mm. 9–16: transition to second descent	mm. 5–8: transition to second descent
mm. 17–25: second stepwise descent, ends F♯-E-E♭	mm. 9–16: second stepwise descent, ends A-G-F♯
mm. 25–32: pivot around E♭, goal of previous descent	mm. 17–24: pivot around F♯, goal of previous descent
mm. 33–48: descending melodic sequence	mm. 25–36: descending melodic sequence

Both compositions, then, share broader melodic design principles. Both are single-section compositions that allow that design to play out on a larger canvas, without the repeated internal subsections of AABA and ABAC song forms. Nevertheless, there are fairly drastic differences in harmonic language. "Windows" relies on fewer chord types than "Song of the Wind," which has an expanded harmonic vocabulary that includes pedal points, modal plateaus, polychords, octatonic (diminished scale) and hexatonic (augmented scale) harmonies, and an avoidance of the evident functional harmonic progressions heard in "Windows." In addition, despite the similar elaborative techniques at mm. 17–25 of "Windows" and mm. 9–17 of "Song of the Wind" (see the figure above: "Windows" elaborates E♭; "Song of the Wind" elaborates F♯), the metric shifts and the climactic m. 24 harmony of "Song of the Wind" enhances its dramatic arc.

To greater or lesser degrees, all three compositions discussed in this chapter make use of axis progressions. "Windows" moves along the P5 axis. "Inner Space" (introduction and Subsection C) and "Song of the Wind" (Subsection D) use M3 melodic axes, while their harmonizations avoid that same axis through alternate harmonies. Such approaches in "Inner Space" and "Song of the Wind" show the extent to which the M3 melodic pathways of "Giant Steps" are retained, but harmonically transformed. And "Song of the Wind" responds to many of the decade's harmonic advancements heard in the works of Hancock, Shorter, and others. Certainly the use of shifting harmonies over pedal points, sus chords, and Aeolian progressions appears in a number of earlier Hancock compositions, as described in the chapter 3. And metrical shifts and hexatonic (augmented scale) harmonies are foregrounded in Wayne Shorter compositions such as "Vonetta."[37]

Unlike the Shorter and Hancock compositions discussed in the previous chapters, the three Corea compositions discussed here reveal a rapid evolutionary arc, particularly in terms of harmonic language. "Windows" relies on traditional tonal progressions to move along its harmonic axis. "Inner Space" relies primarily on major and minor type harmonies, avoids functional dominant seventh harmonies and tonal progressions (although uses a transformed turnaround to return the composition to its m. 1 harmony). "Song of the Wind" uses a widely expanded harmonic vocabulary of chord types.[38] Corea continued to develop multiple compositional approaches well beyond the decade. But his 1960s works offered later composers significant pathways and contributed to an expanded harmonic vocabulary, one that would strongly influence later jazz composers such as Dave Liebman, Richie Beirach, Jim McNeely, and many others.

37. For a detailed discussion of "Vonetta" (from the 1967 Miles Davis recording *Sorcerer*), see Waters, *The Studio Recordings*, 175–79.

38. The overall decline in Corea's use of ii-V and V-I progressions, and the ultimate suppression of explicitly functional dominant seventh chords, matches the gradual evolution of harmonic language through the 1960s. In a statistical corpus study of jazz compositions, Broze and Shanahan pointed out the overall decline in usage of dominant seventh chords, ii-V, and V-I progressions over the broad period 1924–1968. Yuri Broze and Daniel Shanahan, "Diachronic Changes in Jazz Harmony: A Cognitive Perspective," *Music Perception* 31, no. 1 (September 2013): 36.

CHAPTER 5
Booker Little, Joe Henderson, and Woody Shaw

If Shorter, Hancock, and Corea were central to postbop jazz composition of the 1960s, there were additional jazz composers whose work shared some aesthetic principles. This chapter examines three other composers of the decade: Booker Little, Joe Henderson, and Woody Shaw. The chapter focuses on Little's "We Speak," Henderson's "Punjab," and Shaw's "Beyond All Limits." Their compositions, like those of Shorter, Hancock, and Corea, moved decisively beyond the formal and harmonic conventions of tonal jazz.

ANALYSIS 1: BOOKER LITTLE, "WE SPEAK"

Trumpeter and composer Booker Little explored some principles of postbop composition during the late 1950s and early 1960s until his untimely death in October 1961. Like many of the composers discussed in this book, he was steeped in the hard bop traditions of the late 1950s: his recording career began in 1958 as a member of Max Roach's Quintet. Nevertheless, many of his compositions used tonally ambiguous harmonic progressions, unusual formal designs, and mixed meters. His earlier compositions, such as "Larry-Larue" (from Max Roach's *Deeds Not Words*) and "Rounder's Mood" (*Booker Little 4 & Max Roach*), both from 1958, abundantly use chromatic ii-V pairs. In "Larry-Larue," with a 36-bar ABAC form, the chromatically sliding ii-V pairs makes the sense of an overall tonic difficult to assess.[1] "Rounder's Mood" has a 40-bar ABA form (with 16-bar A sections and an 8-bar B section). By 1961, however, in the wake of Miles Davis's *Kind of Blue*, Little's participation in Coltrane's *Africa/Brass* sessions, and his ongoing collaborations with Eric Dolphy, some of his compositions synthesized slow-moving harmonies or pedal point accompaniment with more-rapid harmonic progressions.

"Bee Vamp" (*Eric Dolphy at the Five Spot, Vol. 1*, 1961), for example, alternates a static Bb bass pedal point (in 8-bar sections) with sections that have a more active harmonic progression. Characteristic of many of Little's compositions, "Bee Vamp" has an ABA form. The 20-bar A sections and 8-bar B section constitute a 48-bar form. Additionally, the 20-bar A section itself has a constituent aba form: Bb pedal (8 bars), a progression similar to the opening to Charlie Parker's "Blues for Alice" (FM7/ Em7 A7/ Dm7 G7/ Cm7 F7, 4 bars), and a return to the Bb pedal (8 bars). The overall progression, then, appears as Example 5.1, with the 4-bar "Blues for Alice" progression indicated as "BFA."

Example 5.1. "Bee Vamp," Form and Harmonic Progression

A section (20 bars)			B section (8 bars)		A section (20 bars)		
a	b	a			a	b	a
Bb pedal	BFA	Bb pedal	EbM7 /Am7 D7/ Abm7 Db7/ Gb7(#11)/		Bb pedal	BFA	Bb pedal
8 mm.	4	8	8 (4-bar progression stated twice)		8	4	8

The blend of pedal point (or slower-moving) harmonies with quicker harmonic progressions was a technique to be continued in later postbop compositions such as Wayne Shorter's "Witch Hunt." Little's improvisations during the pedal point sections are oriented to Bb minor. (The head statements during the pedal point sections rely on improvisation rather than a predetermined melody, while the remaining b (the "BFA") and B sections use a predetermined melody for head statements). Example 5.2 shows the four four-note harmonies usually played by the pianist over the Bb pedal. Each colors the pedal point differently: Abmaj7#5 Dbmaj7#5 BM7 GbM7

---

1. See Keith Waters and David Diamond, "Out Front: The Art of Booker Little," *Annual Review of Jazz Studies* 11 (2000–2001): 1–38 for further analytical description of "Larry-Larue" and "Rounder's Mood." That essay also contains a bibliography of additional sources on Little.

(chord symbols refer to root position four-note harmonies above the pedal point).

Example 5.2. Four-chord Vamp in B♭ Pedal Point Section of "Bee Vamp"

To be sure, Little's intervening sections of <u>faster harmonic motion</u> here are tied to tonal jazz traditions. Further, <u>their endpoints make evident</u> <u>B♭ as the overall tonal center</u> (the "BFA" progression ends with Cm7 F7, <u>the bridge progression</u> with G♭7(#11), ♭VI7 of B♭). While those harmonic progressions are relatively unambiguous (particularly the BFA progression), there is a certain formal ambiguity that arises during the A sections. There the interior 4-bar BFA sections undermine the otherwise 8-bar regularity and provide challenges for the improvisers and rhythm section.

Little's "We Speak" (*Out Front*) similarly combines the emerging aesthetic of slow-moving harmony (associated with modal jazz) <u>along with sections of</u> <u>faster harmonic rhythm. And its use of 6-bar sections likewise provides a degree of formal ambiguity.</u> An extended C minor section appears in the interior of the composition, surrounded by 6-bar sections on either end. The following discussion examines the harmonic progression to the improvisations before turning to the head statement, which expands the C minor section. Example 5.3 provides the form and progression for the improvisations. The solos follow the head statement and a linking 8-bar C minor passage in half time.

Example 5.3. Harmonic Progression to Improvisational Choruses of "We Speak"

Fm7		Dm7(♭5)	B♭m7	G13	Gm7	C7
m. 1		2	3	4	5	6

mm. 7–22 (16 bars)
Cm7

Gm7		A♭7	Gm7	E♭7 D7	Gm7	Gm7
m. 23		24	25	26	27	28

The flanking 6-bar phrases have a circular effect by working against an underlying 4-bar regularity. That effect is especially prominent at the end of the form, continuing to the return to the top. Although the final 6-bar passage is secure in its G minor tonality, the final two bars (mm. 27–28) link to the opening two bars as if continuing a process. Example 5.4 shows how that process might be depicted with the following hypothetical progression, depicting a modulation to C minor that would coincide with the top of the form.

Example 5.4. Hypothetical Progression to C Minor at End of "We Speak"

mm. 27–28	"29"	"30"	"1"
Gm7	Fm7	Dm7(♭5) G7	Cm7

hypothetical final 4 bars

The hypothetical progression squares the final two bars into four by placing the mm. 1–2 harmonies at the end of a 4-bar phrase. It also follows up on the harmonic implications of Fm7 and Dm7(b5) by inserting G7: it cadences on C minor at the hypothetical m. 1. That version makes more evident the circularity created by the 6-bar phrases. In fact, on Little's version it is often difficult to *not* hear the continuation of mm. 23–28 into mm. 1–6 as three 4-bar phrases (mm. 23–26, 27–2, 3–6), rather than as two 6-bar phrases.

And the tonal processes support that sense of circularity, with groupings that undercut the 6-bar organization. This is true particularly as the progression repeats during improvisation. The above hypothetical suggested that mm. 1–2 might be heard as part of process, with the Fm7 and Dm7(b5) related to the previous two bars of G minor, possibly implying a modulation to C minor. Yet B♭ minor, rather than C minor, appears at m. 3, creating a tonal rupture.

The progression at mm. 3–6 establishes its own 4-bar tonal process. Tonally the m. 4 G7 harmony, following B♭ minor, suggests the possibility for a chain of dominant harmonies (G7-C7-F7). That progression initially gets underway, as G7 moves to the next link on the chain by means of a ii-V pair (Gm7 C7). Rather than continue, however, the segment ends here. The ensuing 16-bar C minor section then departs from the more consistent harmonic rhythm of the other segments.

The progression at mm. 1–5 is a descending third progression (Fm7 Dm7(b5) B♭m7 G13 Gm7). In one sense, this bass motion outlines or arpeggiates the Gm7 harmony that appears at m. 5 (and so relates to the Gm key of mm. 23–28). But I suggested above that the harmonic move to B♭m7 at m. 3 creates a kind of tonal rupture. Example 5.5 is intended to illustrate this by considering descending third progressions, such as heard at mm. 1–3, in terms of relative closeness. It compares a closely related third progression with Little's. Little's harmonic connection between Fm7 and Dm7(♭5) (mm. 1–2) is close: F minor is included within Dm7(♭5). Thus, although the bass moves, much of the upper structure is consistent.[2] A similar close relation following that Dm7(♭5) requires B♭7 (which includes the previous Dm(♭5) in its upper structure). In contrast, Little's progression uses B♭m7. The m. 3 rupture comes about, then, by negating the M3 of B♭7 (D) and using instead the m3 (D♭) of B♭m7. That rupture further explains the circularity described above, since it allows m. 3 to sound as if inaugurating a 4-bar section.

Example 5.5. Descending Third Progression in Close Relation Compared to Little's Progression

Close relation

Fm7	Dm7(b5)		B♭7
	F minor upper structure		Dm(♭5) upper structure

Little's progression

m. 1	2		3
Fm7	Dm7(♭5)		B♭m7
	F minor upper structure (close relation)		D♭ major upper structure (not close relation)

Fm is still shared.

    The head to "We Speak" similarly involves 6-bar sections surrounding an expanded Cm7 passage. While that single-harmony Cm7 section lasts 16 bars during the improvisations, an inserted 6 bars augments this to 22 bars during the head. The entire head statement, then, groups as 6 + 22 + 6. Two brief interludes link the head with the improvisational form discussed above. Interlude 1 is an 8-bar written interlude, Interlude 2 a half-time interlude with rhythm section and notated horns beneath a trumpet solo. Example 5.6 summarizes the head.

Orchestration !

Example 5.6. Head to Little's "We Speak"

mm. 1–6	7–28	29–34	35–42	43–50
	C minor		Interlude 1	Interlude 2 (C minor, trumpet solo)
6 bars	22	6	8	8 (half time)

2. An alternate close pathway would follow Fm7 with D♭M7. (In that case, Little's third harmony (B♭m7) would stand in a close relation with D♭M7.)

A transcription of the trumpet, alto, and trombone parts (along with chord symbols) for mm. 1–42 appears as Example 5.7. While the discussion above described m. 3 as creating a tonal rupture with the preceding bars, the melodic phrasing supports this with a 2 + 4 grouping during mm. 1–6. That is, following the expanded pickup, m. 1 embellishes C (with upper and lower neighboring tones), returned to at m. 2 with the ascending fourth (C-F) motive. M. 3 starts anew by stating a transposed version of the P4 motive (F-B♭), and mm. 3–6 create a chromatic guide tone line, beginning with B♭ (m. 3), B♮ (downbeat of m. 4), B♭ (downbeat of m. 5), and A (downbeat of m. 6; this pitch is slightly obscured since the alto saxophone is voice a half step above on B♭).

Example 5.7. Lead Sheet to "We Speak"   Swing

Example 5.7. Continued

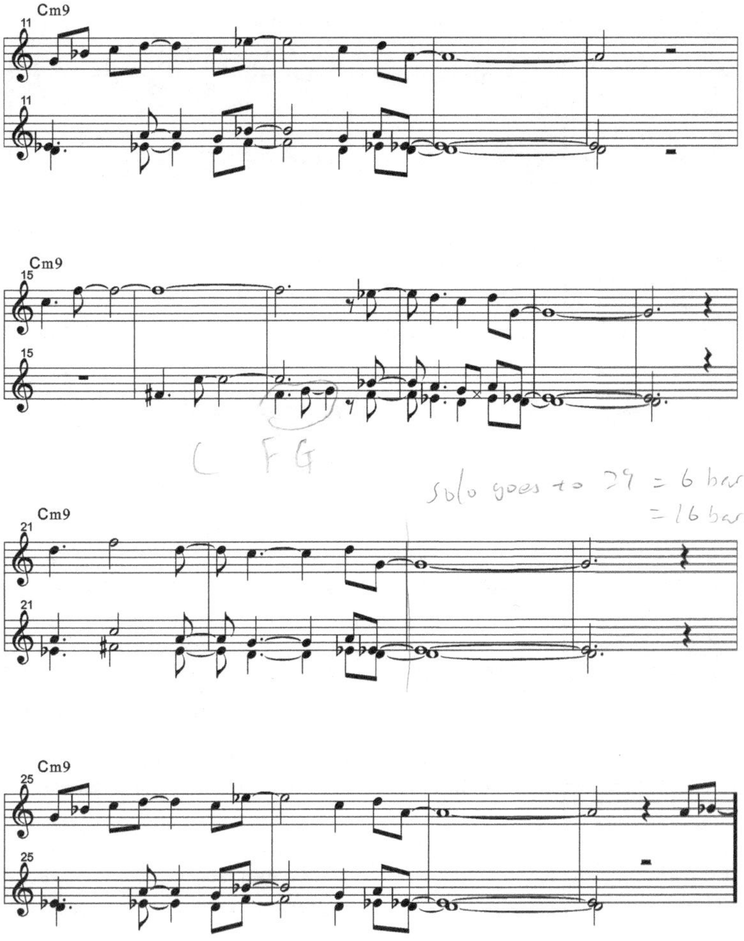

Example 5.7. Continued

The 22-bar C minor section involves an 8-bar segment, a related 6-bar segment, followed by a repeat of the initial 8-bar idea. It shows how certain composers treated a single extended harmony. The three-horn voicings use three primary techniques during mm. 7–28. All occur within the first eight bars of this section. First, Little begins the passage with constant structure planing to harmonize the first two melodic pitches of D and F, forming ninth and eleventh of the C minor harmony (E♭-A-D and F♯-C-F). The piquant F♯ of the second chord provides a colorful sonority, the only horn pitch in the passage that stands outside the C Dorian collection in this section. This then gives way to the second and most consistent technique in the passage, fourth chord planing within C Dorian. Since these preserve the mode, the intervallic construction involves both perfect fourths as well as the E♭-A-D (tritone + P4) spacing that began the passage. Third, the two 4-bar phrases here both end with a characteristic sonority of trombone and alto saxophone creating a D/E♭ half-step cluster below the trumpet melody on G (mm. 9–10) and A (mm. 13–14). The two phrases create a kind of rhyme: they begin differently, but end with a similar rhythmic gesture leading to that final melodic G (mm. 9–10) and A (mm. 13–14).

The ensuing 6-bar segment (mm. 15–20) provides a varied echo of mm. 7–10, the first of the two previous phrases. It begins with an echo effect in the three horns during the first three measures, all repeating the characteristic rhythm (beginning with dotted quarter) heard earlier at m. 7. In comparison with the trumpet melody at m. 7 (D-F), the trumpet at m. 15 now alters the opening pitch (to C-F). The alto at m. 16 (F♯-C) brings back the F♯ heard in m. 7, again standing outside the C Dorian collection. The trombone at m. 17 (F-G) then completes a fourth chord sonority (G-C-F) created by the endpoint of all three voices. The phrase continues (mm. 18–20) with a varied repetition of mm. 8–10, again with fourth chord voicings and ending with the D-E♭-G cluster.

The final 8-bar segment (mm. 21–28) repeats the initial one (mm. 7–14), again with the similar rhyme scheme at the end of each 4-bar phrase.

The main part of the head statement ends with a final 6-bar phrase (mm. 29–34). It differs from the first 6-bar phrase in significant ways, particularly in its tonal orientation, which commits to G minor unambiguously, both harmonically and melodically, underscored by the syncopated rhythm in both rhythm section and trombone/alto saxophone. However, both the opening and closing 6-bar segments feature another rhyme: both end with the same 2-bar idea, heard mm. 5–6 and 33–34.

If the idea of rhyme described above refers to echoes at ends of phrases, Interlude 1 instead *begins* with an echo. That is, its first three melodic pitches (F-D-C) sound as a recollection of the opening of mm. 7–8 (D-F-D-C). Even the common-structure harmonization of F and D at mm. 35 duplicate that of m. 7 (F♯-C-F and E♭-A-D). Unlike at m. 8, Little continues that common-structure for harmonizing the m. 35 C (D♭-G-C). Certainly, the call-to-order rhythmic orientation (1-bar clave rhythm) and back-beat drum accompaniment (and absence of piano/bass) of m. 35 create a dramatic fulcrum. pivot

As Interlude 1 continues, it no longer refers to the earlier mm. 7–8 section. For the remainder of Interlude 1, the upper melodic pitches of the trumpet orient consistently to the diminished scale (or octatonic) collection, proceeding stepwise upward (mm. 36–38), with downward steps chromatically filled in (m. 39), and continuing (mm. 40–42). The harmonization techniques vary here. Common-structure parallel (second inversion) triads prevail mm. 36–37 (ending with a B♭-C♭-E♭ cluster). Mm. 39–(downbeat of) 40 participate in the octatonic melodic activity, with a common-structure harmony descending along the m3 axis. The final harmony of the interlude (and the entire recorded performance) moves to a second-inversion triad (A major), but now the bass enters with G below.

Little's compositions illustrate a keen interest in exploring forms outside the 32-bar song form template, and in developing ways to integrate measure groupings beyond 8-bar phrases, particularly 6-bar phrases.[3] "Bee Vamp" and "We Speak" both place sections of slower-moving harmony (8- and 16-bar) alongside those of faster harmonic rhythm. Further, mm. 1–6 of "We Speak" are characteristic of many of Little's compositions in that they are either tonally ambiguous, or imply certain harmonic destinations left unreached. While Little's death in 1961 cut short his own compositional career, many of those principles were shared by postbop composers as the decade progressed.

ANALYSIS 2: JOE HENDERSON, "PUNJAB" *Five Waters, north indian*

Joe Henderson worked through the implications of the melodic vocabulary of Coltrane's 1960s quartet in a number of his compositions. In "Punjab" he did so while still exploring the axis progressions of Coltrane's earlier works of the late 1950s. Henderson's compositions also share features heard in Monk's compositions, particularly the use of clearly etched and memorable motives, often treated to sequential transpositions or metrical displacement. Many of Henderson's 1960s compositions highlight characteristic sonorities, such as M7#11, that frequently harmonize the melody in parallel motion ("A Shade of Jade," mm. 7–12, from Henderson's *Mode for Joe*; "Black Narcissus," mm. 17–20, from *Black Narcissus*).

Example 5.8 contains a lead sheet to "Punjab" (*In 'n Out*, 1964). Its introduction begins with a harmonic sequence initially moving in parallel motion to the melody. The repeated two-note melodic motive ascends by whole step, using an ascending stepwise sequence of M7 chords. Its predictability is offset by the 3 + 3 + 3 + 4 + 3 eighth-note rhythmic grouping, the melody (which expands to a 3-note P4 arpeggiation in m. 2), and the harmonic arrival up a half step (from BM7 to CM7#11) rather than whole step. Henderson uses similar upward half-step resolutions in the bass as the piece continues, and the final four pitches of the introduction (A-E-B-F#) provide an elaborated P4 design. A varied ascending version of this P4 design provides the opening motive of the head.

bar 1+2

---

3. He used ABA forms in a number of compositions in addition to "Rounder's Mood" and "Bee Vamp," discussed above. The ABA form of "Victory and Sorrow" (*Booker Little and Friend*) consists of 16 + 13 + 16 bars; the solo sections to "Hazy Hues" (*Out Front*) use 8-bar ABA sections, with the A section in 5/4 and the B section in 3/4.

Example 5.8. Lead Sheet to "Punjab"

Following the introduction, "Punjab" forms a single-section 18-bar composition, with two subsections of 10 + 8 bars. The opening four bars create a (2-chord) m3 axis progression of M7 chords, embellished by dominant harmonies that resolve upward by half-step (DM7-B♭7alt-BM7-G7alt-A♭M7; the improvisations omit the G7alt harmony). The result is a m3 (–M3, +m2) double-axis progression. Rather than relying on a more traditional arpeggiation of thirds (F♯-A-C♯-E) to outline the DM7 harmony, the melody instead uses a variant of a P4 arpeggiation (F♯-B-C♯-E), before ending with a descending fourth (F♯-C♯).[4] The trumpet/tenor saxophone harmonization

4. The intervallic design (F♯-B-C♯-E) varies that heard in the final bar of the introduction (A-E-B-F♯).

in P5ths maintains a pentatonic environment for the melody in mm. 1–2. Further, the quarter–two eighths rhythmic gesture that ends the motive recalls that of the opening to Benny Golson's "Along Came Betty," although in "Punjab" it occurs entirely within that pentatonic environment. The chord shifts in m. 2 rely melodically on a common-tone technique in the melody and harmonization: F♯-C♯ is common to all three harmonies heard in the measure.

The motive returns in mm. 3–6, down a m3rd. Relative to mm. 1–2 the motive is extended, forming a 4-bar response to the opening two measures. That extension sets up a motive that becomes the basis for mm. 7–10: B♭-A♭-G-E♭ (m. 4) becomes the point of departure for the B♭-A♭-G♭-E♭ motive heard throughout mm. 7–10. Compositionally, then, the phrase at mm. 3–6 combines both the mm. 1–2 motive with the mm. 7–10 motive. (The tenor saxophone harmonization is voiced a P5th below the melody in mm. 1–2, but voiced a P4th below the melody at mm. 3–4: the tenor saxophone part itself then moves down by half step between mm. 1–2 and 3–4.)

The ii–V pair at mm. 5–6 (Fm7(♭5)-B♭7) avoids a conventional resolution to E♭ by moving instead to a M7♯11 chord a half step above, to E. The harmonization of minor pentatonic (or blues scale) melodies by i and ♭IIM7 became a common compositional design in the hands of numerous composers in the 1960s, and here an E♭ harmony is notable for its absence until m. 10, which—as a dominant chord—then links to the ensuing harmony in the next subsection.[5] During mm. 7–10, the melody recalls the introduction: it uses the same 2-note rhythmic motive that returns primarily every three eighth notes (the eighth-note grouping for the G♭-E♭ motive at mm. 7–8 is 3 + 3 + 3 + 4). Unlike the upward stepwise motion of the introduction, that 2-note motive remains fixed, and stays within the E♭ minor (or black key) pentatonic collection, voiced in parallel fourths.[6]

Unlike mm. 1–10, the second subsection at mm. 11–18 adheres to 8-bar conventions. Even so, there are a number of features that elasticize the sense of meter. For example, the m3 axis movement of A♭M7 to BM7 (with intervening dominant harmonies G7♭9 and G♭7) creates a sense of metric displacement: with a V-I cadence to B, an arrival on B more typically takes place on the downbeat rather than mid-measure. It is easy to imagine two alternative scenarios. The first places G7♭9-G♭7 in m. 12, with the arrival of B the downbeat of m. 13. Or, alternatively, G♭7 occupies an entire measure and B arrives the downbeat of m. 14. Either situation—an arrival on BM7

---

5. While the V-I motion (E♭7-A♭M7) at mm. 10–11 provides a tonal cadence into the second subsection, it supports broader M3 bass axis motion, with EM7(♯11) (mm. 7–10) moving to A♭M7 at m. 11.

6. The m. 6 tenor saxophone pitch E (or F♭) that harmonizes with the trumpet B♭ pitch is not part of the E♭ minor pentatonic collection.

on either the downbeat of m. 13 or m. 14—is easily imaginable, given the (G♭ major) pentatonic environment of mm. 13 and 14, which accords with BM7. In any event, the mid-measure BM7 creates a metrical wrinkle, as do the events of the final four measures.

The harmonies during the head at mm. 14–15 differ slightly from those heard during the solos. Both create metric disruptions, but they differ. In the head, there is an upward chromatic slide occurring during the first two eighth notes of m. 14 (E7-F7), as well as a grouping of quarter-note triplets that ends mid-measure at m. 15. This melodic and harmonic arrival point creates a mid-measure syncopation at m. 15, one that echoes the m. 13 BM7 arrival in mid-measure. But the m. 15 syncopation is made stronger and continues into the next measure: the durational accents created by the longer mid-bar pitches at mm. 15 and 16 enhance the mid-bar syncopation. And the final two bars of the head return to a restatement of the introduction, with its own metric disruption created by the 3 + 3 + 3 + 4 + 3 grouping.

The progression during the solos at mm. 11–18 appears as Example 5.9.

Example 5.9. Harmonic Progression during Improvisation, "Punjab," mm. 11–18

E? M♭6 T

A♭M7	G7	G♭7 BM7	F7	GM7 AM7	BM7 CM7(♯11)
m. 11	12	13	14	17	18

The progression during the solos maintains the mid-measure arrival of BM7 at m. 13, preserving that sense of metric disruption during the solos. But the progression mm. 14–16 remains on F7 for three measures, and eliminates the additional harmonies played during the head.[7] The resultant harmonic rhythm segments the 8-bar phrase into a 3 + 3 + 2 grouping of measures, rather than a 4 + 4 grouping. Thus although the improvisational section eliminates some of the syncopations heard mm. 15–17 of the head, it creates instead some asymmetries of metrical groupings within the 8-bar subsection.

Certainly "Punjab" shares some principles with the melodic vocabulary of Coltrane's 1960s quartet in its use of elaborated fourth chord arpeggiations (mm. 1–3) and pentatonics (mm. 7–10, 12–14). The inclusion of members of Coltrane's rhythm section on the recording (drummer Elvin Jones and pianist McCoy Tyner) further locates the performance within

7. The Aebersold lead sheet to "Punjab" distinguishes between m. 14 (F7) and mm. 15–16 (C-7/F) On the recording, Tyner's accompaniment treats these three measures as a single harmony, often expressed by modal fourth chord planing (alternating left hand E♭-A-D and F-B♭-E♭). See *Joe Henderson: Inner Urge*, vol 108 (New Albany: Jamey Aebersold Jazz, 2004), 12.

that landscape. Yet the use of axis progressions also link to Coltrane's works of the late 1950s.

"Punjab" is, however, far from derivative. It contains many hallmarks of Henderson's compositions. Among them are sequences of M7 harmonies, often stepwise (introduction and mm. 17–18) or along the m3 axis, sometimes mediated with dominant harmonies (mm. 1–4, 11–13). Henderson frequently carries out these details with subtle metrical displacements and phrase asymmetries that defy predictability. Along with other 1960s Henderson compositions such as "A Shade of Jade," "Inner Urge" (*Inner Urge*), "Jinriksha," and "Serenity" (both from *In'n Out*), "Punjab" deeply reflected many of the concerns of postbop composers.[8]

ANALYSIS 3: WOODY SHAW, "BEYOND ALL LIMITS" *[handwritten: repeated harmony of Coltrane's quartet]*

Woody Shaw, like Joe Henderson, worked through many of the implications of the melodic vocabulary of Coltrane's quartet. They frequently appear with progressions—axis and otherwise—exhibiting a regular harmonic rhythm of one or two harmonies per bar. His "Beyond All Limits" (from Larry Young's *Unity*, 1965) is notable for its melodic arpeggiations of P4ths along with pentatonic collections and subsets. The shifts from one pentatonic collection to another often coincide with a change of harmony.

As Example 5.10 shows, "Beyond All Limits" has an AABA form, with 14-bar A sections and a 12-bar B section.[9] The overall sense of a global tonic is *[handwritten: Cloudy]* nebulous, given the wide-ranging progressions. F minor returns as a final chord, ending each A section during the final four bars. During mm. 1–10 of the A sections, melodic cadences coincide with harmonic arrivals on M7 harmonies (mm. 3, 7, and 10, with the melodic cadence delayed by two beats in m. 3). Each of those three harmonic arrivals is approached differently: AM7 (m. 2) leads to A♭M7 (as a V'M7), C♯m7-F♯7 (m. 6) leads to B♭ (as an elaborated ♭VI7), and A♭m6/9 (m. 9) to AM7.[10]

[handwritten: ? / Dm pent.]

8. For further discussion of Joe Henderson's compositions, see David Liebman, "The Compositional Style of Joe Henderson," *The Note* (Winter/Spring 2006): 25–26; and Arthur Lynne White, "Joe Henderson: An Analysis of Harmony in Selected Compositions and Improvisations," DMA diss., University of North Carolina at Greensboro, 2008.

9. The harmonies provided by the Aebersold lead sheet frequently do not comport with those performed by Larry Young on the recording. See Woody Shaw, *Eight Classic Jazz Originals*, vol. 9 (New Albany, IN: Jamie Aebersold Jazz, 1976).

10. The harmony at m. 9 (A♭m6/9) conflicts somewhat with the C♮ played by the horns on the third beat. It operates less conventionally in leading to the M7 arrivals than do the chords at mm. 2 and 6.

Example 5.10. Annotated Lead Sheet to "Beyond All Limits"

In the melodic dimension the technique for the beginning and ending points of many of the phrases use a gapped approach to pentatonics. Even the direct P4 arpeggiations, such as the opening five pitches (A-D-G-C-F), may be considered as a gapped pentatonic collection. This opening (F major or D minor) pentatonic in the melody shifts to another (B♭ major or G minor) pentatonic collection in m. 1. Here the melody creates a pair of gaps immediately filled by the omitted pitch. For example, C-F is filled by D; D-B♭ is filled by C. This idea of gap filling relates to the bebop technique of chromatic encircling, but now transferred to a pentatonic environment. Pentatonic encircling (shown by brackets in Example 5.10) can be achieved by beginning either with upward leap or downward leap, and Shaw uses both techniques, as shown in Example 5.10. That is, the first gap of C-F leaps upward before the filling D; the second gap D-B♭ leaps downward before the filling C. The remainder of m. 1 proceeds directly through the pentatonic collection.

The second measure shifts that pentatonic field down by a half step, and proceeds again by through pentatonic encircling (C♯-A-B). Although the collection is transposed downward, the harmonic progression proceeds differently. A rote harmonization would appear as B-7 (rather than AM7) in m. 2. The result is a fresher harmonization, since the melodic and harmonic dimensions avoid working in lockstep. Further, even though the pentatonic field shifts downward by half step, the first pitch of m. 2 moves upward by half step (relative to the first pitch of m. 1) before the remainder of the measure transposes m. 1 directly.

The phrase continues by shifting the pentatonic field down again by half step (A♭ major pentatonic), and concludes with a melodic cadence to C, achieved through pentatonic encircling. The overall pentatonic progress (from the downbeat of m. 1) thus moves down chromatically, from B♭ major pentatonic (m. 1), A major pentatonic (m. 2), to A♭ major pentatonic (mm. 3–4).

The second phrase (mm. 4–8) returns to the series of melodic P4ths that began the first phase, but now is heard as an afterbeat phrase, rather than as a pickup phrase. Further, the C-C♯ heard on downbeats at mm. 1 and 2 appear directly as the P4ths continue, moving from the end of m. 5 into m. 6. The P4ths continue, now displaced by a half step to C♯-F♯. The phrase concludes by chromatic (rather than pentatonic) encircling, F♯-E surrounding the F that coincides with B♭M7.

This melodic move to F♯-F supports a half-step guide tone line that remains during the A section, with the uppermost melodic pitches progressing F♯ (m. 6), F (m. 7), E (m. 10), en route to E♭ (m. 11). If the first phrase at mm. 1–4 uses chromatically descending pentatonic collections, mm. 6–11 in contrast use chromatically descending guide tones.

The third phrase, a 2-bar phrase at mm. 9–10, varies and compresses the previous phrase by introducing a tritone (G♭-C) into the P4 arpeggiation. The upper pitch F of that arpeggiation (m. 7) resolves chromatically down to E the following measure, coinciding with AM7. Note that both arrivals on the half-step guide tones F and E likewise transpose the harmony downward by half-step (B♭M7 and AM7, mm. 7–8 and 10). But it is illustrative that Shaw avoids a rote harmonization path to A♭M7 as the guide tone proceeds downward again by half step to E♭ at m. 11.

Instead of A♭M7, Fm7 is used during the final phrase at mm. 11–14. The pentatonic field remains on the A♭ major/F minor pentatonic collection in mm. 11–13, recalling the pentatonic subset heard at mm. 3–4. And here the complete pentatonic collection is stated, with pentatonic encircling in mm. 12. Had Shaw used A♭M7 rather than Fm7 in mm. 11–14, he would have continued the process that linked the guide tones F and E to B♭M7 and AM7. Shaw's use of Fm7 (rather than A♭M7) suggests a deliberate substitution, one that bypasses the more predictable A♭M7. So perhaps "Beyond All Limits" requires a more expansive view of key, one that resides within the A♭ major/F minor pentatonic collection. That collection closes the first phrase (attained chromatically via B♭ and A major pentatonics in mm. 1–2) and dominates the final four bars at mm. 11–14. This looser view of key as collection, rather than single harmony or tonal center, allows us to hear that pentatonic collection as a marked resting point within the A sections, supporting either A♭ major (mm. 3–4) or F minor (mm. 11–14).

The B section consists of a pair of related 4-bar phrases, followed by a m3 axis progression. The openings to the first two 4-bar phrases (mm. 29–30 and 33–34) are similar, but not exact. Since the harmonies differ (Gm6/9 and Bm11), the intervallic construction differs, with the pitches of Gm6/9 arpeggiated directly, while that of Bm11 consists of a pair of disjunct P4ths, separated by a fifth (E-A and B-E).[11] Both of these phrases end as a direct transposition (melody and harmony of mm. 31–32 reappears down by half step mm. 35–36). And the melodic material recalls the opening phrase through the fourth arpeggiation (E♭-A♭-D♭) and pentatonic encircling (A♭-D♭-B♭ and B♭-G♭-A♭) at mm. 30–31.

The final four bars of the B section (mm. 37–40) likewise use pentatonic encircling in every bar, but the arrival pitch coincides with a change of harmony along the m3 axis (A-D-B at mm. 37–38, for example). The sequential activity is exact in both melodic and harmonic dimensions, allowing the passage to be heard as transitional. (Shaw used a similar design in the same

11. Porter describes Coltrane's use of similar disjunct fourths in Porter, *John Coltrane*, 237.

formal location—the last four bars of the B section—in his "Moontrane," a direct homage to Coltrane. There the 2-chord passages create a m3 (–M2, +P4) double-axis progression: Gm7 Fm7/ B♭m7 A♭m7 / C♯m7 Bm7.)

The wide intervallic leaps in the melody throughout "Beyond All Limits" are characteristic of Shaw's compositional and improvisational vocabulary. It reflects the expanded pentatonic vocabulary of Coltrane (through pentatonic encircling and other means), as well as an enhanced commitment to P4 construction, arising through arpeggiation or, frequently, through pentatonic encircling.[12] We might imagine Coltrane's inside/outside improvisational phrases and sequences, those originally played over static or slower-moving harmonic frameworks, now reharmonized in "Beyond All Limits" (often with one chord per bar) and reflecting some of their underlying harmonic implications. Shaw's harmonic vocabulary in "Beyond All Limits" relies primarily on m7, M7, and sus chords that progress both conventionally and unconventionally and challenge the notion of a single key. Rather than promoting a focal tonal center, it moves in and among pentatonic collections, with the A♭ major (F minor) pentatonic collection playing a central role.

———————

Little's, Henderson's, and Shaw's contributions to 1960s postbop composition ought not to be underestimated. In many ways, all three explored some implications of Coltrane's music in different manners. If Shorter, Hancock, and Corea ultimately achieved greater visibility and popularity, much of this was due to the success of their jazz-rock fusion music in the following decade. Yet all of these composers shared compositional principles that frequently revoked or altered general conventions of small-group tonal jazz—the song forms, the single-key environment, and the reliance on tonal cadences at ends of 8-bar sections.

12. Some writers also acknowledge the influence of Eric Dolphy, with whom Shaw performed during the early 1960s.

CHAPTER 6
Evolutionary Perspectives

The approaches in this book stress how 1960s postbop compositions transformed or departed from earlier conventions of musical form, harmonic progression, tonal organization, cadence, melody, and other dimensions. As a result, the music requires different analytical techniques. The survey of compositions and ideas in the previous chapters is not exhaustive, and my claim is not that they can explain all postbop compositions. Instead, the aim is to show common threads and overlapping ideas amid a range of compositions. There are likely numerous overlooked avenues; some, if not many, questions remain unanswered.

This final chapter is in two parts. Part 1 offers possibilities for further inquiry. It explores ideas—tonal vestiges, double-axis progressions, and counterpoint—through additional compositions as well as several previously discussed compositions. Part 2 places the book's implications into broader evolutionary frameworks. As discussed in chapter 1, the evolutionary views expressed in this book apply less to questions of musical style (swing, bebop, etc.), and more to questions of compositional and harmonic design. This section, then, discusses syntax and vocabulary, and briefly if skeptically addresses some similarities between the syntactic evolutions of Western European concert music and jazz. It ends by proposing that schematic frameworks (such as axis progressions) exerted evolutionary pressures in tonal jazz works, pressures that motivated some of the syntactic changes that are the focus of this book.

PART 1: FURTHER TECHNIQUES

Tonal vestiges. In considering evolutionary perspectives, we can observe how certain postbop compositions retained vestiges of tonal practice more than others. They did so by retaining the root movements of tonal progressions, but in manners that avoided obvious allegiance to a single key. In particular, direct root movements of P4 (or P5), m2, and tritone often maintain chord-to-chord successions heard in earlier compositions. For example, Hancock's "One Finger Snap" (*Empyrean Isles*) uses the following progression, shown in Example 6.1.

Example 6.1. Progression to Hancock's "One Finger Snap"

C7 (C7sus, C7alt.)	E♭sus13	A♭sus13	Gm7(♭5)	C7alt	Fm7(♭5)	B♭7	E♭M7	Dm7(♭5)	G7
m. 1	5	9	13	14	15	16	17	19	20

Mm. 5–20 use exclusively descending P5 and m2 root motion, and the final chord links to the m. 1 harmony in the same manner. The result creates an ongoing spiral, broken only by the harmony at m. 5. Further, the pairs of m7(♭5) and dominant chords (mm. 13–14, 15–16, 19–20) create conventional ii-V groups. The sus chords act in the manner of conventional dominant chords, resolving either down by P5 (mm. 5–9) or down by m2 (mm. 9–13).

While the reliance on downward P5 and m2 bass motion recall the local directed progressions of tonal jazz compositions, in this Hancock composition larger tonal goals (i.e., the sense of overall key) are not articulated by end-of-section cadences every eight bars. Nevertheless, the direction of the progressions emerges both from the downward bass motion, as well as from the overall downward progression of the harmonic guide tones.[1] In many cases, the chordal 3rds (or 4ths, with sus chords) and 7ths descend by step or are retained as common tones.

Example 6.2 illustrates how the opening 16 bars of Hancock's "Speak Like a Child" (*Speak Like a Child*) operate similarly. The progression at mm. 3–4 creates a harmonic seam, and the following Am7-B♭7 progression moves the bass upward by m2. However, the remainder of the progression

---

1. For a formalized treatment of these ideas, see Sean Smither, "Navigating Simultaneous Syntaxes of Pitch Organization in Jazz Harmony: Transformational Ontology, Voice-Leading, and Guide-Tone Space," MA thesis, Rutgers University, 2015.

spirals downward through a series of dominant type (including sus) chords that ultimately alight on G♭.

Example 6.2. Harmonic Progression to mm. 1–16 of Hancock's "Speak Like a Child"

D♭7alt	A♭7alt	E7sus	Am7	B♭7	B♭7alt	B♭m7	E♭13 (♭9)	A♭7sus	A♭7	G7alt	G♭maj7	G♭ dim(9) (♯11)
	P4 (desc.)	(M3)	P5 (desc.)	m2				P5	P5		m2	m2
m. 1	3	4		5	6	7	8	9		10	11 13	15

The ensuing measures both during the first and second endings depend primarily on descending m2 bass motions. The first ending (mm. 17–22, Example 6.3) reharmonizes the mm. 13–16 melody, before yielding to a transitional 2-bar phrase, consisting of triads over a descending chromatic bass lines, returning the harmony to the Am7, heard last in m. 4.

Example 6.3. Mm. 17–23 of Hancock's "Speak Like a Child," First Ending

E♭sus9	D7alt	C/D♭	B♭/C	C/B	D♭/B♭(=B♭m7)	Am7
m. 17	19	21		22		23

Example 6.4 shows that the second ending differs slightly from the first in its first two harmonies, which reharmonize the mm. 13–16 melodic idea again, this time with bass motion that embellishes the G♭ plateau heard in mm. 13–16. The bass moves down by half step (D♭maj7(♯11)/F, mm. 17–18) and returns back to G♭maj7(♯11) in m. 19. The half step transitional passage remains at mm. 21–22.

Example 6.4. Mm. 17–23 of Hancock's "Speak Like a Child," Second Ending

D♭maj7(♯11)/F	G♭maj7(♯11)	C/D♭	B♭/C	C/B	D♭/B♭	Amin7
m. 17	19	21		22		23

In comparison with "One Finger Snap," the harmonic vocabulary of "Speak Like a Child" is colorfully expanded, particularly with the 2-bar transitional section at mm. 21–22. Yet it retains the same principles. Bass motion by P5 and m2 here emphasizes connections to earlier tonal practices in a more open setting.

Wayne Shorter's "Nefertiti" (Miles Davis, *Nefertiti*) proceeds similarly, with the bass moving by P5, m2, as well as tritone (A4, d5), as shown by Example 6.5.[2]

Example 6.5. Harmonic Progression to Shorter's "Nefertiti"

Abmaj7(#11)	Bbmin/Db	Gmin7(b5)		C7	Bmaj7(#11)			Bbmin7(b5)	Eb13(b9)
Bass interval	P5 (desc.)	d5		P5	m2			m2	P5
m. 1	2	3		4	5	6		7	8

Emaj7(#11)	D/A	Gbmaj7(#11)/Bb	E/B	Bm/E	Eb7(#11)		Eb7alt
m2	P5 (desc.)	m2	m2	P5	m2		
9	10	11	12	13	14	15	16

Although the bass motion is limited to those three intervals, the second half of the composition is given over several times to ascending rather than descending intervals, in particular at mm. 8–9 (Eb-E), 10–11 (A-Bb), and 11–12 (Bb-B). The ascending half-step bass motions form a technique Shorter worked out elsewhere, as in "E.S.P." (mm. 5–8), reversing the more typical downward flow. In "Nefertiti," the A-Bb-B bass motion at mm. 10–12 arises from the harmonic inversions, which camouflage to a degree the mm. 9–10 and 11–12 M2 sequence in those measures, appearing both in the melody and the upper structure harmonies.

The circularity of "Nefertiti" is distinctive. It undercuts the sense of harmonic and melodic arrival at m. 1 that might normally be expected by a composition ending with Eb dominant harmonies (mm. 14–16) and re-beginning with an Ab harmony. Yet the composition relies on traditional bass pathways, at times defamiliarized by the harmonies they host.

These compositions are arguably more closely aligned with tonal jazz traditions, particularly since in most of these cases the presence of an over-arching tonic might be claimed. With "One Finger Snap" and "Nefertiti" the composition ends with a dominant that links back to the m. 1 harmony. Yet the circularity of both, created in "One Finger Snap" by the 20-bar form, and in "Nefertiti" by the melodic sequence that makes the opening bar sound as a continuation of the previous two phrases—all undercut a clear sense of m. 1 as a primary harmonic arrival point.[3] "Speak Like a Child"

2. Shorter's lead sheet to "Nefertiti" provides notated chords (rather than chord symbols) at the beginning, with m. 1 notated as Ab, D, and G, and m. 2 notated as Ab, Db, and Gb. Library of Congress copyright deposit Eu 42288 (March 13, 1968).
3. "Nerfertiti" consists of three related melodic phrases; the first begins with the pitch C, the second with Ab, and the third with Bb. Thus the return to the first phrase

returns to a repeated vamp, alternating A minor and E7sus, that in many ways forms the core of the composition. The long descending passages by P5 and m2 (mm. 5–22 for both first and second endings) departs from and returns to the A minor vamp. That vamp provides a point of harmonic stability that contrasts with the more-active interior progression.

Yet most of the harmonic motion in these three compositions create a sense of perpetual motion, creating environments in which the sense of a clear evident tonic is suppressed, either continuously or for significant portions of the composition. However, the bass motion (and the 3rd/7th guide tone motion of the harmonies) relies on familiar pathways. This links to a longer tradition, heard in AA′BA″ compositions in which each constituent A section is significantly rewritten, such as in "All the Things You Are" or Benny Golson's "Along Came Betty." (Bass motions by 3rd occur at the end of the B section in "All the Things You Are," and twice in "Along Came Betty.") These compositions rely primarily on P5, m2, or tritone bass paths. Yet the continually unspooling harmonic progression creates a broader harmonic arc. In both, the melody of the A′ section returns to the original melodic idea of the first, but not in the same key. Only the final A″ section returns to both melody and harmony of the beginning, and in both compositions the ultimate harmonic goal is virtually withheld until the final section of the composition.[4] Such broader harmonic pathways operate in distinctly different fashion from AABA compositions whose second A sections are more precisely repeated.[5]

Double-axis progressions. Shorter's "Speak No Evil" (*Speak No Evil*) is another composition given over primarily to the bass motions of P5 and m2 described above. The 14-bar A sections begin by alternating between Cm9 and D♭maj7 (mm. 1–8), and end by alternating A7(♭5) and B♭min11 (mm. 11–14). But they are linked by a sequence (mm. 9–10), consisting of a 2-chord progression that then is transposed down by whole step. A sequential melody shadows the harmonic sequence. The result is a M2 (–M3, +M2) double-axis progression (Emin11-Cmin11, Dmin11-B♭min11). Such double-axis progressions, discussed in the previous chapter with Woody Shaw's "Moontrane," allowed postbop composers to further explore axis motion implications. In many of these compositions, their role is transitional,

sounds as a continuation of the second and third phrases. For more on the circularity of "Nefertiti," see Waters, *The Studio Recordings of the Miles Davis Quintet, 1965–68,* 217–19.

4. "All the Things You Are" only briefly tonicizes A♭ mm. 1–4 of the first A section.

5. Horace Silver's "Peace" relies on the same bass pathways, but within a briefer 10-bar composition. ("Peace" also has two progressions that descend by 3rd, at mm. 6–7).

either as a formal link that ends a B section and returns to an A section (in the Shaw compositions), or as a harmonic link (as with "Speak No Evil," moving the harmonic focus from C minor at the beginning of the A section to B♭ minor at the end of the A section (that C minor to B♭ minor ambivalence calls into question the role of a single tonal center).[6]

In some cases, double-axis progressions avoid mechanical treatments, as in Joe Henderson's "Inner Urge" (*Inner Urge*). Mm. 17–24 create a M2 (–m3, +m2) double-axis progression, based primarily on M7 harmonies (Example 6.6). (Compare with Shorter's "Speak No Evil," which used minor quality harmonies moving –M3, +M2.) The second-to-last chord in the sequence (B♭7, m. 23) differs in quality from all the others, avoiding a rote harmonization.

Example 6.6. Double-Axis Progression in mm. 17–24 of Henderson's "Inner Urge"

Emaj7	D♭maj7	Dmaj7	Bmaj7	Cmaj7	Amaj7	B♭7	Gmaj7
m. 17	18	19	20	21	22	23	24

Chick Corea's 62-bar composition "Litha" (*Inner Space*) is given over almost entirely to double-axis progressions. It opens by alternating M7 and m7 harmonies, using a m3 (–m2, –M2) double-axis progression. Its alternation of half steps and whole steps move partially through the the octatonic (diminished scale) collection. Example 6.7 includes the chords and the melody to mm. 1–8. If the 7-chord sequence is systematic, it is remarkably offset by the melody. The brackets in the example show how the melody is sequential with the overall downward m3 arc of the double-axis harmonic progression, but it is so rhythmically offset that its sequential nature is difficult to hear.

Example 6.7. Double-Axis Progression in mm. 1–8 of Corea's "Litha"

(Brackets indicate m3 sequence in melody)

6. Shorter's earlier "Sincerely Diana" (recorded with Art Blakey and the Jazz Messengers, *A Night in Tunisia*, 1960) begins in C minor (m. 1) and ends in B♭ minor (mm. 23–30), taking the same broader pathway as the A section of "Speak No Evil." See Patricia Julien, "The Structural Function of Harmonic Relations in Wayne Shorter's Early Compositions: 1959–63," PhD diss., University of Maryland (2003), 150–75.

M. 6–22 of "Litha" rely on another double-axis progression (Example 6.8). The indirect m3 descents (Dmaj7-Bmaj7-A♭maj) of mm. 1–6 now become embedded within a M2 (−m3, +m2) double-axis progression.

Example 6.8. Double-Axis Progression in mm. 17–22 of Corea's "Litha"

Fmaj7(♯11)	Dmaj7(♯11)	B♭maj7(♯11)	Cmaj7(♯11)
m. 7	11	15	19

Finally, mm. 31–62, the final measures of the composition, alter the 6/8 meter to a faster 4/4 tempo. Overall, the harmonic rhythm decelerates from one chord per measure (mm. 1–6), one chord every four measures (mm. 6–30), to one chord every eight bars. In this final section, the bass movement alternates tritone (with sus chord harmonies) and downward m2 motion (with minor chords), effecting a P4 (+d5, −m2) double-axis progression. The irregular pacing of the melody, and the color shift of the second minor harmony (min9♯5) suppresses the regularity of the double-axis organization. Example 6.9 indicates how the entire section thus creates a hugely expanded turnaround progression that links back to D at m. 1, as shown by the Roman numerals below the progression.[7]

Example 6.9. Double-Axis Progression in mm. 31–62 of "Litha"

Emin9	B♭sus13	Amin9(♯5)	E♭sus13	Dmaj7
ii	V′sus/v	v	V′sus	I
m. 31	39	47	55	1

Example 6.10 shows a 4-chord progression in Hancock's "Tell Me a Bedtime Story" (*Fat Albert Rotunda*), which uses M7 chords to effect a P4 (−M3, −m3) double-axis progression. The bass arpeggiates CM7, the final chord of the sequence, with the melody relying on an F♯ common tone for all four harmonies, forming 5th, 7th, 9th, and ♯11th with the respective harmonies. Initially appearing mm. 9–12 (excluding the 8-bar introduction), the four-chord progression is stated twice each time it appears. It returns again at mm. 21–24 and 41–44, and is used as a closing vamp to end the performance.

---

7. For more on the role of turnarounds in Corea's compositions, see chapter 4.

Example 6.10. Double-axis Progression in Hancock's "Tell Me a Bedtime Story"

Melody	F♯	F♯	F♯	F♯
Harmony:	Bmaj7	Gmaj7	Emaj7	Cmaj7(♯11)
m.	9/21/41		10/22/42	

Another double-axis progression in "Tell Me a Bedtime Story" acts as a transition, appearing mm. 29–32, shown in Example 6.11. Following that progression is a return to the primary melodic idea, each of whose three statements offers a creative study in reharmonizing a blues-scale melody. The m3 (+M2, +m2) double-axis progression occurs with a shift to 5/4 meter, creating a metric deceleration en route to the melodic return. The melody (shown below) shifts upward by m3 (A♭ to B) following the first two chords, highlighting the overall m3 ascent of the harmonies.

Example 6.11. Double-Axis Progression in mm. 29–33 of Hancock's "Tell Me a Bedtime Story"

Melody	A♭	A♭	B	B (Melodic return F♯ A B A C♯)	
Harmony	D♭m7	E♭m11	Em7	F♯m11	(Gmaj7♯11)
m.	29	30	31	32	33

The above examples indicate how postbop composers used double-axis progressions. Nearly all of Corea's "Litha" is organized by those progressions. In Shorter's "Speak No Evil" and Hancock's "Tell Me a Bedtime Story" (as well as in Shaw's "Moontrane"), their role is transitional, linking to other segments. Henderson's "Inner Urge" uses the progression as an ending gesture for the composition. Most double-axis progressions discussed here preserve chordal type, suspending tonal processes. Those that do not may invoke local tonal processes: for example, mm. 31–62 of "Litha" alternate minor chords with sus13 chords, creating an end-of-form turnaround.

Counterpoint. Studies of jazz harmony focus far more on vertical and functional considerations than on contrapuntal ones.[8] The term "counterpoint" has a wide variety of meanings. It most generally refers to the independence of melodic lines operating simultaneously (or in alternation) in different ranges. Thus it can describe a bass line operating melodically or in largely stepwise motion (in tandem with an upper melody), or to multiple voices above the bass, each of which exhibits a

8. One notable exception is Bill Dobbins, _Jazz Arranging and Composition: A Linear Approach_ (Rottenburg, Germany: Advance Music, 2005).

degree of melodic independence. More-specialized meanings of counterpoint arise from the use of contrapuntal devices (such as fugue and canon), or from species counterpoint, a pedagogical method that initially controls the rhythmic dimension of the independent lines: using note-against-note (1:1), multiple notes against single note (2:1, 4:1, etc.), and other textures.[9]

Likewise, ideas of counterpoint figure into postbop compositions in different manners.[10] During the final measures to Corea's "Song of the Wind" (discussed in chapter 4), the skeletal melody moves from one M3 axis path to another, with a harmonization scheme that alternates 9, #11, and 13 until the final chord. Example 6.12a shows the skeletal melody of mm. 29–36. Note that the bass moves exclusively by stepwise motion, either by M2 or m2, passing through a subset of the octatonic (diminished scale) collection. Notably, the inversion with the second harmony (Amaj7(#11)/E) preserves that stepwise motion.

Example 6.12a. 1:1 Melodic Reduction, Showing Axis Motions (G-E♭-B-G and E-C) and Stepwise Bass of mm. 29–36 of "Song of the Wind"

Example 6.12b. Mm. 29–36 of Melody from Corea's Lead Sheet; Mm. 29–32 in 2:1 Counterpoint with Bass (Downbeat M3 Axis Pitches Elaborated with M2 Axis in mm. 29–32)

9. Species counterpoint has been in use since the 1500s, but is most closely associated with the 1725 treatise of J. J. Fux, *Gradus ad Parnassum*. For an historical account of species counterpoint and Fux, see chapter 2 of Joel Lester, *Compositional Theory in the Eighteenth Century* (Cambridge, MA: Harvard University Press, 1992), 26–48. For an introduction to species counterpoint, see Henry Martin, *Counterpoint: A Species Approach Based on Schenker's Counterpoint* (Lanham, MD: Scarecrow Press, 2005).

10. Steven Strunk has examined Wayne Shorter compositions that rely extensively on stepwise bass motion, focusing on how more-fundamental structural harmonies become elaborated by harmonies whose bass is related by step. For example, he explains the final measures of Shorter's "El Gaucho" (Cm9, Dm7, Cm9, Dm7, Em7, mm. 11–18) as a stepwise elaboration of Cm7, which he suggests is a minor dominant to the Fmaj7 harmony at the beginning of the form. Steven Strunk, "Notes on Harmony in Wayne Shorter's Compositions, 1964–67," *Journal of Music Theory* 49, no. 2 (2005): 306.

Example 6.12c. Mm. 29–36 Melody as Played on Corea Recordings, mm. 29–32 in 3:1 Counterpoint with Bass (Downbeat M3 Axis Pitches Elaborated with P4 Axis)

This representation emphasizes the 1:1 (note-against-note) orientation between the upper melodic design and a bass that moves stepwise. However, Corea's copyright deposit of the lead sheet fills in the axis pitches with a single stepwise pitch during the first four bars, providing a 2:1 orientation against the bass.[11] As shown in Example 6.12b, Corea's lead sheet elaborates the analytical reduction of Example 6.12a with a M2 (whole-tone) axis motion in the melody during mm. 29–32. And ultimately Corea's recorded versions drew out the implications of the final four bars of the lead sheet. Example 6.12c shows that mm. 29–32 are in a 3:1 relation with the bass, with each downbeat pitch melodic pitch elaborated by P4 axis motion (G-C-F, Eb-Ab-Db, etc.).

Other 1:1 reductions show additional contrapuntal designs between bass and melody. Chapter 4's discussion of "Inner Space" called attention to the skeletal M3 axis pathway of the melody (during the introduction and mm. 15–18; see Example 6.13) and how the harmonic choices alternate #11 and M7 (formed by bass and melody). The result is a M3 (+m3, +m2) double-axis progression, with the bass moving through a subset of the hexatonic (augmented scale) collection, alternating m3 and m2 (A-C-Db-E).

Example 6.13. Contrapuntal Relationship between Skeletal Melody and Bass in "Inner Space," Introduction and mm. 15–18

Skeletal Melody	D#	B	G	D#
Harmony	Amaj7(#11)	Cmaj7(#11)	Dbmaj7(#11)	Emaj7(#11)
m.	i, 15	iii, 16	v, 17	vii, 18

As with "Song of the Wind," not only do the harmonies avoid a rote M3 (single) axis harmonization, but the bass and melody form a particular contrapuntal relationship. In "Inner Space" the bass here moves in contrary motion to the melody: as the melody descends the bass ascends.

11. Contained at the Library of Congress (Eu 217729, November 17, 1970). The lead sheet for these measures does not include harmonies, only melody.

The 1:1 counterpoint between bass and melody shown in the examples above is intended to be strictly analytical. They call attention to the manner in which the bass moves stepwise ("Song of the Wind") or in contrary motion ("Inner Space") against a simplified skeletal melody. I am not suggesting that these contrapuntal reductions reflected an overt or conscious compositional process, nor that Corea began with them as a starting point. But both examples show the persistence of the M3 axis, along with a contrapuntal bass that avoids parallel M3 axis harmonizations. We might understand that M3 axis as a musical meme, something in the air during this time, that had a certain attraction for creative composers. It thus played an evolutionary role in postbop composition, moving composers beyond tonal jazz conventions. The following section further considers that musical evolution.

PART 2: QUESTIONS OF EVOLUTION: SYNTAX, VOCABULARY, AND SCHEMATA

In many narratives of jazz in the 1960s, postbop jazz is eclipsed by free jazz and modal jazz. Yet for countless practicing musicians and composers, many of these postbop works are crucial. This book's stance is not intended to be staunchly revisionist, but we may nevertheless observe an imbalance between jazz historical narratives on the one hand, and long-standing influences among communities of jazz musicians and composers on the other. Narratives of jazz history frequently rely on tropes of discontinuity and disruption to highlight evident and overt stylistic changes. But musicians and composers frequently mold and fashion musical grammars in dynamic but more evolutionary fashion.[12] Those musical solutions of the 1960s discussed here—postbop compositional practices—are potent and palpable. By attending to them we throw significant cultural and aesthetic achievements of the past half-century into higher relief.

Why do distinctions between 1960s postbop compositions and tonal jazz compositions frequently escape notice? Theories of harmony normally rest on two core ideas—vocabulary (chordal types) and syntax (chord-to-chord successions and techniques of closure).[13] While the postbop compositions

12. For additional insight into how tropes of revolution vs. evolution inform jazz narratives, see Scott DeVeaux, *The Birth of Bebop: A Social and Musical History* (Berkeley: University of California Press, 1997).

13. For more on musical syntax, see chapter 2 of Joseph Swain, *Musical Languages* (New York: W. W. Norton, 1997), 19–43, and chapter 5 of Aniruddh Patel, *Music, Language, and the Brain* (New York: Oxford University Press, 2008), 239–98.

discussed here departed from earlier tonal traditions, changes to syntax and vocabulary were more nuanced and subtle than those of the examplars of modal jazz and free jazz. Although postbop composers explored newer chord types, they also frequently trafficked in conventional ones. Harmonic rhythm is largely consistent. In terms of syntax, conventional chord-to-chord progressions and techniques of closure often differed, but at times harmonic connections and resolutions in postbop compositions altered or muted the conventions of tonal jazz. When more-conventional cadential progressions appear in postbop compositions, they often do so in works that do not express a clear and evident single tonic (as in Hancock's "Dolphin Dance," for instance). In those cases, listeners may at times be more attuned to the moment-to-moment flow of harmonies than to global tonal procedures. As a whole, disruptions to tonal vocabulary/syntax were more starkly evident with modal jazz and free jazz than with postop jazz.[14]

Evolutionary models for understanding changes in jazz composition are convenient if problematic. In some senses, evolution (literally "unrolling" or "rolling out") seems a reasonable metaphor, applied to living beings, languages, and cultural artifacts. Jazz composers adopt and adapt conventions, resulting in progressive and, at times, dynamic changes. The discussion above, highlighting vocabulary and syntax, suggests that language evolution may be a better analog than biological evolution, which describes genetic changes and mutations over far longer historical spans.[15] Musics, like languages, are acquired and transmitted through learning rather than through genetic inheritance. Like languages, musics are not fixed entities but are categorized according to shared architectural principles. Yet those categories may still diverge according to time, region (dialect), social class or group (sociolect), and individual (idiolect). Musics, like languages, fluidly arise through communal practices, but also may be subject to changes by individuals.[16]

14. Nevertheless, some writers have regarded tonal jazz compositions differently from postbop compositions, even if using different terminology and different methods from those used here. Ron Miller uses the term "modal complex" for compositions exemplified by Wayne Shorter. Miller relates harmonies to underlying scalar collections along a brightness/darkness continuum, which creates a "modal contour." Ron Miller, *Modal Jazz: Composition & Harmony*, 2 vols. (Rottenburg: Advance Music: 1996). See also Wayne Naus, *Beyond Functional Harmony* (Rottenburg: Advance Music, 1998).

15. The literature on historical linguistics is vast, but the following two books offer significant perspectives: Roger Lass, *Historical Linguistics and Change* (Cambridge: Cambridge University Press, 1997); and Morten H. Christiansen and Simon Kirby, eds., *Language Evolution* (Oxford: Oxford University Press, 2003).

16. For more on language and music, see Steven Feld and Aaron Fox, "Music and Language," *Annual Review of Anthropology* 23 (1994): 25–53; and chapter 2 ("Music as

It is important to note that categorical distinctions proposed here (such as tonal, modal, postbop, or free jazz), even if they rely on evident differences in syntax and vocabulary, suggest boundaries of perhaps little interest to creative artists. After all, composers such as Shorter, Corea, and Hancock wrote not only postbop compositions during the 1960s, but also others that reflected aspects of tonal, modal, and free jazz.

Evolutionary parallels between the development of jazz harmony and that of Western European concert music of ca. 1750–1925 are intriguing, yet similarities ought not to be overstated. Most likely, both moved from an emphasis on major mode compositions to an increased use of minor mode compositions: for European music, that change appeared during the nineteenth century; for jazz, probably during the late 1950s and early 1960s. For European music, Richard Cohn has proposed a general four-stage path, linking the triadic tonality of the first Viennese school (Haydn, Mozart, and Beethoven), to the chromatic progressions (including axis progressions) of nineteenth-century composers (such as Liszt, Wagner, and Brahms), to the scalar tonality of turn-of-the-century French Impressionist and Russian composers (such as Debussy and Scriabin), to the atonality of the Second Viennese School (of Schoenberg, Webern, and Berg).[17] Those four stages of European music, broadly drawn, loosely correspond to the syntactic changes described above through the 1960s as tonal/postbop/modal/free jazz.

But there are sizeable distinctions, particularly in terms of vocabulary. A reliance on major/minor triads (as with Cohn's first two stages) only comport with ragtime and jazz in its earliest decades, not with the extended harmonies of jazz that began to develop in the 1920s. The same is true with harmonic inversions, far more prevalent in common-practice music than in jazz practice.[18] Additionally, jazz harmony responded to African-American practices in fundamental ways, as with the inclusion of blue notes into characteristic harmonies, such as dominant seventh harmonies with raised ninths (on I and V chords). Moreover, the respective rates of change differed widely. Cohn's four stages were enacted over a period of loosely 175 years. If tonal jazz principles persevered during the first 50–60 years of the

Language") of Kofi Agawu, *Music as Discourse: Semiotic Adventures in Romantic Music* (New York: Oxford University Press, 2009), 15–40. Both also address the degrees to which music has the communicative or semantic properties of language.

17. Richard Cohn, *Audacious Euphony: Chromaticism and the Triad's Second Nature* (New York: Oxford University Press, 2012), 206–8.

18. David Temperley, "Communicative Pressure and the Evolution of Musical Styles," *Music Perception* 21, no. 3 (2004): esp. 327–29.

twentieth century, exemplars of postbop (Coltrane's "Giant Steps"), modal (Davis's "So What" and "Flamenco Sketches"), and free jazz (Coleman's *Free Jazz*) emerged more or less simultaneously, from 1959 to 1960. The differences in evolutionary pacing may be due to many factors, including the development of mechanical means of musical reproduction (recording, radio, etc.). All these factors, as well as other differences—underlying cultural assumptions, social function, systems of patronage, methods of symbolic transmission (such as musical scores), role of through-composed vs. cyclic forms, and provenance—are apt to render extended comparisons between Western European and jazz music overly facile.[19]

How do composers carry forward—and transform—compositional ideas? Composers and performers rely on frameworks at diverse organizational levels. The "head-solos-head" format for the performance of a jazz composition provides an organizational convention at a general level; "12-bar blues" and "32-bar AABA form" are well-learned frameworks. Writers such as Leonard Meyer and Robert Gjerdingen describe such frameworks—schemata—in terms of patterns within grammatical conventions, as abstracted prototypes, or as well-learned exemplars.[20] Jean Mandler defined a schema as "a mental structure formed on the basis of past experience with objects, scenes, or events, and consisting of a set of (usually unconscious) expectations about what things look like, and/or the order in which they occur."[21]

On a more granular level, schemata can describe specific harmonic or melodic traits. For example, "Coltrane changes" refers to a harmonic pattern

19. Other writers have considered parallels between Western European music and jazz. Andre Hodeir labels the evolutionary periods of jazz as "primitive" (ca. 1900–1917), "oldtime" (1917–1926), "pre-classical" (1927–1934), "classical" (1935–1945), and "modern" (after 1945). For Hodeir, similarities between European and jazz music arise from function (with origins in religious vocal music) as well as texture and instrumentation (moving through instrumental polyphony, accompanied melody, and "symphonic music"). They reflect his larger teleological position that art moves from growth through maturity to decline: the final phase (for him, the post-1945 "modern" phase) corresponds to the "division into branches of what was a single trunk." In Andre Hodeir, *Jazz: Its Evolution and Essence*, trans. David Noakes (New York: Grove Press, 1956), 21–36 and 116. See also "The Avant-Garde and Third Stream," in Gunther Schuller, *Musings: The Musical Worlds of Gunther Schuller* (New York: Oxford University Press, 1986), 121–33; and Laurent Cugny, *Analyser le jazz* (Paris: Outre Mesure, 2009), 519–23.

20. Leonard B. Meyer, *Explaining Music: Essays and Explorations* (Chicago and London: University of Chicago, 1973), and Robert Gjerdingen, *Music in the Galant Style* (New York: Oxford University Press, 2007).

21. J. M. Mandler, *Stories, Scripts, and Scenes: Aspects of Schema Theory* (Hillsdale, NJ: Lawrence Erlbaum Associates, 1984), 14.

of major third–related harmonies linked by intervening dominant chords, as heard in Coltrane compositions such as "Countdown" or "Giant Steps." As many writers have observed, Coltrane changes form part of a network of earlier jazz compositions that rely on M3 modulations. And that network extends not only backward but forwards. Earlier works, such as Jerome Kern's "Smoke Gets in Your Eyes" modulate by M3 to begin their bridge.[22] Rodgers and Hart's "Have You Met Miss Jones" contains a progression in its bridge that tonicizes Bb, Gb, D, and Gb. In both, the M3 schema appears within an evidently tonal jazz framework, one that relies on common constraints of tonal jazz (that is, the half cadences at the end of the first A section and the bridge, and the full cadence at the end of the form).

Musical change arises, Leonard Meyer writes, "through the permutation and recombination of more or less discrete, separable traits or clusters of traits."[23] Thus the "Coltrane changes" schema, discussed in this book as a M3 axis progression, heard in earlier tonal works by Kern and Rodgers, was retained and transformed in postbop works without the evident tonal frame. In "Giant Steps," it becomes the central process, in both descending (mm. 1–8) and ascending (mm. 9–16) forms. In Corea's "Inner Space," the schema appears with other melodic and harmonic schemata described as "pentatonic," "Phrygian," and "turnaround." In mm. 1–17 of Hancock's "Dolphin Dance" and the introduction to Corea's "Inner Space," the schema moves to the melody and is elaborated while the harmonies make use substitution principles. In the earlier tonal works by Kern and Rodgers, the M3 axis schema is elaborative, subordinate to the larger tonal frame. In the later postbop works, any tonal processes are subordinate to the M3 axis schema.

Thus this same schema not only operates across different syntaxes, *it can itself be the agent of syntactic change*, particularly when it penetrates to deeper levels of structure ("Giant Steps") or becomes further abstracted or elaborated ("Dolphin Dance" and "Inner Space"). As the constraints of tonal jazz syntax became loosened or abandoned, so too, frequently, did its schematic forms.

Schemata contribute to an evolutionary perspective by suggesting that genetic (or, more properly, memetic) material creates change. Degrees of change can vary. Computer scientist David Cope refines that perspective

22. For a list of compositions that modulate upward or downward by M3 at the beginning of the bridge, see Dariusz Terefenko, *Jazz Theory: From Basic to Advanced Study* (New York: Routledge 2014), 327–28.

23. Leonard B. Meyer, *Style and Music: Theory, History, and Ideology* (Chicago and London: University of Chicago Press, 1989), 148.

through five stages of "referential analysis": "My taxonomy for referential analysis includes Quotations (as in citations, excerpts, or renditions); Paraphrases (as in variations, caricatures, or transcriptions); Likenesses (as in approximations, translations, or similarities); Frameworks (as in outlines, vestiges, or redactions); and Commonalities (as in conventions, genera, or simplicities). . . . Clearly, potential for listener recognition proceeds from strong to weak through these categories, and the potential for stylistic integration proceeds inversely."[24]

strong ↓ weak (margin annotation)

Cope's continuum might underscore why continued use of the M3 schema in patent fashion (as in the second half of Shorter's "El Toro") did not have substantial lasting power. If the indebtedness to Coltrane's "Giant Steps" was too evident (mm. 9–16 of "El Toro" and of "Giant Steps" have a similar harmonic rhythm and both largely use the M3 axis in melody and harmony), "El Toro" would likely be heard at the level of recognizable quotation or paraphrase, derivative because less integrated into the composition, and thus in too direct a dialogue with "Giant Steps." But transformed, the schema still provided a powerful source of organization, operating at the level of likeness or framework, and more integrated into the composition.[25]

Tracing a line of influence from a single influential model or musician can be difficult to wholly substantiate, even for recognizable works such as Coltrane's "Giant Steps." However, the focus need not be placed upon single antecedent compositions, but upon traits that populate different compositions across time. "Giant Steps" became an exemplar of the M3 schema, largely because it worked out the schema systematically, and in ways that challenged many of the constraints of tonal jazz. But if an overemphasis on a single source suggests a causal innovator, a great man view of history, it is possible to reframe the perspective. Rather than focusing on causal effects (single influences), we may instead emphasize how certain schemata prevail: as one writer aphorizes, "a pattern, concept, attitude, and so on is not chosen because it is influential; rather, it is influential because it was chosen."[26] My intent is not to negate the accomplishments of

24. David Cope, "Computer Analysis of Musical Allusions," *Computer Music Journal* 27, no. 1 (2003): 11. For more on a memetic perspective, see Steven Jan, *The Memetics of Music: A Neo-Darwinian View of Musical Structure and Culture* (Aldershot: Ashgate Publishing, 2007). Jan develops a model for schemata through memes, or units of cultural evolution. Jan defines the success of memes through "copying-fidelity," although (like genes) memes are subject to "mutation."

25. Cope's fifth category—commonalities—more properly applies to larger conventions, such as "head-solos-head," or "single-section composition," than to particular harmonic or melodic schemata.

26. Meyer, *Style and Music*, 143.

highly innovative musicians, many of whom richly and powerfully worked out implications of particular schemata—in many ways the innovations of Shorter, Hancock, Corea (and others) provide the recurring theme of this book. We may, nevertheless, see those individuals as participating in and responding to larger historical and evolutionary processes. More attention to those processes is due.

DISCOGRAPHY

Blakey, Art, and the Jazz Messengers, *The Big Beat* (BLUE NOTE BLP 84029, recorded March 1960, reissued 1987 Blue Note Records, with alternate take).

Blakey, Art, and the Jazz Messengers, *A Night in Tunisia* (BLUE NOTE BLP 84049, rec. August 1960, reissued 1989 with alternate take and 1 bonus track).

Blakey, Art, and the Jazz Messengers, *The Freedom Rider* (BLUE NOTE BLP 84156, rec. February & May 1961, reissued 1998 Blue Note Records, with 4 bonus tracks).

Blakey, Art, and the Jazz Messengers, *Mosaic* (BLUE NOTE BST 84090, rec. October 1961).

Blakey, Art, and the Jazz Messengers, *Caravan* (RIVERSIDE RLP 438, rec. October 1962; reissued 1987 Original Jazz Classics with 2 alternate takes).

Blakey, Art, and the Jazz Messengers, *Ugetsu: Art Blakey's Jazz Messengers at Birdland* (RIVERSIDE RLP 464, rec. June 1963; reissued 1989 with 3 bonus tracks).

Bobo, Willie, *Do That Thing/Guajira* (TICO 1108, rec. 1963).

Coltrane, John, *Giant Steps* (ATLANTIC SD 1311, recorded May and December 1959, reissued 1998, with 8 alternate takes).

Coltrane, John, *A Love Supreme* (IMPULSE A 77, rec. December 1964, reissued 1995 Impulse).

Corea, Chick, *Inner Space* (ATLANTIC SD 2 305/ K 60081, rec. August–December 1966; 4 tracks originally released on *Tones for Joan's Bones*).

Corea, Chick, *Now He Sings, Now He Sobs* (SOLID STATE SR 3157, rec. March 1968; reissued 2002 Blue Note Records, with 8 bonus tracks).

Corea, Chick, *Sundance* (GROOVE MERCHANT GM 530, rec. May 1969; reissued 2002 Blue Note Records with *Is* as *The Complete "Is" Sessions*, with 6 alternate takes).

Corea, Chick, *Is* (SOLID STATE SS 18055, rec. May 1969; reissued 2002 Blue Note Records with *Sundance* as *The Complete "Is" Sessions*, with 6 alternate takes).

Corea, Chick. *Piano Improvisations, Vol. 1* (ECM 1014 ST, rec. April 1971; reissued 1994 ECM).

Corea, Chick, and Return to Forever. *Return to Forever* (ECM 1022 ST, rec. February 1972; reissued 1987 ECM).

Corea, Chick, and Return to Forever. *Light as a Feather* (POLYDOR PD 5525, rec. 1973; reissued 1998 Verve, with 2 bonus tracks and 8 alternate takes).

Davis, Miles, *Kind of Blue* (COLUMBIA CL 1355, rec. March & April 1959, reissued 1992 Columbia Records).

Davis, Miles, *The Complete Quintet Recordings 1965–1968* (COLUMBIA/LEGACY C6K 67398, & C6K 67398, rec. between January 20, 1965 and June 21, 1968).

Davis, Miles, *E.S.P.* (COLUMBIA CL 2350, rec. January 1965, reissued 1998 Legacy).

Davis, Miles, *Sorcerer* (COLUMBIA CL 2732, rec. August 1962 & May 1967, reissued 1998 Sony Music Entertainment Inc., with 2 bonus tracks).

Davis, Miles, *Miles Smiles* (COLUMBIA CL 2601, rec. October 1966, reissued 1992 Columbia/Legacy).

Davis, Miles, *Nefertiti* (COLUMBIA CS 9594, rec. June 1967, reissued 1998 Columbia Records, with 4 bonus tracks).

Davis, Miles, *Miles in the Sky* (COLUMBIA CS 9628, rec. January & May 1968, reissued 1998 Sony Music Entertainment Inc., with 2 bonus tracks).

Dolphy, Eric, *Eric Dolphy at the Five Spot, Vol. 1* (PRESTIGE NJ 8260, rec. July 1961; reissued 1991 Original Jazz Classics with alternate take).

Evans, Bill. *How My Heart Sings* (RIVERSIDE RLP 9473, May 1962).

Farrell, Joe, *Joe Farrell Quartet* (CTI 6003, rec. July 1970; reissued 1976 CTI as *Song of the Wind*).

Getz, Stan, *Sweet Rain* (VERVE V-8693, rec. March 1967; reissued 2008 Verve).

Hancock, Herbie, *The Complete Blue Note Sessions* (BLUE NOTE B2BN 7243 4 95569 2 8, rec. 1962–1969).

Hancock, Herbie, *Takin' Off* (BLUE NOTE BST 84109, rec. May 1962, reissued 1987 Blue Note, with 3 bonus tracks).

Hancock, Herbie, *My Point of View* (BLUE NOTE BST 84126, rec. March 1963, reissued 1987 Blue Note, with 1 bonus track).

Hancock, Herbie, *Inventions and Dimensions* (BLUE NOTE BLP 4147, rec. August 1963, reissued 1988 Blue Note, with 1 bonus track).

Hancock, Herbie, *Empyrean Isles* (BLUE NOTE BLP 4175, rec. June 1964, reissued 1999 Blue Note, with 6 bonus tracks).

Hancock, Herbie, *Maiden Voyage* (BLUE NOTE BST 84195, rec. March 1965, reissued 1986 Blue Note).

Hancock, Herbie, *Speak Like a Child* (BLUE NOTE BST 84279, rec. March 1968, reissued 1987 Blue Note, with 3 bonus tracks).

Hancock, Herbie, *The Prisoner* (BLUE NOTE BST 84321, rec. April 1969, reissued 1987 Blue Note, with 2 bonus tracks).

Hancock, Herbie, *Fat Albert Rotunda* (WARNER BROTHERS ST-1834, rec. May–June 1969; reissued 1994 in *Mwandishi: The Complete Warner Brothers Recordings*).

Hancock, Herbie, *V.S.O.P. The Quintet* (COLUMBIA LSP 982152-1, rec. July 1977, reissued 2001 Sony Music Entertainment Inc., with 4 bonus tracks).

Hancock, Herbie, *A Tribute to Miles* (QWEST RECORDS 9362 45059-2, rec. September 1992).

Henderson, Joe. *In 'n Out* (BLUE NOTE BLP 4166, rec. April 1964; reissued 1987 Blue Note).

Henderson, Joe. *Inner Urge* (BLUE NOTE BLP 4189, rec. November 1964; reissued 1989 Blue Note).

Henderson, Joe. *Mode for Joe* (BLUE NOTE BST 84227, rec. January 1966; reissued 1988 Blue Note).

Henderson, Joe. *Black Narcissus* (MILESTONE MSP 9071, rec. October 1974 and April 1975).

Little, Booker, *Booker Little 4 & Max Roach* (UNITED ARTISTS UAS 5034, rec. October 1958; reissued 1991 Blue Note).

Little, Booker, *Out Front* (CANDID CJS 9027, rec. March–April 1961).

Mitchell, Blue, *The Thing to Do* (BLUE NOTE BST 4178; rec. 1964; reissued 1988 Blue Note).

Mitchell, Blue, *Boss Horn* (BLUE NOTE BST 84257, rec. November 1966, reissued 2005 Blue Note).

Roach, Max, *Deeds Not Words* (RIVERSIDE RLP 12-280, rec. September 1958; reissued 1988 Original Jazz Classics).

Shorter, Wayne, *Introducing Wayne Shorter* (VEE-JAY VJLP 3006, rec. November 1959, reissued 2004 Vee-jay, with 5 bonus tracks.)

Shorter, Wayne, *Second Genesis* (VEE-JAY VJS 3057, rec. October 1960, reissued 2002 Collectables).

Shorter, Wayne, *Wayning Moments* (VEE-JAY VJ LP 3029, rec. 1962, reissued 2000 KOCH, with 8 bonus tracks).

Shorter, Wayne, *JuJu* (BLUE NOTE BST 84182, rec. August 1963, reissued 1987 Blue Note).

Shorter, Wayne, *Night Dreamer* (BLUE NOTE BLP 4173, rec. April 1964, reissued 1987 Blue Note, with 1 bonus track).

Shorter, Wayne, *Speak No Evil* (BLUE NOTE BST 84194, rec. December 1964, reissued 1987 Blue Note).

Shorter, Wayne, *The Soothsayer* (BLUE NOTE LT 988, rec. March 1965, reissued 1990 Blue Note, with 1 bonus track).

Shorter, Wayne, *Etcetera* (BLUE NOTE LT 1056, rec. June 1965; reissued 1995 Blue Note).

Shorter, Wayne, *The All Seeing Eye* (BLUE NOTE BLP 4219, rec. October 1965, reissued 1999 Blue Note).

Shorter, Wayne, *Adam's Apple* (BLUE NOTE BLP 4232, rec. February 1966, reissued 1987 Blue Note, with 1 bonus track).

Shorter, Wayne, *Schizophrenia* (BLUE NOTE BST 84297, rec. March 1967; reissued 1995 Blue Note).

Weather Report, *Mr. Gone* (COLUMBIA PC 35358, rec. May 1978, reissued 1991 Columbia).

Young, Larry, *Unity* (BLUE NOTE BST 84221, rec. November 1965; reissued 1999 Blue Note).

BIBLIOGRAPHY

Agawu, Kofi. *Music as Discourse: Semiotic Adventures in Romantic Music*.
    New York: Oxford University Press, 2009.
Baker, David. *The Jazz Style of John Coltrane*. Lebanon, IN: Studio P/R, 1980.
Biamonte, Nicole. "Triadic Modal and Pentatonic Patterns in Rock Music." *Music*
    Theory Spectrum 32 (2010): 95–110.
Broze, Yuri, and Daniel Shanahan. "Diachronic Changes in Jazz Harmony: A
    Cognitive Perspective." *Music Perception* 31, no. 1 (September 2013): 32–45.
Brubeck, Darius. "1959: The Beginning of Beyond." In *The Cambridge*
    Companion to Jazz, edited by Mervyn Cooke and David Horn, 177–201.
    Cambridge: Cambridge University Press, 2002.
Chambers, Jack. *Milestones: The Music and Times of Miles Davis*. New York: Da Capo,
    1998. Originally pub. University of Toronto Press, 1983 and 1985.
Christiansen, Morten H., and Simon Kirby, eds. *Language Evolution*. Oxford: Oxford
    University Press, 2003.
Cohn, Richard. "An Introduction to Neo-Riemannian Theory: A Survey and Historical
    Perspective." *Journal of Music Theory* 42, no. 2 (1998): 167–80.
    _____. *Audacious Euphony: Chromaticism and the Triad's Second Nature*.
    New York: Oxford University Press, 2012.
Collier, James Lincoln. *The Making of Jazz: A Comprehensive History*.
    Boston: Houghton Mifflin, 1978.
Cope, David. "Computer Analysis of Musical Allusions." *Computer Music Journal* 27,
    no. 1 (2003): 11–28.
Corea, Chick. *Now He Sings, Now He Sobs*, transcribed by Bill Dobbins. Rottenburg,
    Germany: Advance Music, 1988.
    _____. *Chick Corea Piano Improvsations*, transcribed by Bill Dobbins.
    Rottenburg: Advance Music, 1990.
Cugny, Laurent. *Analyser le jazz*. Paris: Outre Mesure, 2009.
Demsey, David. "Chromatic Third Relations in the Music of John Coltrane." *Annual*
    Review of Jazz Studies 5 (1991): 145–80.
DeVeaux, Scott. *The Birth of Bebop: A Social and Musical History*. Berkeley: University
    of California Press, 1997.
Dobbins, Bill. *Jazz Arranging and Composition: A Linear Approach*. Rottenburg,
    Germany: Advance Music, 2005.
Duke, Daniel. "The Piano Improvisations of Chick Corea: An Analytical Study." DMA
    thesis, Louisiana State University, 1996.

Feld, Steven, and Aaron Fox. "Music and Language." *Annual Review of Anthropology* 23 (1994): 25–53.

Forte, Allen. *The American Popular Ballad of the Golden Era, 1924–1950.* Princeton: Princeton University Press, 1995.

_____. "The Real 'Stella' and the 'Real' 'Stella': A Response to 'Alternate Takes'." *Annual Review of Jazz Studies* 9 (1997–1998): 93–101.

Gjerdingen, Robert. *Music in the Galant Style.* New York: Oxford University Press, 2007.

Goldstein, Gil. *Jazz Composer's Companion.* 2nd ed. Rottenburg: Advance Music, 1993.

Harrison, Daniel. *Harmonic Function in Tonal Music.* Chicago: University of Chicago, 1994.

Henderson, Joe. *Joe Henderson: Inner Urge,* vol. 108. New Albany, IN: Jamey Aebersold Jazz, 2004.

Hentoff, Nat. "An Afternoon with Miles Davis." In *Miles on Miles,* edited by Paul Maher Jr. and Michael Dorr, 13–19. Chicago: Lawrence Hill, 2009. Originally pub. in *The Jazz Review* 1, no. 2 (December 1958): 11–12.

Hodeir, Andre. *Jazz: Its Evolution and Essence,* trans. David Noakes. New York: Grove Press, 1956.

Jan, Steven. *The Memetics of Music: A Neo-Darwinian View of Musical Structure and Culture.* Aldershot: Ashgate Publishing, 2007.

Jost, Ekkehard. *Free Jazz.* New York: Da Capo Press, 1994. Originally pub. Universal Editions, 1974.

Julien, Patricia. "The Structural Function of Harmonic Relations in Wayne Shorter's Early Compositions: 1959–63." PhD diss., University of Maryland, 2003.

Kahn, Ashley. *Kind of Blue: The Making of the Miles Davis Masterpiece.* New York: Da Capo Press, 2000.

Kernfeld, Barry. "Adderley, Coltrane, and Davis at the Twilight of Bebop: The Search for Melodic Coherence." PhD diss., Cornell University, 1981.

Lass, Roger. *Historical Linguistics and Change.* Cambridge: Cambridge University Press, 1997.

Liebman, David. "The Compositional Style of Joe Henderson." *The Note* (Winter/ Spring 2006): 25–26.

Lynch, Jordan Michael. "Where Have I Known This Before: An Exploration of Harmony and Voice Leading in the Compositions of Chick Corea." Master's thesis, Bowling Green State University, 2012.

Lyons, Len. *The Great Jazz Pianists: Speaking of Their Lives and Music.* New York: Da Capo Press, 1983.

Mandler, J. M. *Stories, Scripts, and Scenes: Aspects of Schema Theory.* Hillsdale, NJ: Lawrence Erlbaum Associates, 1984.

Martin, Henry. "Jazz Harmony: A Syntactic Background." *Annual Review of Jazz Studies* 4 (1988): 9–30.

_____. *Counterpoint: A Species Approach Based on Schenker's* Counterpoint. Lanham, MD: Scarecrow Press, 2005.

_____. "Schenker and the Tonal Jazz Repertory." *Tijdschrift voor Muziektheorie* 16, no. 1 (2011): 1–20.

McGowan, James. "Dynamic Consonance in Selected Piano Performances of Tonal Jazz." PhD diss., University of Rochester, 2005.

Meyer, Leonard B. *Explaining Music: Essays and Explorations.* Chicago and London: University of Chicago, 1973.

_____. *Style and Music: Theory, History, and Ideology*. Chicago and London: University of Chicago Press, 1989.

Miller, Ron. *Modal Jazz: Composition & Harmony*. 2 vols. Rottenburg: Advance Music, 1996.

Naus, Wayne. *Beyond Functional Harmony*. Rottenburg: Advance Music, 1998.

Patel, Aniruddh. *Music, Language, and the Brain*. New York: Oxford University Press, 2008.

Pejrolo, Andrea. "The Origins of Modal Jazz in the Music of Miles Davis: A Complete Transcription and a Linear/Harmonic Analysis of *Ascenseur pour l'échafaud (Lift to the Scaffold)*–1957." PhD diss., New York University, 2001.

Porter, Lewis. *John Coltrane: His Life and Music*. Ann Arbor: University of Michigan Press, 1998.

Ramon. Ricker. *Pentatonic Scales for Jazz Improvisation*. Lebanon, IN: Studio P/R, 1975.

Russell, George. *The Lydian Chromatic Concept of Tonal Organization for Improvisation*. 2nd ed. New York: Concept Publishing, 1959.

Schuller, Gunther. *Musings: The Musical Worlds of Gunther Schuller*. New York: Oxford University Press, 1986.

Shaw, Woody. *Eight Classic Jazz Originals*, vol. 9. New Albany, IN: Jamie Aebersold Jazz, 1976.

Smither, Sean. "Navigating Simultaneous Syntaxes of Pitch Organization in Jazz Harmony: Transformational Ontology, Voice-Leading, and Guide-Tone Space." MA thesis, Rutgers University, 2015.

Strunk, Steven. "The Harmony of Early Bop: A Layered Approach." *Journal of Jazz Studies* 6 (1979): 4–53.

_____. "Harmony." Entry in *The New Grove Dictionary of Jazz*, ed. by Barry Kernfeld. London: Macmillan, 1988.

_____. "Notes on Harmony in Wayne Shorter's Compositions." *Journal of Music Theory* 49, no. 2 (2005): 301–32.

_____. "Tonal and Transformational Approaches to Chick Corea's Compositions of the 1960s." *Music Theory Spectrum* 38, no. 1 (2016): 16–36.

Swain, Joseph. *Musical Languages*. New York: W. W. Norton, 1997.

Terefenko, Dariusz. *Jazz Theory: From Basic to Advanced Study*. New York: Routledge 2014.

Tirro, Frank. *Jazz: A History*, 2nd ed. New York: W. W. Norton, 1993.

Waters, Keith. "Blurring the Barline: Metric Displacement in the Piano Solos of Herbie Hancock." *Annual Review of Jazz Studies* 8 (1996): 19–37.

_____. "Modes, Scales, Functional Harmony, and Non-Functional Harmony in the Compositions of Herbie Hancock." *Journal of Music Theory* 49, no. 2 (2005): 333–57.

_____. "'Giant Steps' and the ic4 Legacy." *Intégral* 24 (2010): 135–62.

_____. *The Studio Recordings of the Miles Davis Quintet 1965–68*. New York: Oxford University Press, 2011.

_____. "Postbop." Entry in the *Grove Dictionary of American Music*, 2nd ed., vol. 6, ed. by Hiroshi Garrett. New York: Oxford University Press, 2013.

_____. "Chick Corea and Postbop Harmony." *Music Theory Spectrum* 38, no. 1 (2016): 37–57.

Waters, Keith, and David Diamond. "Out Front: The Art of Booker Little." *Annual Review of Jazz Studies* 11 (2000–2001): 1–38.

White, Arthur Lynne. "Joe Henderson: An Analysis of Harmony in Selected
    Compositions and Improvisation." DMA diss., University of North Carolina at
    Greensboro, 2008.
Yudkin, Jeremy. *Miles Davis, Miles Smiles, and the Invention of Post Bop*.
    Bloomington: University of Indiana, 2008.

INDEX